S0-CAE-308

FINDING
CHOLITA

**Interpretations of Culture
in the New Millennium**

Norman E. Whitten Jr.,
General Editor

*A list of books in the series
appears at the end of the book.*

FINDING

FINDING CHOLITA

Billie Jean Isbell

To Barbara & Dennis
who have been my
guiding beacon in the
long tunnel I traveled to
complete this book.

Love, B.J.
Feb. 2009

University of Illinois Press
Urbana and Chicago

© 2009 by Billie Jean Isbell
All rights reserved
Manufactured in the United States of America
1 2 3 4 5 C P 5 4 3 2 1
∞ This book is printed on acid-free paper.

Library of Congress Cataloging-in-Publication Data
Isbell, Billie Jean.
Finding Cholita / Billie Jean Isbell.
p.   cm. — (Interpretations of culture in the
new millennium)
Includes bibliographical references.
ISBN 978-0-252-03412-1 (cloth : alk. paper)
ISBN 978-0-252-07606-0 (pbk. : alk. paper)
1. Anthropologists—Fiction.
2. Human rights—Fiction.
3. Latin America—Fiction.
4. Sendero Luminoso (Guerrilla group—Fiction.
I. Title.
PS3609.S26F56   2009
813'.6 — dc22   2008036542

CONTENTS

PROLOGUE: WHY TURN TO FICTION?

Over the forty years that I have been conducting research in Peru, there have been events that have haunted me that I have not been able to forget nor write about in the venues offered in anthropology. In order to gain closure and provide a form of therapy for myself, I have turned to fiction. During the twenty years that I focused on violence, I absorbed the horrific stories told to me and found myself developing disabling infirmities. For example, as I was struggling with whether to publish the testimonies of victims, I was rendered speechless by reoccurring lesions on my tongue that required surgery.

My research has been centered in the southern region of the department of Ayacucho, Peru, that was terrorized by the Shining Path from 1975 to 1992, when the leader of that movement, Abimael Guzmán, was captured. This account of those years is a combination of ethnographic description and ethnographically grounded fiction. Nevertheless, the details and dates of the war are accurate.

I began my research in Peru in 1967 as an undergraduate writing an honor's thesis on the civil-religious hierarchy in the village of Chuschi, Peru. During my first fieldwork, I settled into the village with my husband, my two-year-old daughter, and my mother. The often comical difficulties of that first encounter are described in the introduction of *To Defend Ourselves,* the ethnography of the community of Chuschi first published in 1978. Returning to Chuschi through the decades that followed has allowed me to document the many transformations and changes that have taken place, not only in a remote Andean community that was thrust into the spotlight of history, but transformations in myself as well.

The insurgency, Shining Path, chose to announce their war against the Peruvian state in May of 1980 by burning the ballots in Chuschi for the first national democratic election in seventeen years. That election was also the first that allowed illiterates to vote. That action placed the region in the epicenter of a twenty-year war that cost seventy thousand lives, most of whom were Quechua-speaking peasants. At the time, no one (including me) took the burning of the ballots seriously. No shots were fired, the ballots were replaced, and the election occurred the next day. But later I learned that the burning of the ballots was carried out by teachers and students of the secondary school as a long-term strategy of Shining Path that began in 1975.

When I returned to Chuschi in 1975 I intended to establish a bilingual Spanish/Quechua program in the primary schools with funding from the Ford Foundation and sponsorship of the Ministry of Education. At the time I was puzzled by the opposition from some of the schoolteachers, because in previous years they had been in favor of bilingual education. Later I realized that control of the schools by Shining Path was the vehicle for ideological indoctrination and recruitment for the war to "Establish the New Democracy in Peru." But, rather than a new democracy, Shining Path evolved into a rigid, hierarchical death cult that worshiped Abimael Guzmán, the philosopher turned revolutionary leader who had taught at the University of Huamanga in the city of Ayacucho. He and his followers won the ideological battle that raged in the 1970s between various political factions. Guzmán went underground and Shining Path leadership traveled to China during those years for indoctrination and training in guerrilla warfare before they began the war in earnest in 1980. The heaviest casualties occurred in the southern department of Ayacucho between 1983 and 1985. By the time the war spread to Lima and other parts of the country, it is estimated that Shining Path had close to ten thousand combatants.

As a footnote to this novel, I'd like to mention that Guzmán has been in jail since his capture in 1992, and ironically, he shares a special prison with his arch-enemy, Vladimir Montesinos, the feared right-hand man and head of intelligence who sanctioned numerous massacres under President Alberto Fujimori. Both Montesinos and Fujimori fled Peru within a few months of each other, the president to Japan in November of 2000 and Montesinos to Venezuela a short time later when his own videotapes showing him bribing officials made national news. He was captured in Venezuela in June of 2001 while waiting for plastic surgery to disguise his appearance. After Guzmán's capture, the insurgency faded and only a few hangers-on continued in the coca-growing rain forest region protecting the drug traffic. Guzmán, age seventy-two, is still in prison and has received government permission to marry his second in command, Elena Iparraguirre, age fifty-nine, known as Comrade Miriam, who is also incarcerated.

Alice Woodsley, the narrator of this novel, is a fictionalized anthropologist whose voice grew out of my experiences and those of my women colleagues. The story begins as Alice initiates her career as a young, naïve fieldworker who gradually finds herself entrapped in a growing tornado of violence. The descriptions of the violence are based on interviews with survivors that I conducted during the 1980s and 1990s, when I found myself with a corpus of material that presented a terrible dilemma. What could I publish? How could I fulfill the responsibility of protecting the survivors I had interviewed? What responsibility did I have to anthropology? To wider political issues? This novel addresses and gives voice to those issues. I rewrote the manuscript several times, struggling with voice, finally settling on telling this story in the first person, even though it is perhaps the most difficult voice in which to write. I concluded it was the most appropriate voice for a narrative about what happens to an anthropologist who does fieldwork in a dangerous place. Two other motives guided this book. I wanted to depict how anthropologists can move across ethnic and class boundaries within a society and I also wanted to describe how a researcher can get caught in power struggles she did not foresee.

Some readers might ask, "But if most of the accounts are true then why present them as fiction?" One of the most obvious reasons is to protect people I have interviewed from possible harm. But others might ask, "Hasn't enough time passed? Aren't people safe now?" By official accounts the war in Peru ended in 1992 with Guzmán's capture, but disappearances continued after that date. The families of the disappeared do not feel that the environment in the department of Ayacucho is safe. Many believe they are still under surveillance due to their continuing political actions for personal and legal closure. The mechanisms for such surveillance are still in place. Nor do the victims of gang rape by military personnel feel safe, and they continue to relive their traumas. Nevertheless, the 2008 trial of ex-president Alberto Fujimori for corruption and ordering death squads along with trials and convictions of four death squad members give hope to families of victims. In addition, the National Association of Families Abducted, Arrested, and Disappeared has opened a Museum of Memory in the city of Ayacucho so that "the past is not repeated."

Fiction's place in anthropology has a long but interrupted history that Kirin Narayan (1999), an anthropologist and novelist, has admirably summarized. She points out that the earliest experimentation with fiction was Adolph Bandelier's novel *The Delight Makers: A Novel of Prehistoric Pueblo*

Indians, published in 1870. Elsie Clues Parsons' edited volume of short stories by such luminaries as Franz Boas, Edward Sapir, Robert Lowie, and Paul Radin, published in 1922, is a landmark in anthropological fiction. In 1929, Oliver La Farge's novel *Laughing Boy* won a Pulitzer Prize. Anthropological fiction declined after the initial period of experimentation because scientism dominated American anthropology. Narayan argues that Laura Bohannan's *Return to Laughter* is the best-known novel written by an anthropologist and notes that she published it under the pseudonym Elenore Smith Bowen in 1954, a time when scientism was the most powerful paradigm in American anthropology.

Narayan speculates that Bohannan might have published her novel as a fieldwork memoir today rather than as fiction. Two well-known fiction writers that illustrate the long relationship between anthropology and literature are Zora Neale Hurston, who studied with Boaz, and Kurt Vonnegut, whose novel *Cat's Cradle* (1963) was accepted by the University of Chicago as his master's thesis in anthropology in 1971 after his first thesis was rejected. A more contemporary example of a novelist/anthropologist is Amitav Ghosh, who holds a PhD in social anthropology from Oxford University and publishes in both genres but teaches literary criticism at Queens College as a distinguished professor of comparative literature. Citing this long and complicated history, Narayan argues for maintaining a border between ethnography and fiction but advocates border crossing between the two.

Crossing that border with this volume of fiction draws on my fieldwork experiences, but it is not a fieldwork memoir. However, I have written a short memoir on my fieldwork titled "Written on My Body" (Isbell, in press). On reflection, I think one of the reasons I was drawn to fiction to tell this story rather than memoir or ethnography is that fiction allowed me the freedom to create a conclusion that ethnography could not sustain. The last two chapters of this novel are fictional creations that provide personal, emotional, and aesthetic closure. They are written as an act of hope for the future. Ethnography, in contrast, is never completed in an ever-changing world, and the ethnography on Chuschi, Peru, that I first published in 1978 has gone through republications and additions (1985, 2005), but the final chapter can never be written.

I first crossed the border from ethnography into creative writing in 1994 with a drama titled "Public Secrets from Peru" that was presented as a dramatic reading with masks and a sound montage at a conference at Cornell University on anthropology and performance. I subsequently traveled with the play, along with the Quilt of the Disappeared made by women survivors from Ayacucho, to several universities where students read the play in public presentations and displayed the quilt. The play was never published, but it and the sound montage created by Stefan Senders can be found on my isbell/andes Web site in the Cornell library system. The play drew on interviews I had collected in the late 1980s of the violence of the war in the department of Ayacucho. The dialogue of one of those stories has been reshaped as chapter 4 of this novel. That chapter was informed by feminist anthropology and experiments in writing, especially *Women Writing Culture,* edited by Ruth Behar and Deborah Gordon (1996).

During the years I was struggling with the material on violence, I was not comfortable with shaping the interviews into a publication that would fit into the testimonial literature genre. Rather, I chose to cross the border from ethnography into drama and later into fiction. One of the reasons testimonial literature did not appeal to me is that I did not want to assume the role of researcher as hero. Moreover, I felt that the tone of much of the testimonial literature was nonreflexive. The researchers were frequently invisible. The exceptions to these impressions are firsthand accounts such as Victor Montejo's *Testimony: Death of a Guatemalan Village* (1987) and Alicia Partnoy's *The Little School: Tales of Disappearance and Survival in Argentina* (1986).

Crossing the border into fiction has allowed me to create a voice of an anthropologist who turns the traumatic testimonials she has collected into a fetish and obsessively searches for Cholita. In the process of her long search, she is transformed. In part I turned to experimentation with writing genres because structuralism had failed to account for the rise of Shining Path in the 1970s and 1980s. My frustration at the time was shared by others who found their old paradigms failing them. Many of us turned to Clifford Geertz, who, in *Interpretation of Cultures* (1973), resisted universalizing theories such as structuralism in favor of thick descriptions and interpretive anthropology. That volume brought literary criticism, history, philosophy, and anthropology closer together. The song texts in chapter 12 are an example of my own practice of thick description. Anyone interested in hearing the songs can find the original tapes and Quechua transcriptions on my isbell/andes Web site.

In a 1999 public lecture for the American Council of Learned Societies called "A Life of Learning," which Geertz describes as an exercise of crafted candor and public self-concealment, Geertz refers to the concept of culture prior to the appearance of *Interpretations of Cultures*: "We were condemned, it seemed, to working with a logic and a language in which concept, cause, form, and outcome had the same name." He goes on to explain: "I took it as my task, then, though, in fact, no one actually assigned it to me, and I am not sure to what degree it was a conscious decision—to cut the idea of culture down to size, to turn it into a less expansive affair" (1999, 9). He admits that he was certainly not alone in efforts to offer an alternative view. But that volume had an enormous impact on the discipline, and the results of it have been quite the opposite from his intention. His writing has not cut the concept of culture down to size, rather his writing has facilitated the expansion of the concept of culture to include any meaningful act, no mater how mundane, as fuel for interpretive descriptions in numerous disciplines. In the 1999 lecture, Geertz gave me the distinct impression that he was an "accidental anthropologist" who was compelled to write. He states that his first ambition was to be a novelist, but I have not found evidence that he ever published fiction (some charge that his writing is fiction). Nevertheless, his interpretive framework has done a great deal to reopen the door to fiction in anthropology. In his *Works and Lives: The Anthropologist as Author* (1988) that won the Critics Circle Prize for Criticism in 1989, he introduces the term "faction" for imaginative writing about real people in real places, but the term never caught on. By the decade of the 1990s the pendulum was swinging back to fiction as well as to new hybrid genres of creative nonfiction in anthropology. Narayan (1999) provides a detailed discussion of that development. Therefore, I will concentrate here on her arguments about the differences in the practices of writing ethnography and writing fiction.

Narayan isolates four landmark practices that differentiate writing ethnography and writing fiction: the disclosure of process, generalization versus particularity, representations of subjectivity, and accountability. In terms of process she argues that ethnographers are trained to disclose the methods and analytical tools in their work while novelists generally withhold their intentions from their readers. I have revealed my intentions in this prologue and therefore conformed to the convention of writing ethnography. However, I felt the tensions between the two genres and I confess that I resisted writing this prologue.

I will briefly discuss how Narayan's arguments concerning the other three differences resonate with my experiences. She makes the point that both genres combine generalizations and particularity. "While fiction relies implicitly on generalizations, an attempt to employ stories around generalizable events or people may prove too didactic" (140). As I was writing this novel I continuously had to stifle the didactic voice of the anthropologist, and one of my final acts of editing has been to search for and delete the didactic passages that threaten to overpower the story. In addition, I found it difficult to represent the subjectivities of native speakers of Quechua. At first, I thought my difficulty was based on differences in language, but I think Narayan is correct that the scruples of our ethnographic training make it difficult to represent the inner thoughts of our research subjects who are of a different class and ethnicity. Instead, I concentrated on Alice's foibles and inner thoughts because I felt entitled to represent her subjectivity. When considering accountability outside the text, my experiences also rang true to her argument; I found myself faced with the paradox of wanting to tell a compelling story and to reach a wider audience but also feeling accountable for the particular events of the war waged by Shining Path and especially to the people that the war devastated. I have tried to balance those two frameworks of accountability by creating fictitious characters, utilizing my field notes and interviews, and staying as close as possible to the historical events of the war except for the final two chapters, which are nevertheless ethnographically informed.

I want to make some final observations about the narrator of this story, Alice, the ethnographer. Her drive to find Cholita is extreme and she is initially blind to what motivates her obsession. She embodies many of the characteristics I see as common to practicing anthropologists. She is at times impatient, a bit sanctimonious and preachy. She learns to love many of her research subjects and to hate others. With time she gains insight and more patience, but her obsession remains. In the early days of American anthropology, Boas required his students, Margaret Mead for example, to seek psychoanalysis before engaging in fieldwork. Perhaps we need therapy not only before beginning research but after fieldwork as well, especially if we work in situations of violence. Moreover, just as Alice finds herself being used as a pawn in a larger political struggle, so do many anthropologists, especially in the early stages of their careers.

As is true of all ethnographers, Alice's actions are shaped by her history and her choices. I wanted to create a story where her history was visible. As a young structuralist in the 1970s, she begins her career believing that she was conducting objective scientific research. But it doesn't take long for her to become embroiled in various power-laden situations as she moves up and down the social ladder of Peruvian society. Over time, as violence increases, her work develops into public anthropology focusing on human rights, and all vestiges of objectivity disappear. Of course, my major objective in writing this

ACKNOWLEDGMENTS

I started writing scenes for this novel in 1986 while I was a fellow at the Woodrow Wilson Center in Washington, D.C., as I faced the difficulties of how to publish interview materials of victims of political violence. I wish to thank Catherine Allen and Regina Harrison for our constructive discussions as well as their comments and criticisms on those early scenes and ideas. Encouraged by Barbara and Dennis Tedlock's work on dialogical and narrative anthropology, I continued to work sporadically on scenes and images that haunted my memory, filing them away as scraps of writing.

I returned to those scraps of writing upon retirement in 2002, and I wish to thank Michelle Bigenho and Daniel Goldstein for organizing the panel in my honor at the American Anthropological Meeting in 2003 in Chicago. At the panel, called "From the Andean Kaleidoscope to the Politics of Anthropology," I read from a draft that became chapter 5, "The Autopsy."

In addition, Michelle Bigenho deserves special thanks for her careful reading of the manuscript at its various stages. Her sensitive commentary on the final draft was essential to my final organization of the manuscript. Karen Graubart's and Marigold Walsh-Dilley's critiques of the final draft proved constructive as well.

Others who deserve thanks are Carol Rubenstein for copy editing and advice on the poetry; Freda Wolf, who made extremely pertinent suggestions for translations; and John Miller, who critiqued the manuscript. I would also like to thank the anonymous readers for the University of Illinois Press, whose careful critiques and suggestions guided me in shaping the final version of this novel. Finally, I would like to single out Norman Whitten for his guidance during the final stages of this book. I'd also like to thank Joan Catapano and the editorial staff at the University of Illinois Press.

UNDER THE BANQUET TABLE

Cholita—*The Revised Spanish and English Dictionary,* compiled by Edwin B. Williams, 1962 (New York: Holt, Rinehart and Winston), defines the term as a female half-breed, but the term chola (cholo) is widely used in the Spanish-speaking regions of the Andes of South America for persons of recent upward mobility who participate both in the indigenous and national cultures without being incorporated into either. The word has both negative and positive connotations. It can be an insult directed at those with Indian physical features or at persons of a lower class. With the diminutive added (-ita or -ito), it can also be a term of endearment. Acting like a cholo or chola is a negative appellation for men or women who are crafty and not to be trusted.

AYACUCHO, 1975

Stop sucking on those bones! They're bare, damn it, they're clean!

Cra—a—ck! I heard the bone splintering . . . she was sucking out the marrow. Romulo Rosetti Martinez reached down and handed Cholita another bone. She hungrily grabbed it and continued sucking. The sounds crawled like fingers up and down my spine. I said, "Compadre Romulo, nutrition plays a large part in growth. Cholita would be taller if she had a better diet." Immediately I regretted my Ms. Gringa-with-a-PhD Know-It-All tone. I hadn't touched my plate even though the smell of roast chicken was making me hallucinate.

Romulo looked pleased as he drew himself upright in his chair, stretched his hand toward the center of the table, and pointed downward with an index finger that had a long, thickened nail. He said, "I'm preparing Cholita for the life she will have to face, comadrita. Do you want to pamper her? If she ever gets to eat at the banquet table, she will have to fight for a place." With that, he tossed the last of the chicken bones to the child.

I was at a loss for words. *Why did I rent a room in this household? Romulo had presented a convincing argument for why I needed a room here in the capital city to take a break from fieldwork. As the director of schools in Pumapunku, he seemed to command respect, and his wife was initially so nice to me. But I've learned what they are really like. Grasping, greedy, conniving. I'm learning how much they abuse the Indian population. There are a lot of shitty cholos in this country, but you, dear compadre Romulo, are the worst!* I thought.

I smiled at him and tried to look composed. I folded my hands in my lap and said, "Compadre, please forgive me for not accepting your hospitality. I suddenly find that I'm not hungry. I think that the long bus ride from Pumapunku has made me a little sick." With what I hoped was flourish and ceremony, I put my plate on the floor and Cholita greedily attacked it. As if to protest an act of treason, my stomach gave an audible grumble.

Good shot! It's a game. I just have to remember that he has had centuries to practice. I am learning bit by bit. For just a moment I felt as though Romulo could hear my interior ruminations and was going to debate how much I had learned, but instead he leaned across the table and examined me carefully, ignoring the noise from under the table.

"You know, comadre, you could be Peruvian. You're short, your blue eyes, fair skin and black hair could've come from some lone Spaniard. But you're too skinny for our liking. You have no hips . . . we like our women with hips and breasts you can grab onto! Carajo, like our Indian girls, now, they give a man a handful!" He smacked his lips and cupped his hands around full, imaginary breasts and gave them a little squeeze.

He was just trying to get my goat. I struggled to keep my facial expression calm. I wanted to leap across the table and strangle him. So much for being a pacifist.

"Compadre Romulo, perhaps Cholita could return to Pumapunku with me. The country would be healthier for her. Don't you think?"

Cholita emerged from under the table with a chicken bone in her hand, waving it in the air as she did a little wild dance. She tried to speak, but with her mouth so full, she resorted to bobbing her head up and down affirmatively and tugging at her father's sleeve.

Romulo leaned back in his chair and narrowed his eyes as he shook his arm free from the child's grasp. Taking her cue, Cholita crawled back under the table and chewed noisily. He put both hands on the table, leaning forward, and looking at me directly in the eyes he asked, "Do you see Cholita, comadre Alicia? She's the real revolutionary of Peru. Some day she will grow up and want to kill me!"

2 FINDING CHOLITA

The very idea of being killed by one of his many bastard children seemed particularly funny to my compadre. He rolled his big round head back and roared with laughter. His thinning hair slipped away from his carefully concealed bald spot. He stopped short and inquired, "Alicia, don't you find it funny to think about this little beggar killing me someday? You're not laughing. Carajo! You gringos will never understand our Indians. They're all like children."

It's times like these that I wonder why I've chosen to be a professional voyeur, an intruder, a stranger, a foreigner, an outsider, an anthropologist. I should have become a dentist like my father and gone into practice with him like he wanted me to. Or, I could have become a super volunteer at the hospital, organized charities, or joined the bridge and garden clubs like my mother. I'm comadre with half the shitheads in the department of Ayacucho. I'm godmother to soccer balls, uniforms, basketball hoops, trucks, cars, dogs, even light bulbs. I've sprinkled holy water on the bastard children of bastards. I want to smash his arrogant face in instead of calling him mi querido compadre.

My thoughts were interrupted by Juana, Cholita's mother, as she appeared at the door with downcast eyes. Wringing her hands in agitation, she quietly told Romulo in Quechua that he had a visitor at the front gate. He got up from the table, excusing himself with a slight bow, saying in overly polite tones, "With your permission, comadrita," as if he needed my permission for anything, the bastard. He drew himself up to his full height, tried to suck in his paunch, and struck the pose that had given him the nickname of El Capitán.

Romulo, like most of his cronies, had never complied with the national law requiring military service. Instead, he had received his commission as El Capitán of a brigade of drunken young soldiers of the night whose skirmishes to seduce local virgins terrorized mothers of the city of Ayacucho for years. Their exploits, successes, and a few comical failures became the lyrics of ballads sung all over the region as they, now middle-aged men, nervously guard their own daughters. El Capitán was said to have been the best-looking of the bunch by local standards: tall and lean, with curly hair and large, sad eyes set over an expressive mouth with a slight pout. Years of debauchery had left double bags under his sad eyes. And a beer belly defiantly protruded over his belt, causing him to walk with a slight waddle. Over the years the sensuous pout of his mouth had sagged to become a permanent downcast sneer. Nevertheless, when the occasion demanded, Romulo could still throw out his chest and suck in his belly, set his mouth in a firm line, and become transformed into El Capitán. He turned his back on me and marched out of the room.

I glanced down at Cholita, who was attacking my plate of food. Her mother had prepared two of my favorite potato dishes, papas a la huancaina, small, yellow potatoes topped with a delicious fresh cheese and chili sauce, and white potatoes with a green sauce made from an Andean herb called wakatay. The savory aroma of the sauces blended with that of the roast chicken and made my mouth gush again. For just a moment I regretted relinquishing my plate to the child. As the smells washed over my memory, I realized I had not eaten meat since the fertility rituals were performed for the herds in Pumapunku some eight weeks before. To have chicken during the final days of February, the month of hunger and death, was such extravagance. The moment I arrived, Juana was sent to buy this plump, succulent, mouth-watering, ready-cooked bird from El Pollito a la Brasa, the new, open-pit barbecue in town.

As I sat and watched Cholita eat, I remembered how puzzled I had been when the so-called month of hunger was inaugurated in Pumapunku. We gorged ourselves for three days on animal flesh—alpacas, sheep, even a steer—then we returned to our daily fare consisting of watery soups made with a few potatoes. Later I decided that such feasting was a way to keep the pendulum of scarcity and plenitude in motion.

The rains, now abating, had nourished the crops that had been planted months ago in September. As usual for this time of year, the foodstuffs from the last year's harvest were dangerously low. We were indeed in the time of hunger. I could not expect to see meat in the village until the tumultuous festivities of the Feast of the Crosses in May. I watched Cholita stuff handfuls of chicken into her mouth with both of her filthy little hands while keeping her eyes glued to the doorway of the dining room. She looked like a bright-eyed wolf. Her image, for some reason, gave me a foreboding shudder.

Cholita scampered to her feet and handed me the plate with a small conspiratorial smile. "Gracias, madrina, zui—rico habia sido." The r in rico sounded like a buzzing insect as hissing air passed between her teeth. Quechua had transgressed upon the purring, trilled r of her Spanish. As she sucked the delectable chicken grease off each of her fingers, I sat in gastronomic agony feasting on my own spit. She wiped her mouth with the back of her hand and I noticed that her hands and her mouth were the only clean parts of her body.

"Um, was that good?" I asked. "My God, Cholita, I don't think I have ever been so hungry for meat. Maybe I'll just sneak a small piece of chicken from your father's plate and hide it in my pocket. Romulo will never know."

As I was speaking in a whisper to her, I began to gulp, and I knew that if I opened my mouth again my saliva would run down my chin. My craving for meat had dominated my dreams for several nights now—repetitive dreams in which I was transformed into a puma that always entered an enclosure filled with sheep. I loved the feeling of being the puma, stalking, but just as I sprang into the air toward the sheep, I would wake up hungry.

Last Friday, on market day, I bolted upright from one of my puma dreams to discover that the roof of my mouth was peeling off like a thin glove. My face was also twitching. As I sat up in my sleeping bag, I moved my tongue around and almost swallowed my own flesh. My god, I'm so hungry for meat that I am gnawing on my own flesh. I jumped out of bed and packed my backpack with a few things and headed for the bus that was waiting to take passengers to the capital city of Ayacucho. During the long trip into the city over roads with muddy ruts the size of foothills, I silently argued with myself: *Why is this essential but thus far unnoticed piece of my anatomy falling off?* I held the opinion that my physiological decomposition and facial tics were due to some kind of special fieldworker's fatigue that also caused my hallucinatory dreams. Or maybe the roof of my mouth has fallen off, I thought, from the continual battering my tongue has given it trying to make the god-awful sounds of this god-awful language.

I arrived in the city and immediately went to a doctor and described my symptoms. After several blood tests, the doctor told me that I had beriberi. Jesus, I had moved backward in time. I even had a disease from the last century! Soon I will be in the Middle Ages!

I reached down and tousled Cholita's matted unwashed hair. I realized that even though she was dressed in rags and was filthy with snot running down her chin, she was a pretty child with exceptionally bright black eyes, fair freckled complexion, and slightly curly hair like her father's. As she ran her tongue over her full protruding lips, I could picture what her father must have looked like when he was young. Except that the child's broad forehead and almond-shaped eyes resembled her mother's. She also had her mother's small, flared nose, thank God, and not her father's unsightly protuberance that, by 1975, had achieved an uncanny conquest of the surrounding countryside.

Romulo Rosetti's Roman profile was offered as evidence of the claim that the first Rosetti had arrived from Italy in the sixteenth century to administer an encomienda of one hundred Indians from the region of Pumapunku as a personal reward from the king of Spain. Before long, the conquest of the Incas was visibly overcome by the conquest of the Rosetti nose. The Inca visage, with its characteristic hook that usually occupied the middle portion of the nose, became transformed: it seemed to be slowly migrating up the nose to the bridge. People would look at the curve of a nose and say, "Umm . . . must be a Rosetti." Oddly though, the Rosetti stamp of Roman heritage was evident only on the faces of male offspring. It appeared to be a special manifestation of machismo that for ten generations had nudged its way onto the genetic map for male noses but not for female ones.

"Cholita, you are going to be a beauty, especially since you don't have your father's . . ." I paused and gestured as I switched to English, "Jimmy Durante shnozola." I drew an exaggerated Roman nose in the air and said, "Romulo's nose is more like this." Cholita laughed as I continued in Spanish. "And the next time I surrender my plate to you, Cholita, offer me a bite or two." She looked up at me and smiled with the secret smile of a co-conspirator and nodded her head emphatically up and down. I noticed for the first time that she had an interesting birthmark on the right side of her neck. It was purple in color and shaped like an hourglass. I addressed her in Spanish. "With your features and coloring, Cholita, it will be difficult to classify you as an Indian, especially if you learn to read and write."

"Toma, comadrita. I prepared wakatay just for you," whispered Juana as she stepped across the doorway, lifting her long skirts with one hand and balancing a heaping plate of food in the other. The plate was wrapped in an old but still beautiful piece of hand-woven cloth.

I spread the cloth on the table and dug into the plate of aromatic delights, realizing that I also had been craving some kind of vegetable. "Comadre Juana, you are an angel. I am so hungry I could eat one of those piglets out there—as long as it had wakatay sauce on it," pointing to the sow and her noisy piglets rooting around in the main courtyard of the colonial house.

"I wish you would eat them all and then maybe we could get a good night's sleep," complained Juana in her best Spanish.

"Eat them all," chimed Cholita in Quechua, grabbing at the imaginary piglets and stuffing them into her mouth.

Juana and Cholita shared their space every night with three sows and their offspring, two quackless ducks and their ducklings, and countless chickens

and guinea pigs. This menagerie lived in a separate yard enclosed by a falling-down fence that kept the animals neither in nor out. Mother and daughter slept in the cooking hut just beyond the fence. A rude gate opened into their hut and the sows and their piglets had the habit of intruding in the early morning hours to root around in the kitchen. Behind the hut percolated the pigsty and communal shitting yard.

"My God, eat and conquer. Can we possibly overpower Romulo by eating his largess?" I asked in English.

As I began to wolf down the chicken, I felt a kindred spirit with Cholita. Juana, who had the best view of the front portal, could see that Romulo was still engaged in animated conversation with one of his many compadres. She whispered, "He's still talking, comadrita Alicia. You can finish your plate calmly."

Only twenty years old, Juana's face and body seemed to be battling one another. Her face looked haggard and pinched but her body barely constrained the youthfulness that was trapped in her diminutive, square frame. Barely four and a half feet tall, a fierce energy seemed about to burst forth and stretch her frame to six feet. Her face and body were of different generations and every movement she made dramatized a battle between youth and old age.

I'm betting on her face, I thought to myself.

Juana nodded and said, "Si, no viene."

"No viene," repeated Cholita.

"Good, he's not coming," I said out loud. To myself I thought, *I think I'll go slightly mad if I stay in this house too long.*

I laid my fork and knife across the plate with the knife blade through the fork to signal that I was finished. Juana twisted her skirts into a knot, causing her gnarled mahogany knuckles to turn an angry white. For just an instant, defiance flashed across her face and her square jaw tightened. Her almond eyes narrowed, but then potential rebellion melted into passive defeat. She heaved a big sigh, lowered her eyes, and wiped her hands nervously on the outermost of her five skirts. And after polishing the table vigorously with her second skirt, she turned and started out of the room, saying, "Comadrita, I have to go back to my work. Mama Jesús is returning today. I'll catch the devil if my work isn't done."

Before leaving, Juana smoothed the folded plastic sheets used to cover the furniture. It was Sunday, the only day of the week that the dining room could be used—except for feast days, birthdays, and funerals. During the rest of the week it rested, entirely shrouded in plastic behind locked doors. Even the plastic carnations that perpetually presided over the chrome dining room set were covered, along with the plastic-covered dining room chairs and the plastic Jesus with the "eternal" light in his blood-red heart. The only piece of furniture never enclosed in this protective cocoon was the refrigerator, purchased one year before electricity arrived at the Rosetti compound. Although erratic surges of electricity enlivened the old hacienda structure only about three times a week, the huge Philco refrigerator stood guard over the dining room as silent testimony to progress. Juana ran her hand lovingly over the large square white body. Her gesture captured the sentiment of the entire household. Frequently asked to photograph family members crowded around the gleaming white box, I always waited to click the shutter until someone said: "Smile Sr. Pilco, we're having our picture taken."

During my furtive meal, a silent observer had been squatting on his heels just outside the dining room doorway, passively folding a couple of coca leaves around a small ball of lime made from quinua ash. He carefully put the ball of coca and lime into his cheek and rose to his feet. Gingerly tucking his vara, the wooden staff of office with its ornate silver head, under his arm, he entered the room and offered me a handful of the sacred coca leaves cupped in both his hands. As he extended his large callused hands to me, I noticed that the raw cracks in his thumbs and index fingers seemed to be healing. I accepted his gift with the prescribed Quechua phrase of gratitude: "Diospagarasunki Compadre Gregorio—May God repay you, compadre Gregorio." As I put a few leaves and a bit of lime into my cheek, following Don Gregorio Quispe Cabana's example, he turned to his sister, Juana, and said in flowery Quechua, "Here, little sister, join us. I offer you the most perfect leaves I have. Let us chew together and then I will read the leaves."

Juana looked exasperated as she retorted, "Carajo hermano, you know that I don't chew that stuff! What would people say if I went around with green teeth and lips? I'm not an Indio like you and your wife: I speak Spanish."

"Well," he replied, "if you will not accept my gift, then I will proceed with the reading of the leaves and tell you your future anyway. Comadre Alicia, I had a dream that told me to come to my sister and read her future."

With that, Gregorio, the divinator, the master dream interpreter, the bonesetter, the Alcalde varayoq, reached into his coca bag and took out a handful of coca leaves, a coin, and a small piece of very old, finely woven cloth. Carefully selecting coca quintu, perfect coca leaves that were not broken or blemished, he spread the leaves on the small square of cloth he had spread out on the floor of the dining room near the table and sprinkled cane alcohol over them, while praying his version of "Hail Mary" to Pachamama, the Earth Mother.

Once a year Gregorio led his community as they ushered water from the high sacred lakes and springs down through miles of irrigation canals to moisten Earth Mother's womb so that she may receive the seeds they plant. In his vigilant tending of her, Gregorio had become Earth Mother's familiar, her ever-constant companion. He looked like those dry clumps of sod before they receive the life-giving water from the mountains. And when he dies, Gregorio will be incorporated into Earth Mother's body. He will return to her womb, to rot and give sustenance to new generations.

On long journeys across the high, cold puna with Gregorio and his family, we slept in a huddle like puppies to keep warm. I often felt that the collective bodily warmth emitted by Gregorio, his wife Clotilda, and their children was the only thing that kept me alive in this high, inhospitable world. In the early mornings when we uncurled ourselves from our communal huddle, their bodies gave off steam and a sweet acrid smell that I had grown to regard as my private security blanket. I had come to associate their musty body odors with my survival. Their hands and feet were always warm and clammy while mine were always freezing. Gregorio and his family coined a nickname for me: chirimaki, "snow hands." On those long treks, Clotilda often took my hands in hers and rubbed them brusquely, blowing her warm breath on my cold fingers. It struck me as odd that such a tiny woman could give off so much heat, while my body, larger and better nourished than hers, often struggled to generate enough energy to put one foot in front of the other.

Gregorio continued his incantations with a slow, syncretic version of "Our Father" sung in Quechua and directed to the mountain deities. He began with a slow recitation, "Tayta Wamani Ra—a—zu—u—willka," naming the most powerful of the mountain gods, followed by the names of lesser mountains and ending with an enumeration of every foothill in the region. The prayer was a local geography lesson.

Gregorio asked the deities, "Who placed my sister Juana's clothing, strands of her hair, and fingernail clippings inside of a burial cave? Is that perhaps why she has come to live in this household? Is that how she came to bear Romulo's child?" With his right hand, Gregorio took a handful of the perfect, flawless coca leaves and let them fall slowly onto the cloth, softly singing a prayer that was in cadence with the wafting leaves as they drifted down to Juana's destiny. He repeated the operation six times. He was reading Juana's past and future simultaneously.

One leaf broke in its fall. Gregorio looked up worriedly and exclaimed, "Little sister! Look, the leaves say that you are in danger in this house! Someone has hidden something of yours near the ancestors. You're going to suffer at the hands of those around you. You must return to Pumapunku immediately and visit the cave that is above the village to find what is yours. If you do not, the ancient ones will make you sick and you could even die."

"Gregorio, you're trying to scare me. I don't believe that stuff. You just want me to come home. Besides, it's Sunday and you cannot read the leaves on God's day."

"Yes, I know that I should read the leaves only on Tuesday or Friday, but even Tayta Dios says you should not be here. I want you and Cholita to return with me. Not only do the leaves foretell a dark future for you, I have been having dreams about you. You are in grave danger. Come and live with your family. We will take care of you. We will educate Cholita; I swear we will or may Earth Mother and the Mountain Gods punish me!"

"That's a lie, Gregorio!" Juana jumped to her feet and began to pace in front of me. "Comadre Alicia, when I was sent to school it was too late for me. Our family didn't want to provide education for any of their daughters—only for sons. Besides, the schools in Pumapunku are lousy. Look at what happened to me."

"Quiet, Juanita, for the sake of our mother and father!" admonished Gregorio.

"I begged our parents to send me to the convent of Santa Teresa here in Ayacucho. I remember so well—we came into Ayacucho when I was nine and I was so excited about learning to read and write. I wanted to wear the long, clean, white dress of the sisters. Mama brought five sacks of potatoes and presented them to the convent sisters, but the mother superior said that it was not nearly enough to pay the dowry. So we returned to Pumapunku and I learned to sew baby clothes to sell in village markets."

The word "sew" triggered her hands into activity and she reached into the fold of her top skirt and took out her spindle whorl and bundle of yarn and let the whorl drop. Giving the whorl a rapid spin with both hands, Juana punctuated her tale with its rhythmic spin and drop. "I traveled"; spinning, the thread formed. "Every day of the week"; the whorl dropped and the thread elongated. "To a different market"; she wound the thread back and forth between the thumb and little finger of her left hand rapidly. "Traveling in trucks"; another vigorous spin. "Sleeping in the cold"; the thread stretched out long and fine. "Fighting off abusive men"; and with that statement she furiously wound the thread between her thumb and little finger again.

"Then take a job sewing here in Ayacucho. Leave this house! You fled abusive men to come to live with El Capitán!" Gregorio fell to his knees and pleaded with his sister.

"I never got enough money together sewing to pay the church dowry. How could I support Cholita and myself? Right now I live in the shadow of Santa Teresa in this shithouse; I know that I'll never enter the convent. I'll never wear the dress of the sisters. But I swear to you my dear elder brother, I will never return to Pumapunku! Never! To the devil with everything in that damned place. May it disappear from the face of the earth! Carajo!" With these last words, she gave the whorl a vigorous spin. It bounced up and down like a wobbly top. The yarn was born with uneven lumps and bumps, not the perfectly uniform thread she usually produced. She had to stop and undo several feet of the double-ply thread and start over. She leaned against the doorjamb as if exhausted. Yes, her face was winning. The strength was leaving her tiny body.

"Juana! May Father God, Earth Mother, and the Mountain Gods forgive you! Don't say things like that or you will be struck dead." Gregorio hastily crossed himself and kissed the cross on his staff. As he reached for the bottle in his bundle to pour a bit of the strong cane alcohol onto the ground, he silently offered a brief prayer to Earth Mother, repeating it three times and then repeating the "Our Father," but this time from the beginning to the end in a small breathless voice as if he were in a great hurry. Finally, he named all of the powerful mountains and begged their forgiveness.

Nothing like covering all of your religious bases, I thought to myself. Gregorio seemed to nod in agreement.

As Gregorio finished his prayers, he took a ball of carefully wrapped yarn from his pocket. It was the elaborate, multicolored braid I had tried to produce but had abandoned. As he began to work, he said, "Comadre, let's practice Spanish." He pointed to a chair and said, "silla." I pointed to the table. "Misa," he responded, which means mass and not table.

I enunciated carefully, "M e e sa, not misa."

Gregorio repeated, "Misa," Then slowly, "M i e sa . Carajo, comadre, if I can learn Spanish you can learn this," his fingers working deftly at the jumble of threads.

"No, I can't," I laughed.

I gave Gregorio Spanish lessons three times a week in exchange for all the things he taught me. He desperately wanted to know how to read and write, but his Spanish was so rudimentary that our lessons were slow and difficult. At first he wrote all the words as one long string, making breaks only where he heard a pause in the string of sounds. A logical approach for anyone learning to write, but also the way a phrase in Quechua is built. A phrase can be one string of sounds with twenty syllables, with the root at the beginning and numerous suffixes behind. So it took some clever teaching on my part to get him to think of the Spanish words as smaller units. Our agreed-upon goal was for him to be able to read the historical and legal documents that were in his care as a village elder.

Ironically, Juana's position in the Rosetti household had provided her with the means to learn to read a newspaper. I had seen her sitting near her cooking pots laboriously forming the Spanish words syllable by syllable as she read out loud to herself. Her desire for an education was so great that at the age of fourteen she finally convinced her parents to let her enroll in first grade. Romulo had just been given the job of director of the schools and he moved into Pumapunku, leaving his wife, Beatriz, who had not born him a child, behind in his mother's house in Ayacucho. Juana told me that she had gone to school for no more than six months when Romulo raped her after a drunken fiesta with a bunch of his chums from the city. She didn't quit school nor did she tell her parents, but his sexual demands were the price for what little education she received. When she got pregnant with Cholita about a year later, Romulo brought her to Ayacucho and promised to educate his unborn illegitimate child. Juana was installed as the family's cook, and everyone, especially Beatriz, ignored the child's resemblance to Romulo. Juana had been his servant for five years, enduring the derisive remarks of the household while clinging to the hope that he would keep his promise to send Cholita to school. She told me that the worst of it was not when he loaned her to his friends for their drunken pleasure, but rather when she was used to initiate their sons into the mysteries of sex. Such initiations generally occurred on Sunday mornings while the "decent" women of the family attended Mass. Today was Sunday and Juana nervously eyed the doorway where Romulo continued his animated conversation.

As she stepped across the threshold, she patted my arm and said, "Thank God you are here today, comadre Alicia."

CHAPTER 2

THE SEARCH BEGINS

I stepped off the plane into the waves of heat rising up from the runway. I knew I looked like a grandmother taking a Christmas holiday. My short, gray hair was in disarray and I was dressed for northern climes, not the tropical heat here. I didn't have a free hand to smooth my hair or arrange my clothing; I was struggling with my shoulder bag, camera case and computer. The only clue to my identity was the plastic label on my shoulder bag that read Dr. Alice Woodsley. In the United States, I used the title only in my gynecologist's office, but in Latin America I used Doctora during transactions with all bureaucratic offices. In both situations the title seemed to speed up the business at hand considerably.

The sleepless nights spent in preparation for departure were reflected in my face and body; I knew that I looked older than my sixty-two years. In the tropical heat, my plum-colored sweatsuit clung to my small frame and I felt steam rising from my body. Following the holiday travelers into the hot and humid airport, I went directly to the ladies' room and kicked off my Avia aerobic shoes fitted with orthopedic inserts. Strains of WEL—COME TO JA—MAI—CA. . . . YOUR IS—LAND HOME . . . sung by bored young women waving their skirts at arriving passengers drifted into the ladies' room. Surrounded by others busily transforming themselves for their tropical holiday, I began my own transformation by pulling off heavy woolen socks and wiggling my arthritic toes. The toes took on grotesque proportions as steam rose from my newly liberated feet. I looked in dismay at a metamorphosis of my own feet swimming in vibrant waves and hoped that what I saw was not permanent. My feet took on the form of two giant squids that quickly became transformed into two lakes with tributaries where my toes should have been.

God, I'm hallucinating! No, I'm not. I'm really turning into some kind of jellyfish creature. I've got to head for the mountains; it's too hot here. With a great deal of apprehension, I tugged my top over my head and let it fall on the floor, wondering whether the rest of me would ooze into those tributaries at the end of my legs and eventually flow into the Caribbean. Finally, off came the light aqua silk long underwear that clung to my body like an extra layer of skin. I thought of lazy green lizards sitting on hot rocks languidly shedding layers of skin. Don't lizards eat the skin they shed? No, only toads do that. A toad starts sucking at its own skin as it splits down the backbone and then comes off like a glove. Sloo—oop, the skin disappears into the toad's mouth, and its outside becomes its inside. Strange, wonderful. I remember seeing Mama Jesús's toads doing that. But most of Mama Jesús's toads died in the nightly sacrifice. The ones that survived their ordeal of "eating" her headache ate their own skin. I saw it with my own eyes. Mama Jesús. I'll see her soon. I wonder what she can tell me. Much of it I already know, right? Poor woman, Rodrigo is her only surviving son and since he is a maricón, he will never give her grandchildren. So she is grandmother to hordes of bastards throughout the department of Ayacucho by my favorite compadre, Romulo, but she has no one to stay by her side and care for her in her old age. How old is she now?

Let's see, when Cholita was five in 1975, Mama Jesús was in her forties. So now in December of 2005, she has to be in her seventies: I imagine that she's still selling in the markets and traveling in her truck. I heard that she has hired a driver and taken in a young orphan girl from Pumapunku to teach her the trade. After Romulo was killed by Sendero Luminoso, Shining Path, his wife Beatriz moved out of Mama Jesús's house. A month later, when Ramón was killed in a truck accident, Ramón's wife and children also left the Rosetti house. Mama Jesús was alone with her gay son, Rodrigo.

God, I'm hot! I've got to get out of these clothes.

I reached into my travel bag and took out a cotton skirt, blouse, and sandals; I patted my arms and legs with a damp paper towel and slipped into the loose cotton clothes. As I eased my feet into the rubber-soled walking sandals and glanced into the mirror, I realized that my transformation was almost complete.

Thank God we don't have to eat all of the diverse skins we wear. I wear so many: my professor skin, my fieldworker skin, my "I'm a feminist anthropologist" skin, and my activist skin. I'd be so stuffed by now that I'd have to go on an identity diet.

The flight from New York City to Montego Bay on Air Jamaica had resembled a Caribbean bus trip. People filled every possible space with Christmas gifts. Portable radios of every size and description, decorated with glitter that spelled out the names of reggae groups along with phrases from their songs, were stuffed next to giant boxes of laundry detergent in the overhead compartments and under the seats. During the flight, I had watched with fascination while two tall, slim, beautiful, blue-black women applied tiny decals of tropical flowers to their extremely long, painted fingernails. One of them was over six feet tall and appeared wonderfully androgynous. Centuries ago a mythical artist had chiseled the model for her from stone, and time had rubbed just the right amount of roundness into a few places. But somehow the angular edges of the chisel's gouge had remained: her body was all angles. Her flamboyant dress of bright, flowing sheers was set off by an impressive coiffure of elaborate cornrows made up of tiny braids woven together like an exquisite African textile draped over her high brow. The lower half of the braids were bleached a bronze color and looked like a two-toned silky cloth framing her finely cut features.

On the plane, I had felt pale, washed out, as if I were a bone that had been left out in the sun to bleach white. Almost everyone else on the plane was brown, bronze, dusty black, charcoal black, blue-black, or a kind of rosy bronze. In contrast I was fish-belly white, as one of my black friends described me. Compared to my traveling companions, I had almost a sickly pallor: pale blue eyes, gray short hair and translucent pale skin that never tanned. The rest of the travelers seemed to glow with a dusky zest for life, while my coloring emitted a message that said my inner spirit must have lost its enthusiasm. I felt one step away from becoming a ghost.

Why was I making this trip? What'll I find? I'm a woman obsessed. Do I really want to know the answers to the questions I'm asking? This venture is crazy. My past trips over the last ten years were fruitless and I'm sure I'll hit a brick wall again.

As I stuffed the purple peelings, the silk inner skins, and the space shoes into my travel bag, I said out loud, "No, I'll find Cholita this time."

Several women looked at me and smiled.

The mixture of heavy perfumes, powders, hair sprays, and warm bodies assailed my nostrils and made me feel momentarily dizzy. The pungent odors mixed with the excited chatter of the Jamaican women to give an infectious holiday air. Waiting to use the john, I noticed that the two tall women with the tropical fingernails were next to me in line. I wondered what they did for a living. Dancers, hairdressers, performance artists, or perhaps secretaries or sales clerks? As for me, most people would not even notice me. In the last few years I had become more and more invisible.

At sixty-two, I was thinking about my approaching retirement from my position as full professor of anthropology at American University in the nation's capital. In my early forties I wore a T-shirt that said "Gee, I can't believe that I forgot to have children." After a brief flirtation with the idea of having a child, I decided that an academic career and single motherhood was a very difficult combination to manage. I had watched women colleagues struggling with doing it all—career, marriage, motherhood. Too often their children got shortchanged. I couldn't even manage marriage and a career. I married a mathematics student in graduate school at Harvard; we divorced after my first year of fieldwork for the PhD. My husband had visited me in the field but could not abide what he called the abominable primitive conditions—sharing a cold adobe house with a native family, dirt floor, no plumbing, no running water, no electricity. Our lives simply took separate paths. We remained friends for a couple of years but gradually stopped exchanging Christmas cards. He remarried another mathematician and had three children. I had not remarried, but rather had experimented with a few live-in relationships. Now, at my age, I loved the luxury of living alone with no one in my space that complained, "You're off to Peru again? How long will you be gone this time?"

Adjusting my clothes in the stall of the bathroom in the airport, I read with amusement the lyrical sonnets scrawled by several tourist-bards extolling the size and mobility of Jamaican cocks. Or perhaps airport cleaners had been paid to scrawl the graffiti. By the time I left the stall, I was smiling broadly and laughing to myself. As I splashed cold water on my face and combed my hair, a woman asked:

"First time you come to our island?"

"No, I travel through here a lot."

"People always has a good time and they always comes back."

"I'm sure that they do!" I laughed as I stepped out into the lobby of the airport. I made a mental note to check the additions to the graffiti on my return in six months.

Settling down to wait for Air Peru Flight 601 to Lima, I noticed that the skin tones of those waiting for the flight had changed to golden browns and that the passengers were shorter and stockier than those on the previous flight. A group of Latinos who had arrived on the flight from Miami were sipping their complimentary rum punches and chatting in Spanish. The Air Jamaica Air Peru service to Lima was run something like a Peruvian bus line; passengers had to wait until the connecting flights arrived before the plane left Montego Bay for Lima.

I had developed the habit of flying through Jamaica during the years that Alán García was president of Peru, and I had continued on that route because I loved even a brief glimpse of Caribbean vitality. During García's presidency, the flight agreement between the United States and Peru had been suspended because García would pay only 10 percent of the debt owed to the United States.

The waiting lounge continued to fill up with passengers from Miami. A familiar sensation spread over my body. As I sat, I had the feeling of growing taller and taller as the room filled up with Peruvians returning to their country for the Christmas holidays. Everything around me was changing rapidly: language, tones of skin, shapes of faces. The faces of the returning Peruvians combined the features of their Indian ancestors with those of the Spanish conquerors: high cheekbones, almond-shaped eyes, and straight black hair. Some had broad faces and noses like those depicted on Mochica pottery. They looked like Carlos. *It'll be good to see him again. How many years does this make? My annual pilgrimage to find Cholita? Ten?*

Only a few of the Spanish-speaking travelers were tall and European-looking. Were these "European types" the remnants of the oligarchs who still own more than half of the country's wealth even after the land reforms? I strained to listen to the accents of three men conversing nearby. Yes, their accent was Peruvian and not Argentinean, Ecuadorian, or Colombian. Their clothes were well-cut—tailored, not ready-made. Diplomats? Businessmen? Members of the government? Notables returning from exile? Only one young man among those waiting in the departure lounge had the classic "Inca profile" with the characteristic hook nose that had become a tourist icon. I closed my eyes and pictured him in native dress playing a reed flute with Machu Picchu and a llama in the background. Below the scene in bold print was the invitation:

Fly Air Peru to Cuzco
The ancient capital of the Inca Empire
And receive one internal flight in the country free

He's probably from the southern Andes, either from Ayacucho, Cuzco, or Puno. I'll speak Quechua to him at some point and ask where he's from. I rolled the Quechua phrases of greeting around in my mouth and they tasted musty from long disuse.

Noticing several gringos on this flight, I thought we're no longer in el Manchay Tiempo, the time of fear. It's true, after the terrorism of the 1980s and early '90s many foreigners still feared traveling to Peru, but as I looked around, I concluded that tourism was picking up. There were about twenty tourists in the waiting area. Yes, conditions have improved since Abimael Guzmán was arrested, convicted, and given a life sentence in September of 1992. But people say he is going to be tried again. What repercussions will that have? And the truth commission's list of culprits for human rights abuses had been given to the judiciary. Could there be trials? Elections were coming up in June: Peru was at an important crossroads.

Reaching into my travel bag, I took out my thick manila file folder and began to thumb through notes, charts, and photocopies of articles from Peruvian newspapers and journals from 1980 to the present. I looked for the articles detailing Guzmán's arrest in September of 1992 and pulled out two. One, a front-page article from a Lima daily, featured a large photo of Guzmán wearing a black-and-white striped "prison suit" with the number 1609 on his chest. The suit was fabricated for television audiences to view Guzmán displayed in an iron cage for hours every day for weeks after his capture. He had been located in Lima while attending a party, remarkable because he had not been spotted since 1981. The other article I pulled from my file, my constant companion, my fetish, was a copy of the *Revolutionary Worker* dated April 28, 2002. It featured the same photo of Guzmán but diminished in size and placed in an upper corner. The caption read:

> As of April 21, 2002 Presidente Gonzalo
> Has been held in isolation for
> 9 years
> 171 Days

Below the large caption, the article declared that Guzmán was being held under brutal conditions in an underground dungeon constructed on a tiny island off the coast of Lima for one prisoner—Presidente Gonzalo. The article went on to say that President Fujimori and his powerful head of security, V. Montesinos, have inflicted psychological torture, isolation, and denial of medical attention to the father of Sendero Luminoso. The article also claimed that Fujimori changed the constitution to legalize the death penalty so that it can be used against Presidente Gonzalo and other revolutionary prisoners. It ended with a plea in bold:

> Support the People's War in Peru!
> Support the Communist Party of Peru!

Defend the Life of Presidente Gonzalo,
Fight to Break the Isolation!

Actually, Guzmán was being held in a prison inside the navy garrison in Lima and there is no death penalty in Peru. He enjoyed relative luxury with his sole companion in the special prison—V. Montesinos. What an irony! Montesinos had built the prison. It's rumored that Guzmán and Montesinos play chess together daily. It's also rumored that Montesinos pulled strings so that Presidente Gonzalo (Guzmán) could arrange a meeting with his high command jailed in Puno.

I had started collecting the articles in May of 1980 when Sendero Luminoso had ignited "the Shining Path of Revolution" by burning the ballots for the impending national election in the village of Chuschi, a neighbor to the community of Pumapunku (the door of the puma), where I have worked for years. Sendero Luminoso or Shining Path, the communist party of Peru, obviously hoped that the puma door would open onto a world of utopian possibilities. I opened the thick manila file folder to return the articles and thumbed through several newspaper articles. Stopping, I scanned the report from the Peruvian Truth and Reconciliation Commission.

On the 28th of August, 2003, the Truth and Reconciliation Commission submitted its six-thousand-page final report to President Toledo: Nine volumes with 171 conclusions culminating two years during which the testimonies of 17,000 individuals in 530 villages were tape-recorded and summarized. As he gave the report to Toledo, Salomon Lerner, the president of the commission, declared, "Today is Peru's moment to confront a time of national shame. This report exposes a double scandal—the killings, disappearances and torture on a huge scale, and the indolence, ineptitude and indifference by those able to intervene in this human catastrophe and who did not." The headlines screamed: An estimated 69,280 deaths occurred between 1980 and 2000.

- Statistics put the death toll at 61,700 and 77,552. Thirty-two thousand victims are named and their cases detailed.
- Fifty-four percent of all deaths were caused by Shining Path. Thirty percent were caused by the armed forces.
- Two percent were caused by Tupac Amaru.
- The remaining (14 percent) were caused by government-backed peasant militia (*rondas campesinas*).
- Eighty-five percent of the deaths occurred in the department of Ayacucho and four out of every five victims were native speakers of Quechua.

- Four thousand mass graves have been recorded and the commission recommends exhumations.

Strange metaphor—disappeared. We'll probably never know how many have been made to disappear by the military, even with the Truth and Reconciliation Commission having completed its report estimating the death toll at almost 70,000 and the internally displaced at 600,000. But disappeared? Snatched from their beds at night by hooded military? Or arrested and dropped from a helicopter over the Andes?

A survivor of one such misadventure, an agronomist, recounted his story to me in 1986. He had been picked up by a helicopter as he was walking across the high puna, the plateau of grassland south of the city of Ayacucho on his way to a remote community to inoculate cattle. The helicopter landed; two soldiers jumped out and took him prisoner. Shaking like a leaf, he listened as the air force pilot and co-pilot discussed where to drop the terruco, the military's slang term for terrorist, over the mountain terrain. This practice was fairly common in the early years of the war. As the helicopter soared over the mountains, the agronomist began to cry and plead in Quechua. Lucky for him, an army private who spoke Quechua began to interrogate the agronomist. The private interceded on the poor man's behalf with the pilot and co-pilot, pleading, "Please, sirs, this man is an agronomist with a wife and eight children to support. He's not a terrorist. He's just a simple man doing his job. Here are his papers. He works for World Neighbors."

"What," exclaimed the pilot. "That can't be true! He is too short to have eight children!"

The agronomist responded in his loudest, most authoritative voice: "Height has nothing to do with it sir!" They landed and released him. Their laughter echoed behind him as he ran across the high, treeless puna. Three days later he was captured by Shining Path and held for a week in a herder's hut. The agronomist recounted how his captors bombarded him with lectures: "Mao says . . . , President Gonzalo says . . ." They placed a large poster on a low stool outside the hut and lit a candle. The poster showed Guzmán dressed in a suit, white shirt with the neck open and no tie. His dark hair was neatly combed back from his square, clean-shaven face; his horn-rimmed glasses framed his serious stare as he displayed to the viewer a book bound in red with the inscription: DEVELOP THE POPULAR WAR SERVING THE WORLD REVOLUTION. A red flag with a black hammer and sickle framed Guzmán's figure. Presidente Gonzalo Thought—Mao Thought—day and night. The lectures, recalled the agronomist, were more like religious chants that the Senderistas sang out in chorus over and over: "We give our full and unconditional submission to the greatest living Marxist-Leninist-Maoist on earth: our beloved and respected President Gonzalo, chief and guide of the Peruvian revolution and the world proletarian revolution, teacher of Communists and party unifier. We give full, unconditional submission to the scientific ideology, the infallible ideology that illuminates our path and arms our minds. We give our submission to the world proletarian revolution. We give our full and unconditional submission to the quota. We will cross the river of blood to victory."

"The quota?" I had asked. "The river of blood?"

The agronomist explained that each Senderista had to pledge to give his or her life and blood for the revolution. No compromises, no giving in. Destroy in order to create the new democracy of Peru. That's what they told him. In the end, he never knew why they let him go. Perhaps because all he kept chanting back to them was "I want to go home to my wife and children! I want to go home to my wife and children! I want to go home!"

The agronomist had been afraid to tell the Senderistas that he belonged to an evangelical church because he knew about the massacres of his brethren in the Apurimac Valley. He prayed that they didn't know that World Neighbors, his employer, was a Protestant nongovernmental organization with headquarters in the United States. They examined his ID card over and over, saying "hm—m—Vecinos Mundiales? World Neighbors? Who are they?"

When he was released, he raced to Lima with his wife and children and quit his job. Like so many other refugees, they lived in Lima from hand to mouth for several years. Shortly thereafter, World Neighbors withdrew from the Peruvian highlands altogether.

As the number of deaths and disappearances climbed in the mid-1980s, people demanded concrete evidence. Therefore Amnesty International and other human rights organizations published concrete lists of names. A large bureaucracy sprang up in Peru to document the violent events of the undeclared war. International agencies were on the alert. A computer system was set up in Peru with international funding to record violent confrontations between the guerrillas and government forces. Categories were created to tally the deaths of guerrillas, civilians, military personnel, elected officials, appointed officials, labor leaders, teachers, lawyers, peasant leaders, political opposition leaders, women, men, children.

Every month the computers churned out lists and categories of "actions" and deaths. The tallies showed that most of the fatalities were Quechua-speaking peasants who were not participating directly in the war. One impassioned Peruvian writer declared, "Our people are caught under the grindstone of the political process. They are the husks and chaff on the mill floor of history."

One human-rights document listed eighty-five names of "disappeared" persons from the small village of Pumapunku, with a population of two thousand, that I had studied: Names like Ccallocunto, Quispe, Carhuapoma, Tucnu, Vilca, Huamani, Achalma, Pacotaype, Machaca. Names that appeared on my kinship charts. Ancient names. Quechua names as common as Smith and Jones.

An official report from a member of the Peruvian Congressional Human Rights Commission named the orphans from the region; another report listed the villages where only children and the aged remained. Many of the villages in the document had Quechua names like Pumapunku—Quispiqocha, Canchacancha, Pomabamba, Vilcashuaman. Another listed villages totally destroyed and abandoned.

Lists, sworn documents, testimonies, investigations, analyses, often compiled at considerable risk to the authors.

In order to concretize the facts in my own mind, I gathered every piece of evidence that I could find. I gave an academic paper in 1985 at the American Anthropological Association in a session designed to discuss the comparisons of political violence in Peru with political violence in Guatemala. The meeting took place in the grand ballroom under the dimmed chandeliers of the Washington D. C. Hilton Hotel on Connecticut Avenue.

I outlined the concrete events and gave concrete statistics. I even showed slides "of where it all began." I dutifully documented a concrete case. One hundred fifty people made a concrete noise: they applauded. I was dumbfounded—applause? On the verge of tears, I barely survived the questions from the floor. As the session ended, many people stopped me to congratulate me on my presentation. This was all wrong. Congratulations? *We should be organizing to do something. But what?* I joined the postsession group at the bar and one close friend and colleague asked, "How do you know concretely that people in your village are dead? You haven't even been able to get back in there."

Ah! The impeccability of empiricism. Anthropological authority—you must see it to believe it! Someone else said, "You have to decide whether you have primitive violence, state violence, or religious violence."

He must be a goddamned visiting political scientist; we anthropologists did away with the concept of primitive violence ages ago.

An archaeologist asked, "How do you feel about the cultural remnants of the Inca Empire being destroyed? There is so much we do not know yet."

"Jesus Cristo!" I answered. "You would think that we were discussing an ancient textile from a mummy bundle that has been accidentally torn before it has been analyzed. What if we convince ourselves that we have analyzed all of the essential parts of ancient Andean culture? What would you say then? Your question summarizes the major problem with cultural evolution: You don't give a shit about humanity!"

I was getting drunk. I stood up and slurred, "You basars—urr—so—o—o full o academic shi—i—t !"

I made it to my room before losing what little composure I had left.

• • •

The flight attendant's voice announcing that we would board in twenty minutes broke my reverie. Before putting the articles back into my worn leather portfolio, I paused and reread for the hundredth time one article dated February 18, 1985. It was dog-eared and the smeared headlines read:

Former Director of Schools Is Executed by Shining Path Guerrillas

In the small, remote village of Pumapunku in the Department of Ayacucho, Province of Cangallo, three women Shining Path guerrillas held a summary trial and shot Romulo Rosetti Martinez, the former district director of schools, for being abusive to students and for stealing school funds. Two other village officials were tried and threatened but they were allowed to flee the community. The two community officials who escaped with their lives reported the incident to the officer in charge of the temporary military garrison in Cangallo, the province capital. They reported that after shooting Romulo Rosetti M., one of the women embraced one of the other assassins and shouted, "Carajo, Cholita, at last we've finally killed the old bastard."

I kept staring at the newspaper and translated over and over. *Carajo, Cholita, at last we've finally killed the old bastard. At Last. Killed. Killed. The old bastard, at last. Damn, did she kill him? She certainly hated him enough. And with good reason. But shoot him in the plaza like that? God, I wonder.*

A soft Jamaican voice with a lilting Caribbean accent interrupted my internal dialogue to announce that Air Peru Flight 601 was boarding for departure from gate three. I closed the manila folder and put it back into the flight bag with the plastic identity tag.

I stood up and smoothed my skirt and my hair and absent-mindedly followed the holiday travelers to the gate. Settling into my seat on the aisle, I was pleased to see that the young man with the Inca poster profile was seated in the window seat. I smiled and nodded a silent greeting; no need to rush. We have several hours together. Accommodating my carry-on belongings and sinking into my seat with a sigh, I buckled my seat belt and closed my eyes.

An hour later, I opened my eyes and turned to Señor Poster Profile, and in Quechua gave the traditional greeting, told him my name, and asked his: "Imanaylla kachkanki taytalla? Noqaqpa sutiy Alicia. Imata sutiki?"

The greeting in Quechua no longer felt musty in my mouth; rather the words tasted good, like my favorite potato dish.

The young man returned the salutation and, speaking Quechua, answered my question: "My name is Felix Roncalla Nuñez and I'm from the department of Ayacucho, from a small town called Puquio in the Province of Lucanas. The town of Jose Maria Arguedas's novels *Deep Rivers* and *Yawar Fiesta*. Do you know his work? He is considered a national treasure."

"He is my favorite Peruvian novelist," I said, smiling and extending my hand. Felix's handshake was firm and warm. I explained that I greatly admired the novels of Arguedas because he tells us more about Andean culture than any of our anthropological studies.

I added, "I know the area well. I have lived and worked in the next province of Cangallo in the River Pampas."

"My family lives near the River Pachachaca that Arguedas describes in *Deep Rivers*," Felix said. He went on to describe where his village was located. His eyes became wistful and moist as he talked. His voice cracked and he stopped and looked at his hands, which were clinched into fists.

"Pachachaca means bridge over the world, doesn't it?" I inquired softly. "You have taken that bridge to reach another world, haven't you?

"Yes, indeed I have," responded Felix as he looked out the window.

"My favorite work of Arguedas is *The Pongo's Dream*. Do you know it?" I asked.

"Oh, yes, we studied it in school. I had to learn it because we gave it as a play in secondary school. I played the pongo and his words are engraved in my memory."

Switching to Spanish, I commented, "If I recall the story correctly, the

great lord of the manor made the poor servant, the pongo, run through the halls of the hacienda on all fours like a dog, fetching things in his mouth to bring to his master."

"True," responded Felix. "But then one day the pongo tells his master that he had had a dream that they both had died. The lord of the manor demands to know the details of the dream and the pongo, dressed in rags, bows his head and relates his dream."

Taking on the whimpering, halting voice of the pongo, Felix continued the story: "Since we were dead men, my lord, the two of us were standing naked before our dear father, St. Francis, both of us, next to each other. St. Francis looked at us closely with those eyes that reach and measure who knows what lengths. He examined you and me, judging, I believe, each of our hearts, the kind of persons we were . . . the kind of persons we are. You confronted that gaze as the rich and powerful man you are, my father."

In the deep voice of St. Francis, Felix boomed, "May the most beautiful of the angels come forth. May a lesser angel of equal beauty accompany the Supreme One. May the lesser angel bring a golden cup filled with the most delicate and translucent honey."

Now in the voice of the humble pongo: "My owner, as soon as our great father, St. Francis, gave his order, an angel appeared, shimmering as tall as the sun. He walked very slowly until he stood before our father. A smaller angel, beautiful, glowing like a gentle flower, marched behind the supreme angel. He was holding in his hands a golden cup."

I nodded excitedly and motioned for Felix to continue. He again assumed the voice of St. Francis and said in a deep commanding voice, "Supreme angel, cover this gentleman with the honey that is in the golden cup. Let your hands be feathers upon touching this man's body."

Switching to the whimpering voice of the pongo, Felix continued: "The lofty angel lifted the honey with his hands and glossed your whole body with it, from your head down to your toenails. And you swelled with pride. In the splendor of the heavens, your body shone as if made of transparent gold."

"Now we get to the good part!" I excitedly exclaimed, laughing. "What does St. Francis command next?"

Felix lowered his voice to the register of the voice of St. Francis and intoned loudly, "From all the angels in heaven, may the very least, the most ordinary come forth. May that angel bring a gasoline can filled with human excrement."

"Yes, yes," I squealed, clapping my hands as if I were three years old listening to my favorite bedtime story. Several of the other Spanish speakers had joined in listening to the story and they nodded approval.

Felix, as the pongo, continued: "A worthless, old angel with scaly feet, too weak to keep his wings in place, appears, carrying a large can."

Now in the authoritative voice of St. Francis, Felix boomed again, "Smear the body of this little man with the excrement from that can you brought. Smear his whole body, cover it all the best you can. Hurry up!"

Felix, as the humble pongo, lowered his head and whispered, "So the old angel took the excrement with his coarse hands and smeared my body unevenly, sloppily, just like you would smear mud on the walls of an ordinary adobe house. And in the midst of the heavenly light, I stood and was filled with shame."

"Just as it should be!" I responded, taking the part of the great lord and folding my arms across my chest as if to signal the end of the story.

Felix, as the pongo whimpered, "But, my lord, St. Francis, took another look at us. First at you, then at me. With those eyes that reach across the heavens, I don't know to what depths, joining night and day, memory and oblivion. Then St. Francis spoke."

Felix paused and looked around at his audience, and in the voice of St. Francis authoritatively proclaimed, "Whatever the angels had to do with you is done. Now, lick each other's bodies slowly, for all eternity."

Everyone roared with laughter. Even the Peruvian stewardesses laughed and clapped.

"I love that story! It captures the Andean sense of sweet revenge," I laughed. "Quechua speakers are the best storytellers in the world. They always embody and enact the various characters in stories with such delicious accuracy."

"Yes," responded Felix, "and I've never forgotten those lines that I learned so many years ago."

Our conversation shifted back and forth from Quechua to Spanish and did not slip into English until I asked Felix where he lived in the United States. He answered in almost flawless English, without the characteristic breathlessness of Spanish speakers.

"I live in Paterson, New Jersey. There's a lot of Peruvians. We even have a club for Serranos from Ayacucho, called Club Huamanga."

He went on to say that he had lived in the States for almost fifteen years and that he worked as a waiter, making enough money to send a little home each

month and be able to return to Peru every couple of years. When I asked how he had arrived in the United States, he explained that he had flown directly to Canada, to Montreal. But he was stopped at the border and was deported right on the spot and flown back to Lima. His family teased him, saying he just wanted a free vacation to Canada. He saved money for two more years and traveled overland to Mexico. It took three months to get to Mexico City. He paid some guys five hundred dollars to get him across the border into Los Angeles, where he spent almost a year living in the house of Ayacuchanos, a man from Lucanas who knew his father. Finally, he made his way to Paterson, New Jersey, where he has a cousin, a wawqey—that's what brothers and first cousins are called. He married a Huamangina, a girl from the city of Ayacucho that he met in Paterson at the club, and they have two children. He smiled and declared emphatically that they didn't want any more.

"You mean you don't want the traditional twelve apostles?" I inquired.

"My God, no, two children are enough if you want to educate them. We took our kids back to Ayacucho and to Puquio last year. They loved it but they were saddened by the poverty."

I asked why he was returning to Peru, and he recounted that he had a sad obligation to attend to because he had to visit his sister who was sick. She was arrested by the navy in 1984 and taken to the stadium of Huanta. She's in Larco Herrera, the state mental hospital.

I felt a chill run up my spine. The stadium of Huanta was converted into a torture center during that time. I whispered, "What happened to her?"

"She was almost killed. Do you believe that her mother-in-law accused her of being a Senderista? Actually her mother-in-law was trying to help my sister's husband, Faustino, that no-account bum, sneak off with another woman. So she told a lie to the navy's paid informer and got my sister arrested—hoping she could get her 'disappeared'! What's worse, her mother-in-law took María's two small children and Faustino and fled to the jungle. If I ever get my hands on him I'll do the same things to him that the navy did to my sister! I swear I will!"

We both remained silent for a time, but then Felix took a deep breath and recounted that his sister was in the hospital again, deeply depressed and tormented by nightmares of her children being tortured. He planned on seeing his sister in the hospital and then traveling to Ayacucho to see if he could locate his sister's children.

As we gathered our belongings, I reached for his hand and had to choke back tears. We exchanged phone numbers before deplaning and heading for

MEMORIES OF LIMA

I gathered my bags, went directly to the taxi counter, and gave the address of Carlos, my long-time friend and former lover. As I settled into the back of the taxi, I was so engrossed in thinking about the people I planned to see in Lima that I hardly spoke to the driver. Usually, I engaged taxi drivers in avid conversation because they were willing to share their observations on current politics. The first image to come to my mind was not Carlos, but Francisco. Not Francisco in his sixties, but the young, impulsive Harvard student I had known decades ago. He was the progeny of a union between two of Peru's remaining aristocratic families. His father had owned one of the largest haciendas in Puno—about the size of Rhode Island—and his mother had inherited wealth from the exploitation of silver mines. She shopped only in New York and Paris and refused to set foot in that "savage world of Indians" that was the other half of her husband's life. They were both beautiful people of Lima society: she was tall, willowy and blond; he was a modern taller version of a Spanish conquistador, dark and bearded, intensely black eyes and chiseled features. They gave their only son all the advantages they could afford: private, or rather public, school in England, Oxford, and finally graduate school at Harvard.

I pictured Francisco as six feet three inches tall, with curly black hair, piercing black eyes, square jaw, and firm mouth. His lean, muscular physique made him look like a model for a comic book version of a Latin Lover—a role he accepted at Harvard with gusto.

I had met him in 1969 during my last year at Harvard at a presentation I gave on the Peruvian agrarian reform that had been enacted that year. My interpretation was especially harsh on the landowners of Peru who were attempting to block the massive land reform being carried out by Velasco's military government. Francisco had argued fiercely with me during the discussion period after my talk, taking the position that the agricultural sector would collapse if land were distributed to the Indian population. Our argument continued over beers with a small group of students and later over several dinners and meetings. I knew he was taking the position of his father's class—paternalistic about "their Indians" at best or downright racist and abusive at worst. Our attraction for one another was nourished by our political disagreements.

After we left Harvard, our encounters always included passionate sex as well as passionate arguments. One took place in New York City; Francisco convinced me to meet him two days before the beginning of a professional meeting. He had booked rooms at the Waldorf Astoria, and I still remember being greeted by the smell and sight of a suite filled with red roses. Another memorable rendezvous was a trip from Lima to Paris, with Francisco arriving at the airport in his pajamas and slippers for a redeye flight. At his expense, I joined him in first class where we drank champagne all the way. His family had a large share in the airline. In Paris we enjoyed lots of good food and wine and of course lots of passionate sex and passionate politics.

Perhaps the most memorable liaison was the one that took place in 1970 in Francisco's ancestral home that had been converted into a national museum. The colonial house stood in the old center of Lima. It had been built in 1890 at the beginning of the "Aristocratic Republic," when both sides of his family amassed great wealth. To keep the wealth within a small circle of elites, many "cousin marriages" took place in the intervening generations, causing their genetic stock to suffer. In Francisco's generation, there were few viable, reproductive families. Perhaps that was the Indian population's ultimate revenge: they simply outreproduced their former lords.

When I arrived to conduct research that year, the museum was closed for the day, but Francisco had keys. Overcome by the dusty splendor and history of the place, that encounter entailed innovative sex on the French dining table, on the kitchen table, on a large, ornate oak and silver desk, but not on the small canopy bed that didn't appear stable enough for our athletic grappling. Passionate political arguments were notably absent.

Now I reflected back to that time and wondered why. Were we just too exhausted or did we both have a glimmer of our future?

I chuckled out loud when I remembered having been taken to Francisco's palatial home for dinner that evening and horrifying Francisco's mother by speaking Quechua to the uniformed maid serving dinner. I had simply wanted to know if the maid was from Puno. Without thinking, the maid replied in Quechua that yes, she was from the señor's hacienda.

I remembered that a stony silence had fallen over the dining room until Francisco made a weak apology, explaining that I was an anthropologist, implying that I couldn't help myself. I had smiled and shrugged my shoulders as if to agree. Several days later we returned to his parents' home; they had traveled to Europe. While Francisco looked for a particular first edition in his father's library, I took the opportunity to talk to the five household servants, all from the hacienda in Puno: two married couples and their daughter, who had served dinner on my first visit. I found out that they had understood Lima society's class structure via the instructions that Francisco's mother gave for setting the table. Very important people were served on antique dinnerware from France and silver table settings from her great-grandmother's trousseau. On those occasions, the finest linens were also used and different wines were served with each course. "How many courses?" I asked. "Always five," they responded.

"Has President Prado ever had dinner here?" I asked.

"Many times," they answered. "He's a relative of the señor."

"How are the other groups served differently?"

"There are four groups and they are ranked from high to low," my native observers offered.

"What group do I belong to?" I maliciously inquired.

"The last," the daughter blurted. But one of the men quickly offered, "But only because you are so young."

"Perhaps," I retorted. At that, they all laughed nervously, knowing it wasn't true.

I related the story to Francisco and commented that his parents' servants had come up with a class structure based on his mother's table settings. Now that would be a fascinating article, I had said without a trace of a smile. When he gave me his most serious frown, I reassured him I wouldn't write it. He had responded with a comment I will never forget.

"My mother doesn't know that she's an endangered species. She and her kind will disappear before long." I wondered if he would survive the tumultuous changes taking place. At that moment, I had known that our love affair was over.

We never saw each other again after his mother took her remaining wealth and moved to Paris. Within five years, his father's hacienda was expropriated along with his other massive landholdings in Peru. His father died soon after. Land redistribution moved slowly but wealth didn't move at all. A small number of elites continued to control the majority of the wealth of the country, but Francisco's family lost out in the lottery of national and international realignments. Perhaps due to his father's untimely death and the departure of his mother, Francisco couldn't keep his family businesses afloat. The state of the economy in the late 1980s didn't help. Banks were nationalized and businesses went belly up under President García.

Before his mother left for Paris, she had arranged an appropriate marriage for her only son with a distant cousin, but the marriage was doomed; Francisco's extravagant lifestyle and increased drinking plunged him to the bottom of the social heap. By 1990 he would not have been invited to his mother's table, even as a fourth-category guest. I heard he was literally on the street, a derelict, a drunk. How sad, I thought.

Now Carlos, he was a different kettle of fish altogether. As a young student he had joined Hugo Blanco's guerrillas in Cuzco in 1965, but he was more of an intellectual than a fighter, so the insurgents sent him to Cuba to attend Castro's First World Congress. He claimed that he practically had to go around the world to get into Cuba, because he couldn't get a visa in Peru. In 1968 he left Peru when the military, under army General Juan Velasco, took power, and he didn't return until the democratic election of 1980. During those years in exile, Carlos lived in Madrid and Paris, teaching as well as writing fiction and poetry and political essays.

I had met Carlos at a reading of his most recent novel in Washington, D.C., in 1979. I was immediately attracted to him. He was smart and his writing was compelling and humorous. He was also the opposite of Francisco in every way; he was only five feet six inches tall, just a couple of inches taller than me, which made him short even by Peruvian standards. He was endowed with the square physique typical of mestizos from the north coast of Peru: long, broad torsos and short legs. Sitting at a table with a group of men who measured over six feet in height, Carlos appeared to be as tall. But if he rose to a standing position, you could see that he was short. He also had the flat face and broad nose of the Mochica, revealing his northern Indian coastal heritage. His face looked exactly like those on Mochica precolombian portrait vessels. However, his dusky complexion and slightly kinky hair suggested a black contribution to his physiognomic hybridity. Physically, he looked like a coastal map of Peru's history.

I broke my reverie for a moment to look out the window, and I noticed that we were passing a line of gambling casinos. Do casinos appear in a country when an economy goes under or when it improves? As we climbed over the barren desert mountain to La Molina, I noticed that the casino's glitzy

exteriors contrasted sharply with the stark poverty of the squatter settlements. The straw mat houses of migrants from the highlands crept over the hills between the walled, barricaded, middle-class houses like a swarm of ants following a trail of food. So even Carlos, the old leftist, had fled Lima. Interesting. I wondered if the car bombs drove him away. Or maybe he left when Sendero blew up the shopping mall near his apartment.

I gave instructions to the cab driver through the labyrinth of winding streets with private security cabins stationed in front of gated communities. It was not at all like the old days when Carlos returned to Peru in 1980 after twenty-two years in exile having to live in other people's apartments, moving every few weeks to a new location. He was, perhaps rightly, paranoid about military surveillance. He returned with Alán García, whom he had met in Paris. Both men had fled Peru when the military took power in the late 1960s. Carlos became García's major speechwriter when he ran for and won the presidency in 1985. Strange how so many world leaders return to their countries after decades of exile to assume power.

Carlos stepped out into the driveway. I had always thought that his expressive, twinkling brown eyes were his most attractive feature, and to my delight I saw that they hadn't dimmed since my visit last year. He gave me a bear hug and the obligatory kiss on each cheek. He looked good, hair thinner on top, but hey we're all getting old. He ushered me into the living room; a maid took my bags to the guest room.

As I watched him, I thought. *We've not shared the same bed for how long? Almost twenty years? My God, has it been that long? But we have become better friends than we were lovers.*

"Back again with your annual quest? Your mission? Your own holy grail?" chided Carlos. "How are you feeling? You look great. You had knee replacement surgery, didn't you?"

"Yes, I'm fine. My titanium knees are fantastic except they set off the alarms when I go through airport security. Right now, my feet are killing me. I've got to get these shoes off."

"I'm always happy to see you, querida," Carlos said as he smiled and handed me a pisco sour. "I see your portfolio has grown fatter since last year." He gave me an exaggerated frown and shook his finger at me. "You have been searching for Cholita for ten years. Don't you think it's about time to give up and move on?"

"No" I responded as I accepted the drink, lowering myself wearily onto the sofa. "I'm going to find Cholita this year, or at least find out what happened. My portfolio is fatter because I added information from the Truth and Reconciliation Commission. What do you think of the widespread denial of the number of people killed in the war? I think the number is probably higher than the seventy thousand estimated." I set my portfolio on a side table as I kicked off my shoes and reached for my drink.

"You're probably right," answered Carlos. "Limeños denied the war until it came to Lima and disrupted their lives. As long as Sendero stayed in the highlands and killed peasants, it didn't really concern us here," he said, settling in beside me on the sofa and continuing.

"Do you remember when we worked to get peasant leaders out of jail in the early '80s? I'll never forget that we actually had to pay for each bullet shot at them by the armed forces when they were arrested. How much did a bullet cost? I can't remember."

"I can't remember either," I answered as I searched his face, watching his eyes cloud over as he commented with a frown.

"I see your country is traveling the same path: Holding prisoners without charges or access to attorneys. Our great democracies have so much in common. Holding terrorists without formally charging them and trying them in military courts? No civil liberties? No habeas corpus? The next step is to charge defense lawyers with terrorism."

His eyes brightened and he broke into a large grin. "Say, to change the subject to something cheerier, do you know who came to see me last week?" he asked as he took my empty glass and carried it into the kitchen to prepare another drink.

"One of your old girlfriends, I suppose. Who?" I asked, following him into the kitchen. "There must be hundreds in that category."

"You exaggerate just a little. Mary Elizabeth, the historian. I think you two were great friends in the mid-1980s. Weren't you?" Carlos turned on the blender to mix the ingredients of the drinks.

"Oh yes, we were friends. Don't you remember? She and five other women were having dinner with me when you dropped by my apartment in Miraflores."

"Sure, that was a nice party. My God, to be in a room with seven beautiful women was so delicious!" Carlos's expression and devilish smile made me want to crawl inside his head as he journeyed back through twenty years to that evening. He handed me my drink and turned and strutted back into the living room, doing a little jig.

Aha, I thought, *he's like the Cock of the Rock. That beautiful Andean bird with the red feathered hood, black body, and white-tipped wings who engages in a competitive dance to attract females, strutting and bobbing his fluffed-out hood back and forth, up and down, until females gather around. Once copulation occurs, the females hatch the eggs and raise the offspring while the Cock of the Rock immediately abandons his mate to repeat his perpetual dance. I remember this particular Cock of the Rock bobbing and weaving around each of us all evening, all puffed up, hoping to attract our attention.*

"Thanks," I said as I accepted the glass. "Do you remember that you left early?"

"Yes? And?"

"Well," I replied with a devilish smile of my own, "after you left, we looked at each other and burst out laughing when we realized that all of us had slept with you. So as the evening and the wine wore on, we began to compare our 'Carlos' stories. We decided that you were the 'welcome basket' for female intellectuals doing research in Peru. Then we began to compare your basket."

"My basket?"

"Tu paquete, hombre," I answered. "Basket means the same thing in English. Didn't you know that? By the way, how *is* your little brother, Juan, these days? We told stories of how you called your penis Juan, your little brother, and recited your own poetry to him, not to us, when you made love. We dubbed your dick Don Juan."

"My God, you didn't!" Carlos laughed good-naturedly.

"Oh yes, and I think it was Mary Elizabeth who asked, 'Have any of you noticed how Don Juan seems to turn to the left? He has a little crook at the end,' and then Joyce, the archaeologist, asked, 'Have you noticed that one of Carlos's balls is much bigger than the other?'"

"Women don't really talk about such things, do they?" Carlos exclaimed.

"Oh yes, we do. All the time! Men never realize what women really say about them, do they?"

"I guess not."

"How is little brother Juan these days?" I playfully made a sad face and reached as if to grab for his crotch, but did not touch him.

"My little brother is very lonely these days. No one comes to visit him. Do you want to make him feel better?" Carlos asked, spreading his arms and his knees wide.

"No, Carlos. I bid your little brother Juan good-bye many years ago. By the way, does your ex-wife still set a place at her dining table for you when she entertains? And does she still make apologies that you are late to dinner? I remember shortly after you were divorced how she somehow got into your apartment and slashed all of your clothes but left them hanging on the hangers. And then she stole your book manuscript. And that was before the days of computers."

"Don't remind me. She was a real terror. Our son says the table setting has become a permanent mesa, you know, a ritual table, where she performs witchcraft."

"Well, a woman scorned and all that." We both laughed and gave each other a fond embrace and went to our respective bedrooms.

The next morning at breakfast, I was anxious to know Carlos's opinion about the upcoming election. I asked, "Do you plan to write speeches for Alán García again?"

"Probably," Carlos answered. "He needs my help and we have remained good friends, even during his exile in Colombia. I visited him several times in Bogotá. I think he has a chance of winning this election. He came back and breathed life into APRA."

I closed my eyes and leaned back and rested my head on the sofa while Carlos cited statistics from the departmental elections that APRA had won. *How could people support García? Inflation rose to almost 8,000 percent at one point and then Fujimori and Montesinos tried to prosecute García for corruption. García fled the country under a hail of gunfire and just recently returned. No one seems to remember the chaos of his administration. I guess we can conclude that democracy has no memory.* I opened my eyes as Carlos was saying:

"Still, foreign debt has to be restructured. There's a movement in Latin America now to demand it. Those loans were pushed on us by the global elite and now with the election of Evo Morales in Bolivia, and with Chavez threatening to cut off oil from Venezuela to the U.S., Latin American leaders may become unified in demanding a dialogue. There is more and more resistance to the global banking system."

"Is that one of his platforms? Won't people remember how ruthless the IMF and the World Bank were before?"

"Maybe not," Carlos said very slowly as he finished his coffee, fruit and bread. "Most Peruvian voters are too young to remember any of that. Alán is still a hell of an orator. But I doubt that he will oppose the banks again."

"It sounds like you have been doing your homework for his speeches. Can he control the military?"

"Who can?"

The maid appeared and told me my cab was at the door. I gulped down my coffee and took my bread and cheese with me as I rose to leave. I called out to Carlos as I started for the door, "By the way, were you in the country when García battled it out in a gunfight with the military in '92 and narrowly escaped? I'll bet you helped him when he was in hiding for two months. Did you help him get to the Colombian embassy?"

"Alice, I liked you better when you studied Andean symbolism and religion," Carlos said with a short laugh. "Now go, your cab is waiting. Where are you going, by the way? Remember what I taught you, always tell people where you're going and call frequently so I know you are safe. God, I sound like your father or brother. You have gotten into serious trouble in the past with your insistent questions." He held me at arm's length and waited for an answer.

"I'm going to Larco Herrera, the mental hospital, to interview a woman whose brother I met on the plane. He called me this morning and I am going to meet him there."

"To put in your portfolio of horrors no doubt. Don't you have enough of these stories?"

"Bye." I gave him a peck on his cheek and flew out the door.

I tumbled into the back seat of the waiting cab and mused: *Sure, you liked me better as a young, politically naïve twit. Carlos and I have traded places. I have become more political and he has retreated into his writing. Has he given up his passion for history? He used to lecture me about doing ahistorical ethnography. One advantage of getting old; you're forced to live history even though you ignored it in your youth. Is Carlos living in the past or the present? Or perhaps he is living in a fantasy world of his own creation using his memories to shape his stories. Somehow, I feel like I'm living more in the past probably because I keep reviewing my portfolio. Perhaps I can return to the present when I find Cholita.*

As the cab crawled through the congested traffic of La Molina, I took inventory. I got out a notebook and pen and formulated questions I wanted to ask. I had decided not to bring my digital tape recorder because I didn't have permission to record Felix's sister's story. A deep melancholia overcame me: *Why do I feel so compelled to collect these stories? No one wants to hear them. They've made me a professional pariah. I must be emitting an invisible signal that says, "Tell her! Tell her—she wants to hear your story!" So many strangers approach me to unburden themselves and I listen and record their accounts.* I sat staring out the window for a moment and then turned my attention to the cabbie. Taxi drivers were the pulse of the Peruvian nation and they always had opinions.

"How are things in Lima these days? Has the economy improved since Toledo took office?" I inquired.

"He keeps claiming that the economy is growing but none of it shows up in my pocket. I thought driving this cab was going to be temporary, now it looks like I'm stuck with this job. At least it's a job."

"What did you do before?"

After a long pause, he looked into the rearview mirror and our eyes met. "I was a sergeant in the guardia, the national police, with nineteen years of service. I resigned after I was assigned to duty in Huanta, Ayacucho."

"I've been to Huanta. I've worked for years as an anthropologist in the department of Ayacucho. In a small village called Pumapunku in the Cangallo province." My heart was pounding and my anthropological antennae buzzing. I added, "Huanta was really raked over the coals by both sides in the conflict."

"We saw everyone as an enemy. I was a member of an interrogation team in the stadium in Huanta. I helped stoke that fire, but I did something even worse. Señora, I want to tell you a story." He spoke slowly as we pulled up in front of the hospital, stopped, and shut off the engine. He turned to face me and said, "I was ordered to search for and kill two children, a boy ten years old and a girl twelve, exactly the same ages as my son and daughter. Ya' see these two kids were suspected of bringing a bomb into the barracks that exploded and killed two men. The kids came into the garrison every day to sell fresh fruit. We trusted 'em."

I waited transfixed and slowly removed my hand from the door handle, waiting for him to continue. Examining his face, I saw that he was probably in his mid-forties and his eyes, dark and deep-set, communicated a profound sadness. The lines etched at the corners of his eyes continued like tear stains down his cheeks and ended at his mouth. He sucked in his lips and bit his lower lip to try and stop them from quivering as he spoke. Then he turned away from me and faced the front of the car, clutching the steering wheel.

"I found 'em in the early morning hours in the market helpin' their mother set up her stall. I waited all day and followed 'em home. I killed 'em . . . and their mother. God forgive me." He began to sob and leaned his head on the steering wheel. He told me he had a complete breakdown, screaming in his sleep at night, "I've killed 'em! I've killed 'em!" calling out his children's names, convinced that he had killed his own children. The commander ordered him to Lima for a two-week leave. He was at home for about a week when he realized that he couldn't look at his children's faces because slowly they were transformed into the faces of two Huantino kids he had killed. So he stayed away from home during his leave and drank himself senseless. When it was time for his leave to be over, he couldn't face going back. He ended up here at Larco Herrera. But servicemen who had breakdowns were treated only for two weeks and then they were sent back to Ayacucho. He couldn't go back, so he quit. He continued to sob with his head on the steering wheel.

"My God, here." I reached into my briefcase and brought out a small address book, pen, and paper and scribbled a note. Handing it to the taxi driver, I urged him, "This is the name and phone number of a psychotherapist friend of mine. I am sure she can help you."

He accepted the paper and, reaching into his pocket, pulled out an insignia pin with his name, unit number, and a representation of the Peruvian flag and seal on it, saying, "Here, señora, please keep this and pray for me."

I took the insignia, noticing that his name was Juan Gonzalez. I held the man's hand for a moment and put my other hand on his shoulder. He was trembling. "I will pray for you and may God forgive you. Please call my friend. She can help you." I gingerly put the pin in my bag and thought, *another addition to my collection.*

I tried to pay the fare, but Juan Gonzalez just waved me on and whispered good luck. I exited the cab with a heavy sigh and waved good-bye, watching the cab pull away slowly. Before ascending the steps, I thought, *Why me? Why am I such a magnet for these stories? What am I going to do with them? God, I hope he can find some peace of mind. I'm sure his story never reached the Truth and Reconciliation Commission and that it never will. How many such stories are there?* An image flashed before my eyes of thousands of words flying toward me in the form of vibrating arrows. I could hear the buzz of voices as I felt the arrows pierce my body. I almost fell to the ground. Pulling myself upright, I stood in front of the building and wondered what I would find inside. What would Felix's sister tell me? How many of the patients here are tortured souls who were caught up in this war?

I went into the courtyard of Larco Herrera. It didn't look like a hospital, but rather resembled a turn-of-the-century manor located on ample, manicured grounds, except that patients in pajamas wandered about. I assumed that those few people dressed in street clothes were either doctors or staff. I pushed open the door of what looked like the main building and entered to find Felix, the young man I met on the plane, waiting for me.

"Thank you for coming, Doctora." He shook my hand firmly and said, "My sister, María, is waiting for us. She seems pretty good today. Some days, she's too far away to talk. But let me warn you she repeats her tragic history as if she has an internal tape recorder that is on automatic play."

I only nodded. I had not recuperated from the taxi driver's story, and I realized that I would have to call on all my psychic energy to hear yet another tale of horror. *How many years have I been collecting these tales? Since 1983 or 1984? How many have I recorded? Perhaps a thousand.* We made our way to a day room with barred windows that obstructed our view of the courtyard. Eight tables with four chairs each filled the middle of the room, and the ubiquitous television blared in one corner. A long table filled with games stood against one wall. There were only three other visitors: a woman and two children waiting at one of the tables.

I wondered about the taxi driver's wife. Had she come to visit him here when he was hospitalized for those brief two weeks? Was that woman waiting for a husband who had been similarly traumatized?

Felix interrupted my thoughts. "That's my sister, María, sitting over there. María!"

María was resting her head on her arms on the table closest to the window. She was staring outside and mumbling to herself. When she raised her head, I studied her face: María looked about twenty-five, dark-skinned with Andean features. She could be anybody's maid in Lima. Her black eyes were deep-set and hollow, expressionless. Her hair was braided in two plaits that were tied together and hung about half way down her back. Dressed in a black cardigan sweater, black blouse, and black pleated skirt, she nervously looked down at her rubber shoes. The shoes appeared to be too narrow for her feet. She lifted her bare feet in and out of them, resting the soles on top of the shoes, wiggling her toes. She repeatedly wiped her hands on her skirt. Then María slowly raised her head to look at us. Placing the index finger of her right hand to her lips, she turned her head to slowly sweep the room with her eyes. Her left hand clutched her skirt. As she gazed at us, she spoke in a low voice.

"Sh—sh—sh, I have a secret to tell you. I am so ashamed and I don't want people to know, but I must tell someone." Felix rushed to her side and put his arms around her. She didn't seem to recognize him.

"My name's María Roncalla and I'm from Puquio but I was working in Huanta . . . when I fled here, to Lima, after, after . . . it . . . it . . . happened."

"María, it's me, Felix, your brother."

María nodded slowly and looked through him as if to read the scenes of her own past somewhere on the opposite wall of the sparse room. She shifted her feet in and out of her shoes, wiped her right hand on her skirt, and continued. "It was about two in the afternoon when the navy come t' get me. I was workin' in the restaurant—n—I had ma' baby, Justa, ya' know on ma' back. In ma' liklla. Ma' other child, Joselito, was sittin' on the floor in the kitchen. They told me to leave my children—n—come with 'em. Joselito was only two—he began to cry—that woke up the baby. They both began cryin'. Joselito callin' out 'Mamá! Mamá!'"

She paused and looked over her shoulder nervously and continued in a hushed, confidential tone. "My husband escape to the jungle. On Thursday, those navy men took me away and on Saturday they were gonna kill me along with the others."

"María, I'm here. I'm here," Felix murmured softly as he cradled his sister in his arms. He turned to me and said, "She'll now repeat the whole sad story from beginning to end. She can't seem to stop herself."

She paused briefly and then continued. "At seven in the evening . . . that's when . . . they . . . five . . . they was five men." She covered her face with her hands and then looked up and spoke very slowly. "There was five men in the same tent with me. Los marineros, tol' us ta undress . . . The navy men shout and cuss . . . so we took 'em off. They tie our hands behind our backs—n—made us sit on the col' ground. Then they left . . . with our clothes. We didn' speak o' look at each other al'night cuz we was so ashamed. The men just stare at the ground. I keep ma' eyes shut—n—try to cover ma'self by huggin ma' knees."

"Hermanita calmate, calmate," Felix said with tears welling up in his eyes. Rocking his sister back and forth in his arms, he stroked her hair and tried to calm her.

Felix was right: She continued as though she was on auto-play with no stop button. "The next morning one of marineros came back and shout 'Carajo terruco'! Now ya'll tell us where your comrades are hidin'!' I peek out'ta from under ma' arms and saw him draggin' an old man out'ta the tent. The poor man cry in Quechua, 'Ma' son ain't no terruco! He's gone ta' Lima ta' find work.' But the marinero kick 'em and shout, 'Ya' miserable piece of cholo shit, ya'll tell us where your son's hidin'!'"

Felix continued to stroke his sister's hair while her history seeped out of her soul. "With ma' head down, I stol' a peek at the man sittin' across from me. He look about ma' age. A nice lookin' fella. Probably married, two or three kids like me. He jus' stare at the floor. But when they took 'im away, he look at me and say, 'May Tayta Razuwillka keep ya' safe and return ya' to your children.'"

Felix began to weep silently while María's memory marched on, struggling up the mountain of tormented visions. She suddenly raised her head and cried to the mountain god, "Tayta Razuwillka! Hear our pleas!"

I looked on and the old feelings of helplessness washed over me. I, too, began to sob as María's story relentlessly poured out of her. "One by one, they took the men away . . . I was save for last. I remember I look at the ground and saw lil' broken pieces a'teeth near ma' big toe." She marked a spot on the floor with her bare toe and bent down and picked up an imaginary piece of tooth and looked at it.

"I pick up a tiny piece o' tooth and hold it in ma' hand." She stared for a moment into her empty palm and added, "That lil' tooth remind me of ma' baby, Justa . . . She just begin'in' to get her first tooth. I stare at tha' tiny piece o' tooth and wonder if I never see ma' baby again. A great pain shoot through ma' breasts n' milk drip down ma' stomach, down ma' legs. I open ma' eyes cuz El capitán was shoutin' at me. He come this close to ma' face"—she put her hand a few inches away from her nose. Then she cupped her hands and cried in a loud voice: "He shout: 'Wake up lil' terruca, we've saved you for dessert.' Two of his men com inta' the tent after 'im. They was drunk. The youngest one say, 'Capitán, look'a wha' we gotta here! We gotta lil' vaquita! Anyone, wanna' a drink of leche fresca?'"

"My God! He call me a Lil' Cow! Those men gotta be foreigners! They can't be Peruvians!"

Felix cried, "Please, María, stop, stop! I can't stand to hear this again!"

But María couldn't stop; she stared at the drama being projected on the back of her mind. "The milk wudn' stop'a comin'. Que verguenza, I was so scared that . . . that . . . I . . . I . . . wet myself. They all laugh. I cover my breasts, but the milk justa kept drippin' through ma' hands. Ayee—e—e—e Díos mío, Madre santissima!" She covered her face with her hands and sobbed. "El capitán push one'a his men on top o'me—I fell backwards!" She fell out of her chair onto the floor in a spread-eagle position. Panting, she stopped for a moment and slowly placed her right hand on her left breast and continued: "One'a the marines grab ma' hands and force ma' arms out like this . . ."

She looked into her brother's face and spread her arms out, palms up to show him before continuing. "My God! He sat on me and suck on ma' breasts! Then he bit me so hard that I bleed and scream. When I scream, he slap me. I try to get away but I cud'n move. He turn his head to the other marines— n—began to sing 'Arroz con leche, yo quiero casar . . .'" After singing a bit of the song, María jumped to her feet and demonstrated his stance—hooking her thumbs in an imaginary belt and swaggering, she screeched in a loud voice, "con una muchacha. . . . que sepa ballar." Her voice trailed off to a whisper.

Felix stood slowly and wrapped his arms around his sister. Shaking herself free of his grasp, she whispered, "The other marineros, they laugh-n-slap 'im on the back. The other prisoners, ma' llaqtamasikuna, was gone. They dun' been disappear. I was alone."

She covered her face with her hands and sank slowly into her chair, but suddenly looked up as if an idea just dawned on her. "I wish I'da ask their names. They was Serranos like me. I bet their families're still lookin' for 'em. We never even spoke."

She began to rock back and forth in her chair and her eyes became wide as she stared at some frightful scene being projected on the beige, cracked wall of the day room. She hugged her own shoulders and stuffed her hands between her knees and continued to rock back and forth. "They drug me off t'a buildin' by ma' hair and hung me up by ma' feet. The blood rush t'ma' head—n—I felt sick. They kick me yellin' 'Who are they? Carajo! Puta terruca de mierda! Quienes son?'"

"'But I dun' know any terrucos,' I cry. 'All I do is cook—n—serve food—n—go home ta'ma' kids.'"

Her tone changed and she shouted in a low, male voice, "You give Sendero food. We know ya' do." She covered her face with her hands, but then she looked up and continued in her own voice. "Then they cut me with knives. Just lil' cuts . . . see? Here," pointing to her legs "—n—there," pointing to her breasts. "They cut ma' breasts . . . But I dunno a thing. How cud'I?" She began to sob softly, hugging herself and rocking back and forth.

Suddenly María stopped and looked at me as if seeing me for the first time: "Did ya' ask me why they come to arrest me?" She shrugged her shoulders and laughed sardonically. "I dunno. I swear to God, I dunno. Ma' husband run off with his lover to the jungle—n—his mom wanna get rid of me—n—take ma' kids. So she tol' the navy capitán that I gave food to terrucos. I dunno any terrucos! Ma' suegra always hate me. She pick out'ta girl for her son ta' marry. A Serrano divorce. That what it is. Ma' children! Felix, where are ma' children?"

Felix answered, "Don't worry. I'll make sure they're safe. Maybe I can take you and your children to the States."

María emerged from the grasp of her memories and grabbed her brother's arm and pleaded, "I haven't seen 'em for years. Please bring 'em t' see me, Felix, please."

"I will, I will bring them here, but first we have to get you well. I am going to make an offering to Pachamama."

María's moment in the present dissolved and suddenly her eyes clouded over again and she resumed her tale. "On the second day they hang me up by ma' feet again and bring inna huge bucket of filthy water. Really filthy! It had al' kina' shit in it. Human, llama, donkey . . . even pig shit. Then they lower the rope." She paused and her face twisted into an ugly grin as she imitated the voice of the capitán: "'Listen, terruca, we're gonna kill ya' if ya' don't tell us who they are.' When ma' head's force in'ta tha-bucket o shit, I think I gonna die. That filth went in'ta'ma mouth and I can't breathe. They haul on the rope and ma' head come out'ta the mess. Then they laid me on a table. I stay very quiet—n—keep'ma eyes close. But then, and then . . ." She covered her face with her hands. "I guess I pass out. I, I . . ." She paused and started rocking back and forth again faster and faster, twisting her skirt in her lap. Suddenly she stopped and stuffed her skirt between her legs, looking skyward and wailing, "Why's God punish me so? Wha'ta I dun'ta deserve this?"

For a moment María was quiet, but, searching the corners of the room for her torturers, she whispered, "Later, as if from a long way off, I could hear 'em say, 'She's dead, you just as well dump 'er with the rest of the cholos de mireda.' They throw me on the ground like a sack' a potatoes—n—one a'em kick me in the stomach—n—say, 'You mean our little vaquita's dead, too bad, no more leche fresca.' He give me 'nother kick-n-all the water gush outta'ma mouth: I cough—n—I hear the capitán say, 'Well, lookka that, you're one lucky puta terruca. We thought you were done for. I guess you're not a terrorist after all!'"

"One of his men grab me by ma' hair-n-pull-me to ma' feet. Ma' arms—n—legs'r numb—n—I fall to the floor. El capitán throw a bundle of clothes at me—n—I crawl like a dog outta the door.

"'Leave Huanta—don' come back,' el capitán shouts. 'If you do, we'll kill ya' next time, carajo!' That man, you know the one who sat on me? He start laughin' and call out, 'MO—OO, MO—OO. GO HOME LITTLE VAQUITA! You need milkin' again! Carajo, stupid chola!'"

"When I got outside, I try to stand up but I couldn't. Then I saw that I was bloody—n—al'kinda bruised down here." She covered her crotch with her hands and began to sob.

I finally ventured a question. "Felix, ask her what her attackers looked like."

María heard me and answered, "Wha'd ma' torturers look like? . . . Casi Peruano . . . almost Peruvian. El capitán was blond . . . blue eyes and glasses. Yes, almost Peruvian. But ya' know somethin'?"

She leaned forward and looked me in the eyes and whispered, "He look justta' like you."

I felt as if I had been shot. I jumped up and rushed out of the day room and leaned against the wall. My heart and head were pounding. I felt a constriction in my chest. My vision was blurred and I couldn't form words. Felix came out and embraced me, saying, "Doctora, I am so sorry."

I tried to speak but only a moan escaped. I gasped, "You have nothing to be sorry for" as I handed him the name and phone number of the same friend to whom I had referred the taxi driver. "I hope she can help your sister. She's got to rid herself of these phantom memories."

"If we were in Puquio, one of our curers could help her, but these people in the hospital haven't helped at all."

I replied, "I hope my friend can. She is an anthropologist as well as a therapist and lived for years in the highlands. Also, I think that reuniting your sister with her children would probably help. Good luck."

We walked to the front door together in silence. We embraced good-bye and a double kiss on each cheek. I stuffed my notes into my briefcase and my hand began to tremble as my fingers brushed the taxi driver's insignia.

As I stepped out into the eucalyptus-filled courtyard and hurried toward the street, a gust of wind blew the medicinal scent of the trees into my face. Along with the strong odor were images of the terrifying events of 1980 in Pumapunku rising before my eyes. *Am I hallucinating like María? She saw the horrifying events of the past in front of her eyes like a never-ending movie being repeated over and over again. Have I acculturated to Quechua language and culture to the point that the past is forever in front of me as it is for her, a native of this traumatized culture?*

The figure of another rape victim loomed large in front of me as I was carried back twenty-odd-years to the graveyard of Pumapunku. *Will I ever be able to gain of glimpse of the future? Or is the future for me as it is for puechua speakers, behind my head and out of view? Will perpetually facing the past prevent me from imagining the future free of the terrifying events I witnessed?*

CHAPTER 5

THE AUTOPSY

"You can't do this, compadre! For God's sake, she's the mother of your child! What's wrong with you? Are you mad?" My words are hardly audible as they whistle past my clenched teeth. Just then a large gust of wind make the eucalyptus trees surrounding the cemetery rustle and their pungent perfume wash over me.

"No, comadre, I'm not mad. It's the law. The law requires an autopsy in the case of suicide." His words are slurred but there is no trace of emotion on his face or in his voice.

The law my ass. Jesus, how I detest this man! I think to myself. I can smell the alcohol on his breath. He's been drinking all night. He and his buddies had a fiesta last night. They're here watching this macabre display of machismo. He's doing this to impress them.

I feel an electric charge as I grab his wrist with both hands, applying all the pressure I can to prevent him from raising his arm. Like blood poisoning, whiteness from my fingers moves up his arm. As he raises his right arm, I feel myself being pulled forward over Juana's body, and my fingers begin to tremble. My throat is so constricted that I find it difficult to speak; I hear the voice of a small child as I say, "Compadre, it may be the law, but not with twenty students watching! This is barbaric." I let go of his wrist and my hand drops to the burial litter; our eyes remain locked together for a few seconds. Finally, with my eyes filled with tears, I lower them to the dark pit in front of me.

The gravediggers nervously smoke cigarettes and blow the smoke on each other for protection against the cadaver as they cross themselves and begin mournful incantations when they comprehend what Romulo is about to do. All eyes except mine are focused on the knife in his right hand. I begin to weep soundlessly and slowly rock back and forth.

Bemused, Romulo turns to the group of students huddled together at the head of the newly dug grave and gives a military salute to his hung-over buddies standing behind them. Just at that moment, I hear a plaintive moan from the large wooden doors to the cemetery. I look up to see Cholita using all her strength to open the massive doors just as a gust of wails from the assembled mourners rushes in ahead of her and falls on Juana's body. Cholita stands near the doors, not approaching the grave. From where I am, she looks like her mother's headstone as she raises her arm and points to Juana. She lets her arm drop lifelessly to her side as she whispers, "Mamá, Mamá."

Romulo barely glances at Cholita as he begins his science lesson for the day. "Students, we have an excellent opportunity to study the human body. It's tragic that Juana committed suicide, ya' know it's a mortal sin. That's why Juana's being buried on the edge of cemetery. In cases of suicide the law requires an autopsy. Since we have no doctor in Pumapunku, I'll do it and file a report with the prefect in Ayacucho."

A collective crescendo of wails from Juana's women kinfolk ascends the high walls of the graveyard and falls on his words like hornets in falsetto.

"Students," he continues, "it is a rare opportunity to be able to examine the human body en vivo, well, almost en vivo." His buddies giggle in appreciation of his joke, but the students look more alarmed. "Please take out your notebooks and take notes as I proceed. You'll have an exam tomorrow."

I can't move. Even though tears are flowing down my cheeks, I seem incapable of sound or movement. *En vivo, shit. He's trying to be clever. Oh mother of God, he's about to dissect her. I wonder if he will stick tags in the organs with numbers on them like my anatomy professor did. Those tags haunted my dreams for months and I saw that woman's dissected body every time I went to the meat market. Women are meat to Romulo. I remember when he told me I didn't have enough fat on me. I've heard him discuss how much fat he likes and where it should be. Women are marbled steaks to him. Shit, I'm having a nightmare. This can't be happening. I'm cold all over and I seem to be experiencing everything in slow motion, but I can't move. I feel faint.*

Frozen in a kneeling position beside Juana's body, my hands are still gripping the burial litter. I force myself to look at Juana, whose face bears the pain of all the generations of women before her. I imagine the rat poison working its way through her system. For some reason, the poison is iridescent green as I see it coursing down her throat, into her stomach, intestines, rushing into her blood stream, and finally invading her heart and lungs. Mesmerized, I notice that instead of blood in Juana's veins, bright chartreuse sand glows and shimmers.

How long had it taken? She must have suffered terribly. Her hands are clenched into fists and her face is contorted. There are severe burns around her mouth and chin caused by the regurgitation of the poison and stomach acid. She must have taken the poison right out of the bottle. I can see the round mark of the bottle on her swollen lips.

She has on her best "go to town" dress, not the usual white shroud. Her brother Gregorio washed her body, chewing coca and drinking trago, cane alcohol, during the necessary preparations. He was the only person willing to touch her. After dressing Juana, he tenderly slipped the special burial slippers made from llama skins on her feet. When Gregorio wrapped a beautifully woven alpaca coca bag around her neck, Juana was ready for her journey to the world of the dead. Did he put the sweater on her thinking it would give her warmth in the grave? No, the sweater is for her journey to the underworld. This is day two of her five-day journey and she will be facing her first dangers. I wonder what those dangers will be. Gregorio hasn't performed the divination to foretell her journey. I guess he's afraid of her tortured spirit. Everyone is afraid that her spirit will cause crop failure or an earthquake. We are at a dangerous time between the rainy and dry seasons. The social world must be in order for the transition to the dry season.

I force myself to look at Juana again. Shit, what a way to end a short, bitter life. She's still beautiful with her high cheekbones and thick black braids, but I can't see her almond-shaped eyes because they are so black and swollen. Her skin has turned a strange gray color, and I look at the red burn around her mouth and left cheek. What should her epitaph be? I sit down on the lip of Juana's grave, close my eyes and conjure up an image of her headstone.

> Here lies Juana Quispe Cabana
> Died by her own hand at the age of twenty-six on April 25th, 1980
> Daughter of Alejandro Quispe Vilca and Margarita Cabana Tucno
> Survived by one brother, two sisters and Cholita
> Her 12-year-old illegitimate daughter

. . .

The high-pitched keening of the women mourners in the entryway of the cemetery evokes images of the many funerals I've attended in Pumapunku. Twenty years ago, in the first six months of my fieldwork, I was called "the undertaker," but nothing has prepared me for today. I had arrived in the village with newly acquired language skills, a tape recorder, and a camera, with great expectations of documenting the culture, only to discover that no one would talk to me or even direct a brief glance in my direction. I became desperate after six weeks of silent avoidance from everyone except the mestizo shopkeepers and two schoolteachers. One morning I heard the death toll from the church bells and raced to the church and waited out of sight. A group of men entered the church to rent the burial litter, a tattered black cloth to cover the body, a large silver cross, and two incense burners. I followed them at a discreet distance and once the men entered through the makeshift gate of a family compound, I took a deep breath and followed.

The deceased was laid out on a table under the portal of the house with candles at his head and his feet. A woman was kneeling at the foot of the table saying a prayer. Other mourners were preparing to carry the deceased to the cemetery. A momentary shock passed through the mourners when I slipped inside the gate. All eyes gazed at me, and I returned their gaze with a mumbled greeting in Quechua. Finally a woman got to her feet and ordered an old man to serve me trago, cane alcohol cut with water that serves as the social lubricant for all rites of passage. The drunken old man lifted a bottle to a glass and filled it, stumbled to his feet and downed the liquor in one swallow, filled a second glass from the same bottle, and extended it to me, slurring in Quechua, "I drink to you, señora, thank you for paying your respects to my dear brother."

Trying not to show my excitement, I accepted the glass. Those were the first words spoken to me in Quechua since my arrival. I accepted the glass and extended it to the old man, offering the appropriate Quechua response: "I drink with you in memory of your brother, sir." As I raised the full glass of clear liquid to my lips, the odor that assailed my nostrils was not the strong odor of cane alcohol. It was kerosene. The old man had drunk the fuel without so much as a twitch. I closed my eyes and poured the kerosene down my throat and hoped for the best. I performed the next prescribed social act and poured the woman who seemed to be in charge a healthy drink of the same stuff. The woman put the glass to her lips and exclaimed, "Carajo, this ain't cane alcohol, you ol' drunken fool; it's kerosene." With that, she threw the drink onto the dirt floor and boxed the old man's ears, calling him a string of names in Quechua. She put her hands on her hips, threw back her head, and roared with laughter, explaining to everyone that the gringa preferred kerosene to trago. People pointed at me and laughed. The woman patted me on the back and invited me to stay for the rest of the wake.

At the precise moment that I meekly took a seat on the floor with the other women, a loud gaseous belch issued forth from my poor stomach. The young woman next to me tapped me on the shoulder. I swiveled around to look, and as I did so, she struck a match, held it in front of my mouth, and said, "poom!" A burst of hearty laughter shattered the barrier that had excluded me, and I felt accepted at last. Only when I returned for my second year of fieldwork was I invited to participate in other activities. I had entered the culture of Pumapunku through the door to the underworld.

.   .   .

And here I sit now on the edge of a grave, trying not to fall into its depths. Romulo's voice brings me back to the horrific scene before me.

I open my eyes to see Romulo unbutton Juana's sweater and blouse tenderly as if she were his lover. He pulls her skirt down to expose her bloated belly, raises a knife, and gingerly starts his incision above her pubis, continuing until her clavicle stops his ascent. Withdrawing the knife, he doubles his fist and hits Juana's sternum once, twice—and on the third blow, a loud crack announces that the clavicle and sternum have broken. He continues by making an X-shaped incision across her clavicle.

Feeling faint and grabbing onto the edge of the grave, I notice that green iridescent sand is leaking out of Juana's body, and I stare at it as it falls and think of an hourglass. The chartreuse grains land near my feet and a few of the iridescent bits of silicon drift with the wind onto my feet and legs. As if sprinkled with a magic powder, I feel my body shrink until I'm on a green sandy beach looking up at a giant cadaver. Romulo's enormous figure looms above me and his voice descends on me like acid rain, each word stabbing my diminishing frame.

"I'll begin with the womb, that hollow home where every human being begins life and is nurtured for nine months," Romulo declares as he puts his hands into the base of the long gash at the pubis and feels around for the organ. "Ah hah, here it is!" Keeping his left hand in the body cavity, he carefully cuts the uterus away with his right hand and lifts it for the students to examine. In doing so, the bladder, intestines, and stomach spill outside of the corpse and more bright green sand drifts down on me. A gasp and a flutter of movement arise from the huddled students clustered together at the head of the grave.

Romulo continues. "Students, make a circle around me so that you can see better." The twenty students become one giant amoeba that engulfs the grisly scene as they cautiously inch forward. His drinking buddies look like a hungry snake encircling the scene.

Oh no, don't let them come any closer. I'm going to be trampled, pushed into the grave! Help! Don't let me shrink any more! What's happening to me? I'm disappear-

ing! My body is still here, huddled by Juana's cadaver, but I see myself: I'm weeping and holding onto the litter. Have I split into two parts? Or do I have a disembodied double that is observing me from above. My God, there I am! I feel this green stuff falling on me. I see Juana's butchered body! Yes, I'm sitting on her dried blood. Am I the only one who can see the luminous green poison? I have to calm down, to return to sanity. I can clearly see myself scramble onto the beachhead of "operation science" as Romulo drones on.

"This woman's purpose in life is here in my hand. To reproduce! To provide the oven to bake the bread; men provide the yeast for life to rise. Look at it," he demands as he cuts open the pear-shaped uterus and spreads it apart to reveal the inner structure. The amoeba transforms itself as the students shuffle and jostle one another, trying to retreat, but the snake encircles them and prevents their escape. I open my eyes to see Cholita standing motionless, staring at Romulo. A thousand-year-old hatred gleams in her eyes. She clenches her fists, sets her jaw, and in that instant becomes a woman.

Romulo glances at Cholita for a second but quickly returns his gaze to the organ in his hands and continues. "The womb, not very impressive is it? Just a vessel? An envelope?" He puts the mutilated uterus and bladder on a plastic seed sack and goes on. "Now I'll remove the heart and the lungs."

Keening from beyond the cemetery wall reaches a fevered pitch as dark clouds cover the sun. I shudder and timorously move toward the enormous pear-shaped womb, glistening with that peculiar iridescent green glow. I overcome a corner of my fear and inch forward. I gingerly reach out and touch the womb. Cold, hard, and green. As I remove my hand, an apparition rises and floats upward. Can this be pachachaca, the bridge to reach another world?

> Juana's womb takes flight
> a winged pear-shaped uterus
> a wounded butterfly
> an iridescent kite
> with a luminous fetus
> still attached
> by a green umbilical cord
> reaching and grabbing at the empty air.
>
> The kite, with its fetal tail, catches on a gust of icy breath
> as Juana's face and outstretched arms
> form a prismatic rainbow
> that covers the sun.
> Rising to fit into the prism

her iridescent heart
with lungs flapping
float in the wind.
Stomach, liver, intestines
race after the womb-kite
with its flaying fetus
born higher on a gust of wind.

The great green vessel glows
as the iridescent rainbow
gathers the mutilated organs
into her crystalline body.
Juana tenderly places the fetus,
fully formed and crying, into her womb.
Folding her arms protectively,
the apparition disappears.

I am transfixed and I see Cholita slowly pointing to the sky. As the apparition fades, she turns her burning gaze on Romulo. I feel a current of cold, deep hatred wash over my tiny body. As the image fades in the sky, my body returns to its normal size, and I raise my eyes to the sky just in time to see the prismatic cloud move southward toward the land of the dead. I think that I still discern the outline of Juana's folded arms over her infant.

Romulo has finished his science lesson. He instructs the students to file past the organs and sketch them in their notebooks. He barks orders to the gravediggers to begin lowering the body into the grave. They balk, saying, "But Don Romulo, we can't bury her without her insides. She'll be angry and search for them."

"Nonsense! Bury her! I'm going to preserve the organs to teach biology classes in the school."

The two men whisper together for a few moments, nervously look at the body, then at Romulo. Crossing themselves and putting fresh coca into their mouths, they gingerly pick up Juana's body from the burial litter and climb into the grave. Smoke rises as they furiously bathe each other in its protective cocoon. Their rhythmic incantations fill the air with dread. The mourners receive the news of Romulo's intentions as the whispering students file out of the cemetery. A rising chorus of protest outside responds with cries of "No, no, he can't do that! She'll never rest in peace."

Gregorio pushes his way through the coagulated students and confronts Romulo at graveside just as Romulo is putting Juana's organs in the plastic seed sacks. He laughs and chats with his buddies; they, as his army of the night, help him carry the harvested organs.

Without any verbal formalities, Gregorio angrily demands in Quechua, "What desecration of my sister's body have you performed now? Haven't you caused her enough pain? All of the Lords of the Mountains and Pachamama will have revenge for this savagery!"

"I'm performing what the law requires! Who are you, indio bruto, to call me savage? Out of my way!" Romulo picks up two of the sacks and pushes past Gregorio with his buddies behind him.

Gregorio is left standing at the side of the grave with his staff of office in hand. He kneels beside the grave, and the rhythm of the gravediggers shoveling dirt on Juana's body provides percussion to his sad song. "Sister Juana! Please forgive us. We are powerless in the face of this evil. Please leave us in peace. Do not punish us for what has been done to you! I beg of you leave this place." He sings his peculiar Quechua version of the Lord's Prayer and lets perfect coca leaves drift down into the grave on top of Juana's body, now partially covered with dirt. He speaks to the gravediggers, stands up, and extends his hand to help me rise to my feet.

"Comadre Alicia, we must go home and make preparations. We are in grave danger. Juana's soul is angry. Did you see the sky? She will visit us tonight." We walk to the door where Cholita is waiting.

I reach for Cholita, but the child backs away, turns, and marches out of the cemetery doors away from the village toward the hills. I walk to Gregorio's house, which is in turmoil with women weeping and keening the high-pitched funeral dirges. More alcohol than usual is being consumed, given the bizarre events of the day. Clotilda, Gregorio's wife, rushes forward, tension and strain plainly visible in her face and diminutive frame.

"Comadre Alicia, husband, what can we do? Juana's soul was already angry after the suicide and now she is missing her organs! She will bring calamity upon us for sure!"

Gregorio, taking his wife's small hands in his rough brown paws, says, "We'll prepare a watan misa."

"But that's done at the first anniversary after death, not the day of burial. We should be performing the—"

Gregorio cuts her off and says, "I know, I know, but perhaps her soul will believe it is time to leave us if we send it off properly. We must try, or someone else will die from her vengeance. But first we must get her organs back, especially her heart and liver."

"Not her womb?" I ask, remembering the gigantic winged apparition I had seen ascend into the sky.

"I've never heard of a womb being stolen. Heart and lungs, yes, but a woman's reproductive organs? Never!" Gregorio looks worried.

"But doesn't that mean that the womb is even more important to return to her body?" I ask.

"Yes, you're probably right. We'll have to return all of her organs to her before she will rest in peace." Gregorio crosses himself and mutters a prayer before putting more coca leaves into his mouth. He extends his cupped hands filled with the leaves to us. We accept the offering and the three of us stand chewing together in deep contemplation. Gregorio's face brightens; he carefully returns the remainder of the leaves into his coca bag, reaches for the bottle of trago, and serves us, saying, "Salud, may God be with us on this dangerous endeavor." He obviously has an idea. He turns to his wife and, using the formal Quechua address, declares, "Mamay, prepare the table with Juana's clothes, the candles and the cross. Alicia, once it's dark, you'll come with me to search for the organs."

"Yes, compadre Gregorio," I respond. But silently I whisper to myself, *Oh God, I don't want to do this. Hunt for Juana's organs and return them to her body?*

Entering my room in Gregorio's household compound, I immediately shudder when a cold wind hits my face. These rooms always remind me of a tomb, there's always a cold wind inside. How can a cold wind blow inside a stone and adobe room even when it's warm outside? Out loud I say, "Compadre, I'm going to lie down. I think I could sleep through the end of the world." Before my nap, I stick my head into the cooking hut and ask my comadre, Clotilda:

"Have you seen Cholita?"

"No, she probably went up to the pastures," Clotilda answers. "Her cousin Teresa is tending the herds in Ranga Cruz."

"I hope she's all right, Clotilda. The look on her face scared me. Did she say anything to you as she left?"

"No," answers Clotilda. "The only thing I heard her say during the whole thing was 'mama' and then she just left."

As I stretch out on the bed and look up through the ichu grass thatch, I can make out the eyes of the family of weasels that live in the rafters above my head. When I had first discovered my housemates, I had been frightened by those beady black eyes that had peered down at me, but now I regard them as friendly co-residents. I wonder if they are related to the weasels that live in the rafters of Mama Jesús's house. Or maybe that family moved in here with me. Do weasels migrate with their human companions? This room is large and windowless, one of the largest in the compound and usually used for food storage. It measures twenty feet long and twelve feet wide and has three-foot-thick stone walls, as well as a dirt floor and an ichu thatch roof soaked after six months of heavy rain. The room smells of musty vegetation and wet earth. The damp darkness embraces me like a hungry lover who makes me shudder at his touch. Gregorio and his family think it strange that I sleep in the storage room, saying, "There's bad air trapped in there." Everyone else sleeps under the portal roof. I let out a long slow breath and a cloud of frost appears before my mouth. For some reason that makes me smile and think, *Well, there's still a sign of life in there somewhere.* I feel as though I have been entombed. I pull my sleeping bag up around my ears and drift into a fitful sleep.

The dream descends upon me immediately, not even waiting for deep sleep. It's more of a vision than a dream. I'm back on the iridescent green sand and I hear my name being called. I look up into the sky to see the shape of Juana with her infant tucked in her womb. Juana reaches down and scoops me into her hand and asks:

"Comadre Alicia, how could you let him violate me like that? My brother's correct. I'll take my revenge on all of you if my body is not whole when it's consumed by the earth."

"Comadre Juana, look at me, I'm so small and helpless. What could I do? I promise we will get all of your organs back and return them to your body. I promise, I promise." The giant figure of Juana takes a breath and blows me out of her hand. I drift slowly to the ground like a coca leaf. I wake with a start, muttering, "I promise, I promise."

After my nap, I step outside, where thirty relatives are roaring drunk. Carlos, Juana's cousin on her mother's side, is standing over the set of Juana's clothes that has been laid out to represent her body: a pair of shoes, skirt, blouse, and sweater. He's holding a bottle of trago and a glass, but he's so unstable that he spills the booze all over the table and extinguishes one of the candles at the foot of the effigy. His wife grabs his arm and tries to get him to sit down, but he continues with his diatribe against his dead cousin.

"Juana, how cud'ya commit suicide? We took care of ya'—n—Cholita. We gave ya' a home, food. Ya've committed a grave sin against Pachamama, and al'o'the sacred mountains who'll take their revenge on us. Pachamama'll send earthquakes! She'll send floods! Away, go away! Be off with ya'!" With that, he begins to wave the bottle wildly over the image of Juana's body. Gregorio and three other men force him to lie down in one of the stone niches that serve as beds along the outside wall of the portal. They pour more liquor down his throat and force him to lie back and go to sleep. Gregorio looks knowingly at me and we step outside. It is dark but a full moon provides ample light to navigate to our destination, so Gregorio decides to leave his lantern behind and we set out on our organ hunt.

We reach the plaza of Pumapunku and approach the school, cautiously keeping to the shadows of the church. We pass the two stores and finally reach the municipal building that stands adjacent to the school. Gregorio slips inside the municipal building to speak to the night watchman, who is his nephew. After explaining our mission, the watchman is more than amenable to unlocking the doors of the school. The entire village is fearful of the consequences of Juana being buried—incomplete.

Upon entering the school, we go directly to Romulo's classroom, where we locate the empty feed sacks on the floor beside his desk. With a small pen flashlight, I sweep the room with a small circle of light that finally catches the reflection of large glass jars on a shelf in the back of the room. The organs are submerged in some kind of liquid and I notice they have lost their green glow. Gregorio lifts the jars and carefully carries them to Romulo's desk. After a tense whispered discussion, I roll up my sleeves and reach into the jar, but upon contact with the heart, I give a start and jerk my hands out, spilling the liquid on the desk. The smell of cane alcohol almost overpowers me. "My God, Romulo has put Juana's organs in trago!" I rasp in a loud whisper. Gregorio whispers back, "Comadre, be quiet!" as he wipes the liquid up with the edge of his poncho. I can only nod as I shut my eyes and gingerly reach into the jar again, removing the heart, womb, liver, and stomach. Reaching into the second jar, I recoil when my fingers encounter the intestines, and I have to use both hands to lift them from the jar. Wiping the sweat from my face with my sleeve, I whisper to Gregorio that all the organs are in the sack. Before lifting the sack to his shoulder, Gregorio crosses himself and sprinkles trago on the sack with words of prayer for Juana. We scurry out of the school as fast as thieves and make our way to the southern path exiting the plaza that descends gently to the cemetery. Since the dead must be placed in the earth at the union of two sources of water, the cemetery is located below the juncture of two irrigation canals. We move stealthily along the dirt path that I have traveled so many times before documenting countless processions of the dead to their last career.

Isn't it interesting, I muse. *We would say "their final resting place," but the dead of Pumapunku don't go to their resting place: They go to work. In the world of the dead, time is reversed, their day is our night and their rainy season is our dry season, but they do everything the living do: They plant, harvest, and tend animals. I wonder if they make love. Yes, they make love to the living in dreams. The soul and body are separated at death and we know how mischievous souls can be. Their bodies rot and return to the earth and fertilize the fields of the living. That's why the cornfields for the saints are so close to the cemetery. The dead are like seeds for new generations of the living. Their souls visit us in our dreams.*

Gregorio breaks into my anthropological wanderings and whispers, "There aren't many houses on this side of the village, but keep to the shadows of the trees anyway. We don't want anybody to see us. Somebody'll think we're condenados wandering around in the middle of the night."

"Yes, but we're not in our animal forms."

"The condenados can wander at night in human form and suddenly turn into animals any time they want. Didn't you go on nightly patrols last year with Don Luciano, our condenado catcher?"

"Yes, but we didn't catch anyone. We only heard their bells and followed the sound. When we got behind Doña Julia's house, the bells stopped and we found her donkey standing in the corral. Don Luciano said, 'I knew she's one. I always suspected she committed incest with her brother.' Do people really believe they are incestuous?"

"Yes, now be quiet. We're almost there."

As prearranged, the gravediggers have left the doors to the cemetery open and have propped their shovels beside Juana's unfinished grave. Upon seeing what was waiting for us, I let out a moan.

"Jesus, Mary, and all the saints! Now I'm truly the Undertaker. Why didn't I study dentistry?"

"Comadre, we both have to get into the grave. You have to tell me where the organs go. They must be in their right place."

"Compadre," I whine nervously, "I can instruct you from up here, can't I?"

"No, you know how sound carries from here. We'll be heard in the village," Gregorio whispers nervously.

"Oh shit," I mutter in English as I climb into the grave. "Díos mío, there's not much dirt on her is there?"

"No. I told the gravediggers not to cover her up because we had to return her organs."

"O.K. let's do this quick—n—get outta here." For the first time, I feel uneasy

in the graveyard. My mind wanders and I remember the many times I came for burials, to put out food for the day of the dead. With special fondness, I remember a very pleasant afternoon I spent with Gregorio and two other officials of the village to tidy up the graves. They chewed coca as they lined up skulls and bones into floral patterns to make room for new graves. The same graveyard has been used for centuries; land is better utilized for crops. I remember watching with astonishment when people handled the bones tenderly, calling them by the names of their relatives and reminiscing about their lives. It had been such a pleasant afternoon, sunny and warm, that I fell asleep on one of the graves next to a skull surrounded by vertebrae and other small bones arranged to resemble a sunflower. Now I have a feeling of foreboding as we put Juana's organs back into her body cavity. Our grisly work is made more difficult by rigor mortis, as if Juana is rejecting her own organs. But at last, her heart, liver, womb, and finally the intestines are once more in their proper places and we begin covering Juana with dirt. Damn, I'm not sure whether we placed her bladder beneath her uterus or not. Oh well, I giggle and mutter in English, "Maybe she'll develop bladder trouble." Gregorio looks at me puzzled.

Both of us are drenched with sweat when we finish, even though the night air is cold. Gregorio offers me coca leaves and trago, which I gladly accept. We kneel at the head of the grave and pray, first to Juana, asking her forgiveness, then to Pachamama, the Virgin Mary, the local mountain deities, and finally to Tayta Dios, God the Father. Gregorio sprinkles the grave with trago, ushering me out of the graveyard hurriedly as the dawn breaks on the horizon.

Entering the household courtyard quietly, we take seats along the wall and share another trago and chew coca. Sitting silently together, I feel closer to this illiterate peasant than I do to any other human being. It isn't sexual attraction, but rather a filial love that sweeps over me as Gregorio reaches in his coca bag and brings out another handful of coca leaves. Now, with all of Juana's organs returned to her body, he can perform the required divination to foretell Juana's journey to the land of the dead. He begins with a prayer, then lets the coca leaves flutter down to the beautiful textile that is the ritual space for his performance, and begins to read the leaves.

Clotilda and several children are sleeping together on llama hides in one of the bed niches, curled together like vines. Clotilda stirs as Gregorio begins his prayer and greets us in a hushed voice, "Qosay, husband, comadre, were you successful?" We both nod affirmatively. Clotilda responds with a sigh of relief and crosses herself. Gregorio continues with the coca divination. The next step requires that he "toss the bones" to read Juana's future in the world of the dead. Clotilda and I patiently watch, hoping that Juana's journey will take her to the world below. We both ask, "Does it go well?" To which Gregorio responds, "It's unclear. We'll have to wait." With heavy lids and aching limbs, I excuse myself and enter my tomb-like room and fall across the bed. Within minutes I descend into a fitful dream.

> Falling, falling
> down a spiral of water to the center,
> into the crystal cavern of creation.
> Blue, green, gold, silver luminosity
> of a sumptuous living cloak,
> the warp and weft alive with
> llamas, alpacas, yutus, pumas, viscachas.
>
> Pachamama's two-headed snake,
> the amaru, swims in the river of time:
> Pacha, earth, this place, this time.
>
> "Where am I?" I ask.
> "In ukupacha,
> in my domain, the world below."
> The vast, stupendous, enormity thunders,
> "Why are you here?"
> I answer,
> "To find Juana's organs,
> her heart, lungs, liver, womb.
> To return them to her body,
> to make her whole again."
>
> Pachamama turns,
> and I see two faces,
> one stupendous body
> with emergent tubers.
> Earth, stone, water, flesh.
> One face, benevolent, luminous,
> the face of creation.
> Corn in her right hand,
> a condor in her left,
> a baby llama suckles at her breast,
> a puma crouches at her side,
> fish swim at her feet.

The other face, malevolent, dark,
the face of destruction.
A skull suckles at her other breast,
a fox crouches at her left side,
a lizard sits below.

I kneel in front of her. She is female and male, good and evil, creation and destruction. She gazes at me and opens her mouth and says, "Go! You don't belong here!"

"No, no, she's going to—" Just at that moment a forceful jet of water sweeps me upward and into a water spiral. The force of the water is overpowering and I lose consciousness for a moment. When I come to, the crest of the water spiral has carried me to the surface of the earth. "Her spit carried me here! But this isn't saliva; it's spring water!" I'm sitting in one of the springs that feed the irrigation canals of Pumapunku.

I wake up laughing. I am back in my dank and musty room, damp but rested. Surprisingly, I feel totally refreshed and hungry. I have slept well into the afternoon. Jumping out of bed, I open the door of my room and call for my compadre, Gregorio.

"Compadre! Pachamama is pleased that we returned Juana's organs to her body. Pachamama told me!"

"Comadre, what are you saying?" Gregorio and other members of the family crowd around me as I recount my dream. Gregorio sets out an especially fine piece of ancient textile and begins the divination of Juana's journey for the third time. After the toss of the bones, he announces, "Yes, she has crossed the river of blood and is in the village of dogs. We must burn her clothes and she'll choose a black dog to carry her to the village of the dead. Hopefully she'll be at peace until the day of the dead when we must feed her."

"I think we should set out food for her every day, just in case," Clotilda declares worriedly.

"It certainly wouldn't hurt," Gregorio agrees. With that decision made, he prepares to burn the effigy of Juana that is laid out on the table, but stops short after setting fire to her clothing. "If one year had passed, we would be changing our mourning black to new attire. Should we do that or keep on our black out of respect?"

A general buzz arises from the twenty or so relatives who have kept vigil all night. The general agreement is to keep their mourning black on for the year and repeat the entire watan misa on the anniversary of Juana's death.

I help serve bowls of soup to everyone, and Gregorio assures the mourners that Juana's organs have been replaced and they are in no danger. As Gregorio finishes his story, a knock at the gate silences the crowd. Everyone waits for whoever is on the other side to announce their identity and their business. Silence, then a louder pounding.

"Open the door! This is the police!" Juana's clothing flares in a burst of bright flame, and everyone stares at it and then at the gate as Gregorio picks up his staff of office, puts on his hat and goes to let trouble into the sanctity of his home.

Romulo and two national policemen step through the gate and survey the wake. Romulo quickly catches the significance of the burning clothes. "A year early, aren't you? You know why we've come. A very serious matter. Someone's stolen what belongs to the state, the nation."

Jesus, now Juana's organs are national patrimony. Maybe they'll put them on display in the national museum. But he has to find them first. Will he dig her up again? I wonder. They won't dig her up, I'm sure. Look how nervous they are; the two policemen are just a couple of young kids from the coast who wish they could go home.

Romulo approaches me and puts his hand on my shoulder in a fatherly manner. "Comadre, I hope you're not mixed up in this. A serious crime has been committed," and with that he turns to Gregorio and begins rapid-fire questions in a low voice in Quechua that neither the policemen nor I can follow. Gregorio's denial of any knowledge is echoed by his kinfolk. This is the part of the game they have perfected over the centuries. The policemen are up against a solid, stone wall built stone by stone by polite resistance over centuries. Romulo gives the two young men a nod and they step forward. One says, "Señora, you will accompany us to Cangallo. The prefect is coming from Ayacucho and the secret police investigator wants to take your statement." With that, they march me out the door to the plaza and into the waiting pickup truck. Romulo gives a short military bow that declares a victory for El Capitán in the first of many scrimmages that will follow. His small army of drinking buddies is on the path outside waiting for him. They snap to attention and salute him as we pass.

I primly take my place in the cab of the truck between the two national policemen, guardias as they're called locally, and try to engage them in chitchat that fails miserably. They think I am some kind of gringa body snatcher. I finally learn that José Martinez is from the coastal city of Trujillo and Martín Hernandez hails from a small town north of Lima. Neither has ever been to the highlands before and they feel like they are in a foreign country. Strange language, inedible food, and, most of all, sullen Indians. This incident of organ snatching confirms their suspicions that "these Indians" are savages. I do my best to explain that Romulo performed a barbaric act by holding an autopsy at graveside with the mourners outside the cemetery wall and with more than twenty students watching.

"Where are the organs now?" demands José. "What if that guy, what's his name with the staff of office, has stolen them to do some kind of witchcraft?"

"My compadre Gregorio? No, I know that's not true," I reply. "If he took the organs, it was because he wanted to return them to his sister's body so she could rest in peace. Otherwise, she could do a lot of mischief and harm for everybody."

After a moment's pause, I add, "Besides, there's more witchcraft in Trujillo than here."

"Really? I don't believe it," counters José.

"It's true," I try to use my most authoritative professorial tone. "Trujillo has more curanderos, shamans, and witches than anywhere else in Peru. Right?"

"I suppose so. But . . . well, they don't steal organs."

"Witches do. They may not actually steal the organs. But they symbolically remove them to make victims sick, don't they?" I look at him and see that small beads of sweat are forming on his upper lip.

"Well, I've heard of that . . . but. . . ," sputters José.

Martín cuts in. "If she's right . . . they stole the organs to put them back in some woman's body. Right? Shit, I don't want to dig up a woman who committed suicide. That's scary. I want to be back in the cantina drinking and dancing with Josefa."

Right, we all want to be somewhere else. I want to be in my garden in Washington, D.C. I wonder what awaits me in Cangallo.

CHAPTER 6

AN ENCOUNTER WITH THE STATE

The truck bumps along the dirt road from Pumapumku to Cangallo. José, the driver, lights a cigarette and opens his window to let the smoke out, allowing the dust from the road to pour into the cab, clinging to our clothes and our hair and clogging our nostrils. This dust smells as though generations of ancestors have been recycled to become these specks of dust. *Maybe the generations of ancestors who have returned to the earth give the dust this special odor. The people here in the Andes have the same odor, not a body odor like ours but an odor that is old and earthy,* I muse as I pull out a tissue and dig the dust of the ancestors out of my nostrils.

José asks, "Do you want me to close the window, señora. Is the dust bothering you?"

"Yes, that would be great," I reply, looking at the clog of dirt I have just extracted from my nostrils. Now it looks like the dirt in the fields after it rains. I could plant a small garden in this dirt. They say that the dead become condensed and tiny and everything in the world of the dead is diminutive: the people, the fields, the animals. With the dust of the ancestors and a little water, I can plant a tiny plot for the dead.

As we pull into Cangallo I can see that a fiesta is in full swing.

"What's the celebration?" I ask.

"They're celebrating the one hundred-year anniversary of Cangallo as the province capital," explains Martín. "I bet it hasn't changed much since then."

The plaza is rectangular with a five-foot concrete statue in the center that is a replica of the obelisk commemorating the battle of Ayacucho in the Pampa of Quinua when Peru won its independence from Spain. The sixteenth-century church dominates one side of the plaza and the governmental buildings the other. A small pitiful park and garden surrounds the obelisk, which is encircled by wire fences protecting the struggling flowers from wandering pigs, goats, sheep, llamas, and children. In spite of all these efforts, the little garden of geraniums and a patch of violets look pretty sad. The rains are extremely late and the garden is suffering, as are the crops, for lack of water. Makeshift bleachers have been constructed at one end of the plaza between the two streets that exit the town. A platform stands in front of the municipal building for the dignitaries, who are seated watching the bullfight that is taking place in the streets.

Bullfights in Andean towns do not resemble their parental form, the bullfights of Spain. Cattle that are usually kept in the high puna, the tree-less plains above the villages and towns, are brought down by their owners to the town centers and dedicated to the bullfight by having a godmother or godfather chosen for the bull. The godparents' responsibility is to spit cane alcohol in the animal's eyes to give it enough spirit to fight. Most of the bulls are actually cows, because history has taught the locals that cows make better fighters than bulls. The animals are never killed or harmed and they are usually victorious over the drunken contestants who are fool enough to stagger into the plaza and wave their ponchos in the animals' faces. Injuries are common.

At the moment of my arrival, several men seem to be trying to distract an especially ferocious cow standing over a man who is covering his head with his arms. His fallen poncho lies on the ground, and the cow is stamping on it and sweeping her head and horns from side to side over the man's body. The men succeed in attracting the cow's attention and two men drag the injured man out of harm's way. His wife marches from her stall where she sells beer and sodas and begins to berate her husband's foolhardiness in a loud voice. The crowd laughs and claps approvingly. This episode has held the attention of the dignitaries high above the crowd on the balcony of the municipal building, but now that it is over, they turn their attention to our arrival and the mayor of Cangallo leads a small procession of men to greet me.

"Doctora Woodley, we are so pleased that you could join our small, poverty-stricken celebration." *I don't think I'll correct his mistakenly calling me Woodley. Maybe they had Woodley instead of Woodsley in the police records, better no one knows.* I take a deep breath and manage a smile.

"I am so pleased to be among your most distinguished guests, Señor Al-calde." *As if I have a choice. Now which one of these bastards is the PIP investigator, the secret police representative who is going to interrogate me? Aha! That's him, the guy with the slicked-back hair, tailor-made charcoal gray suit, new shoes, white shirt, and long narrow tie. He looks about thirty-five. Not bad-looking, but not as good-looking as he imagines. He's a macho dandy, I'm sure.*

"Doctora, let me present the prefect of the department of Ayacucho, Doctor Luis Zarate, who traveled from the capital to preside over our humble festivities."

"Con mucho gusto," the prefect says as he extends his hand and then kisses me on each cheek. "I hear you are conducting anthropological research in Pumapunku. Correct? That's close to Chuschi where Sendero Luminoso burned the ballot box for the election last May. But the election was held when new ballots were flown in. Were you in Pumapunku then?"

"No, Doctor Zarate, our semester doesn't end until mid-May, and I was teaching in Washington, D.C. I didn't arrive until the first of June."

Mr. PIP, of the Peruvian Investigative Police, approaches and introduces himself. "I am Oscar Bustamante from Lima here to look into several recent events in this part of the department of Ayacucho. I'm sure you can be helpful in my investigations." He smiles and shakes my hand firmly, first looking into my eyes, then sweeping his gaze slowly up and down my body.

I've got to be careful with this guy. He's probably dangerous. I've always been told to avoid the secret police like the plague. I'm really in the frying pan now. Better watch what I say. He has an agenda for sure.

The mayor rushes over and grabs my elbow and exudes, "Doctora Woodley, we have a special honor for you" as he leads me to the municipal building, recently whitewashed for the celebration. We climb the stairs to the second floor and proceed out through a door to the low balcony that looks out onto the plaza. The prefect takes his place in the center front row and the mayor has people move over to make room for me next to his place in the first row of chairs. After much shifting and readjustments, I am seated between the prefect and the mayor, who calls to an indigenous official, a staff holder or varayoq, who is in the back of the congregated dignitaries leaning against the wall of building. The varayoqkuna are not allowed to sit with mestizo dignitaries; they hover around the peripheries waiting for orders. He receives his instructions and takes off at a trot, his staff of office bouncing under his arm and his poncho flying. In a few minutes he returns with what looks like a silver vessel from the church.

"Here you are, Señor Alcalde," he says as he carefully hands the vessel to the mayor. It is half full of holy water.

The mayor looks at me in anticipation. "Doctora Woodley, we ask you to be the godmother to our new dump truck and to baptize it with this holy water. Please, come this way." With that, he hands me the vessel. I look down and see that, indeed, a new dump truck, shiny and black, has been driven to the front of the municipal building. A small crowd has gathered to watch the proceedings. I step forward to the railing of the balcony and, dipping my right hand in the vessel of holy water, sprinkle the truck, intoning in a sing-song voice, "I baptize this dump truck for the town of Cangallo."

Good God, now I can add a dump truck to my list of godchildren. What's worse is that the mayor as the father of the truck is my compadre and can ask me for a contribution when the truck needs new tires or repairs. Or he'll ask me to perform a Mass and baptism of health for one of his children so he can request that I educate his kid in the U.S., or maybe he'll ask me to become the godmother of one of his children's weddings. I have ten godchildren already and people expect so much from me. I've got to put a curb on these ritual relationships. But how? I—

Oscar Bustamante breaks into my thoughts and asks, "Doctora Woodley, would you step into the mayor's office, please. I have just a few questions to ask you."

Here it comes, I say to myself as I enter the mayor's office and sit on a long bench against the wall. Bustamante pulls a chair in front of the bench to face me, his knees almost touching mine.

"May I see your passport, please?"

"I only carry this photocopy around with me, and here is my research permit issued by the Ministry of Culture and stamped by the mayor of the community of Pumapunku."

"Let's see, you reside in Washington, D.C., and you are a professor of anthropology. Your birth date is 1933 so that makes you—"

"I'm forty-seven," I answer.

"But not married?" he asks, raising his eyebrows.

"No, I am not," I answer.

"I was informed of the bizarre events in Pumapunku. Organs from an autopsy were stolen? Is that correct?"

"Well, not really stolen. The peasants of Pumapunku broke into the office of the director of schools to return the organs to the body of a woman who had committed suicide. You see, they believe that she will not leave this world until her organs are buried with her body. In addition, they believe that natural disasters, such as earthquakes, droughts, floods, or crop failures, will occur if the woman is buried without her organs."

"I see. Superstitious bunch if you ask me. Did you take part in the theft, Doctora Woodley?"

"Well, I went along as an observer. To see what they would do. It was a very interesting event, anthropologically."

"So you know who the culprits are?"

"I don't know their names. They drew lots to see who would fetch the organs. They believed that to touch them could do them great harm. I watched from a distance, but I didn't ask anyone's names because they wouldn't have told me."

"O.K., Doctora, now I have a few more questions for you." He stands up and sits next to me on the bench. Then with a great flourish, he stretches his left arm out and lays it on the back of the bench behind me. I move forward to avoid bodily contact. He continues. "You are aware that last May a group of delinquents burned the ballots in the village of Chuschi, not far from Pumapunku, aren't you?"

"Yes, I was not in residence in Pumapunku until the first of June, but people who were at the Friday market in Chuschi brought back the news." I answer.

"Do you have any idea who could have done this?"

"No, señor, I have no idea. People say they were hooded and came in the night."

"We think they are members of Sendero Luminoso, Shining Path, a communist group operating out of the city of Ayacucho, mostly university students. But locals could be involved as well."

"I have no idea who could be involved locally. I haven't heard any communist speeches or seen any posters in Pumapunku."

"You'll keep me informed if you see anything suspicious, won't you, Doctora? If I were you, I would plan to leave Pumapunku. It's very hard to keep you safe in such a remote place." And with that statement, he slips his left hand over my right one, picks it up and places it on the handle of his gun that is tucked in the top of his pants. He squeezes my hand so that my fingers curl around the handle of the gun. With his right hand, he reaches across my body and grabs my left hand and places it in his crotch. He has a hard-on. *I'm holding his cock and his gun!*

I avert my eyes and try to think of something to say, but can't. I wrench my hands free of his grip and gingerly lift both hands in the air and shake them as if I've been burned. I want to shoot his johnson off and flee, but I'm trapped. A long, awkward moment passes while he just leers at me. I'm frozen, so shocked I don't know what to do. I know my face is flushed beet-red. I hear a noise on the stairs and look toward the door beseechingly.

The mayor bursts into the room calling out, "Doctora Woodley, ahora eres mi comadre — you are my comadre; we are co-parents of the dump truck.

I've come to take you to the festivities. We've prepared a wonderful meal, a Pachamanka, meat, potatoes, habas, ocas, and other vegetables roasted in an earth oven. Have you been to one before?"

"Oh yes, the people of Pumapunku gave one for my birthday last year. Pachamankas are wonderful!" *But you, my dear mayor, are more than wonderful for rescuing me! You are splendiferous!!*

"Then afterward," the mayor adds as he takes my arm and hustles me toward the door, "we're having a dance. I'm sure you know how to dance the wayno, don't you?"

"Oh yes, I do. It sounds like a grand fiesta."

The mayor turns to Bustamante, El Señor PIP with the hard-on, and says, "And Señor Bustamante, you must come as well." As I rise to leave with the mayor, I look back and see Señor Hard-On trying to rise and compose himself. The mayor and I leave the office and cross the plaza, littered with bottles and plastic bags from the crowd that has dispersed after the bullfight. The pit for the earth oven has been dug in the schoolyard and one of the secondary school rooms is set up with long tables. The wives of the traditional authorities, the varayoqkuna, are serving the mestizos—mostly bureaucrats and schoolteachers, and a few local merchants. None of the traditional officials are seated at the tables. They are fed outside after the mestizos are served. Social hierarchy and separation are carefully observed. Even though the indigenous population has "donated" the food, labor, and service for the festivities, they are excluded from the table. The old feudal system has been modified, but it perseveres. Mestizos no longer own Indians like chattel, but they own their records. An Indian peasant cannot acquire a birth certificate or voters' card without the pen, ink, and signature of mestizo bureaucrats. The written word is as powerful as the sword.

The schoolyard is filling up with invited guests and we are ceremoniously ushered to the table reserved for dignitaries. The mayor introduces me as the godmother of the dump truck and everyone applauds, except for Señor PIP—Mr. Hard-On, Oscar Bustamante, who looks amused. I'm seated between him and the prefect of the department. We drink several glasses of beer as one after another of the mestizo bureaucrats gets up to make a toast: To me, to the new dump truck, to Bustamante, to the prefect, to the local priest, to the mayor, and finally to the town of Cangallo for its one hundred years as a province capital.

We are served a heaping plate of guinea pig, potatoes, corn, and a variety of other root vegetables that have been included in the stone-lined fire pit and roasted slowly for six hours. Communities in the surrounding region have been called upon to provide food for almost one hundred guests. The prefect of the department of Ayacucho leans over and asks me if I have eaten guinea pig before, and I answer, "Oh yes, it's delicious isn't it?" I pick up the half guinea pig with my fingers and tear off one of the legs, saying, "I must confess, I never eat the head." He laughs, picks up his half guinea pig and crunches the head with his teeth and says, "But the head is the best part!"

The prefect, as a political appointee from Lima, must belong to the same party as the president, Fernando Belaunde Terry, who was ousted from the presidency in 1968 by the military. His election earlier this year in 1980 was the first democratic election in seventeen years. Spirits are high in Cangallo as the appointed bureaucrats celebrate. The beer begins to flow more freely after the meal, and the prefect and Bustamante begin to talk openly about the burning of the ballots in the village of Chuschi. The prefect is of the opinion that it is nothing to worry about, but Bustamante thinks otherwise. He declares, "Radicalism and Marxism are widespread in the university in Ayacucho. I'm sure that this act against our return to democracy is the work of one of the Marxist groups."

"But," the prefect laughs, "there are so many competing Marxist groups that fight amongst themselves. How can they organize to do anything?"

"I think they're up to something big. Mark my words. I'm here to try to find out what's going on in this province," Bustamante responds with a frown as he stares pointedly at me.

"I'll do whatever I can to help you," the prefect replies. And with that he turns to me and asks me to dance. A brass band has entered into the courtyard and has begun to play. The prefect is short, fat, balding, about forty-five with sagging jowls and puffy eyes. His suit is ill-fitting and stained. I keep staring at his tie because it looks like someone cut it off with scissors. It only reaches the second button on his shirt and has a huge grease spot on it that looks like an eye.

Oh well, I think as we stamp and pivot to the wayno music, *perhaps he's a good administrator.*

As the evening wears on, the men, who are seated in clusters, are getting drunker and louder, and the women, who are seated along the wall in a straight line of chairs, cross their arms and look on disapprovingly. I try not to drink and take refuge in the line of women along the wall. Señor PIP asks me to dance and I beg off, saying I'm tired from the last energetic wayno.

"Oh come on, it's a slow waltz," he says as he pulls me to the center of the floor.

Several women call out, "Yes, dance, Doctora, you must have a good time." On the dance floor, he holds me very tight and I can feel the pistol tucked in his belt. I can also feel his other gun swelling. He begins to whisper in my ear, "Doctora, I bet you've never had a good Peruvian lover before. I'll show you what a real man's like."

Before I can say anything, the prefect cuts in and slurs, "If the gringa goes wif anyone, it'll be me."

Bustamante growls in a low drunken tone, "The hell you say" as he pushes the prefect away.

I put my hands on my hips and yell, "Why don't you filthy bastards go fuck each other and leave me alone!" The music stops and everyone stares. Some of the women cover their mouths in shock.

At that moment, there is a commotion just beyond the entryway to the school. My compadre Gregorio and four of his subordinate officials are standing just outside the circle of light of the courtyard. Gregorio steps onto the dance floor, holding his staff of office with his four officials behind him also displaying their staffs of authority.

"Comadre Alicia, we are here to escort you back to Pumapunku. Your business here must be completed by now. The moon is full and it will be no difficulty to walk." He makes this declaration in his most carefully enunciated Spanish as he reaches for my arm and pulls me forward to give me the traditional greeting. Standing and facing one another, we raise our right arms over each other's shoulders and place our left hands on each other's backs at the waist, and go pat pat pat. Reversing our arms, we repeat the gesture on the other side, pat pat pat.

From here on, I'll always associate the sound and feel of those pats with safety. I quickly move toward the door with my phalanx of protectors, the varayoqkuna.

The municipal mayor comes forward and says, "Nonsense, that's a four-hour walk. I'll send the National Guard truck to take you back."

"Gracias alcalde, muy amable," I hurriedly say as we move further beyond the door. I look back to see Oscar Bustamante drunkenly talking to the prefect, who is waving his arms and pointing at us. The National Guard post is only fifty yards from the school and we reach it quickly. The mayor gives one of the guards on duty quick instructions and the six of us climb in the back of the truck.

"Doctora," pleads the mayor, "I am so sorry this has happened. Don't you want to sit in the cab?"

"Oh, no, I'm fine in the back with my compadre and his officials," I answer as I settle down beside Gregorio. *They really saved my ass this time,* I think. *How am I going to ever repay them?*

CHAPTER 7

THE PRISONS

I was jolted back to the present.

The smell of eucalyptus that had assailed me outside of Larco Herrera after visiting María, Felix's sister, had again returned me to the cemetery in Pumapunku. During the hour-long cab ride to Carlos's house, I remained silent, afraid of what the cab driver might reveal. I'd heard enough for one day. I fingered the insignia in my brief case and pondered the unimaginable ways people have gotten tangled into the web of the war with Shining Path.

The taxi driver broke into my thoughts and said, "We're here, señora." I opened my eyes and paid him. When I entered Carlos's fortified house in La Molina, he came into the hall to greet me.

"Querida, you look terrible. What happened at the hospital?"

I told him about María's story, and Carlos led me into the living room and we sat on the sofa. I felt bone-tired. Carlos put his arms around me and gently asked, "What are you going to do with these stories, Alice? You have been collecting them for years. At first you were reluctant to publish them for fear of endangering the individuals and then you published several because the victims thought it was important to do so. But now, during the reconciliation process, what purpose will publishing such stories serve?" Tears were now running down my cheeks.

"Carlos," I sobbed, "when I asked her what her attackers looked like, she look right at me and said, 'Almost Peruvian, but you know? El Capítan? He was fair-skinned, blue-eyed, wore glasses.' She paused and took a long look at me and then said, 'He looked just like you.' I felt a stab in my heart. JUST LIKE ME! Just like me!"

My sobs grew louder and Carlos began to rock me as if I were a baby. "Alice, please, you are destroying yourself. You are not responsible for what happened to María. You have got to move beyond this war. We as a nation are moving beyond it. You must as well." He stroked my hair and held me tenderly.

After a long silence, I confided. "That dream has come back. It rears its ugly head every time I come to Peru."

"What dream?" Carlos asked.

"I'm in the countryside near Pumapunku and I'm building a huge wall with adobes. But no one helps me. There are crowds of people in the distance carrying placards with pictures of their dead loved ones on them. I work hard and fast, but if I look away for even a moment, the wall crumbles into a muddy heap. I curse and stamp my feet and start all over from the beginning, calling out to the people in the distance to come and help me. It's exhausting and I wake up so-o tired."

Carlos gently pushed me away from him, held me at arm's length and looked into my blurry eyes, and said, "I think you are building a memorial wall to the dead. Do you know what you will do with it when it is finished?"

"Maybe you're right, Carlos. I think I'd put the pictures of the dead and disappeared . . . the placards that relatives of victims carry . . . you know on the wall."

"And create a monument to them. Right?" observed Carlos. "But each time you build it, it crumbles. You obviously feel that you are failing to build the monument that they deserve."

"Well yes, the wall is a monument to the dead and I do feel that I have failed to commemorate them."

We sat in silence and Carlos commented in a soft voice, "Maybe if you build your monument, you can return to the present."

"Could be, but I know that I will move beyond the war when I find Cholita," I responded as I wiped my eyes and blew my nose. I moved toward the telephone and picked it up, saying, "I have to call Carla and tell her that I have given her number to María and to the taxi driver. I have to convince her to treat them. I'll pay her fee. I know neither of them has the money and institutional treatment will do nothing. Also I have to make arrangements to get into Santa Monica, the women's prison in Chorrillos. I think Teresa Quispe, Cholita's cousin, is there. I hope she is not in Puno, because I don't want to travel to the coldest place in the Andes."

"What taxi driver?" Carlos asked.

"I'll tell you later," I answered as I walked toward the phone.

As Carlos followed, he commented, "I think only the leadership of Shining Path is imprisoned in Puno. Seven hundred rank-and-file members are dispersed throughout the prison system. Alice, I wish you luck in your quest, but querida, it's taking a severe toll on you." He shook his head and went back to his study to weave his fantasies into poems and stories. He paused at the door and turned. "I think you should see Carla and explore your dream with her. There's obviously a lot more there."

"You're probably right," I said as I picked up my portfolio and carried it into my room to add my notes to my twenty-year archive. I picked up the taxi driver's insignia and cradled it in my palm and suddenly remembered that I had not tape-recorded his story. I had to write down my notes immediately. As I stood picturing him, I ran the digit finger of my left hand along the left side of my tongue where a lesion had been excised. A large section of my tongue was missing. The surgery had left me speechless for weeks. For a few days I worried that the stories I had collected had given me cancer of the tongue, but the biopsy had been negative. What year had that been? Wasn't it 1983, during the height of the violence? It had been a particularly difficult time, when I was trying to decide which stories of the war were safe to publish and which had to remain secretly guarded in my portfolio. Now, twenty years later, I can publish all of them. Or can I? I ran my finger along the incision on my tongue again and reached for the phone.

I spent the next three days confirming that Teresa Quispe Huamán was in Santa Monica prison in Chorrillos, along with five other members of Shining Path. Political prisoners were no longer held together in large groups because in the mid-1980s they had run the war from the prisons. I remember going into Lurigancho, El Frontón, and Canto Grande prisons in May of 1986 with a Belgian film crew. It was only a year after Romulo had been assassinated, and I was looking for any evidence of Cholita's involvement with Shining Path. In the women's prison, Canto Grande, I learned from a young woman that at the same time she had joined Shining Path, two young girls that fit the descriptions of Cholita and her cousin, Teresa, were recruited into the ranks of the insurgents. That was in 1982, a year and a half after Juana's suicide. Evidently, the two girls had fled Pumapunku the day of Juana's burial and traveled to the city of Ayacucho, where they came into contact with university students, who won them over to Sendero's cause. Cholita was twelve and Teresa was thirteen at the time.

One of those students was Edith Lagos, the eighteen-year-old daughter of a prosperous shopkeeper. The popular myth is that on the second of March of 1982, Edith Lagos was arrested and jailed in the city of Ayacucho. Lagos, along with 130 other inmates, was liberated from the prison by a column of one hundred Shining Path insurgents. Cholita and Teresa were rumored to have taken part in that action, and they became members of the column that Edith Lagos commanded. Later that year, the story goes, Edith Lagos was captured, some say while learning to drive a car in Andahuaylas, but the official story is that she was captured in a battle between Sendero and the guardia. The popular myth is that Edith was brought back to Ayacucho, interrogated by the PIP, the secret police, and tortured to death. Shining Path members stole her body from the PIP headquarters in Ayacucho and put her on display in a funeral procession that drew a crowd of 100,000 people.

Edith Lagos took on the status of a mythical heroine after her death. Her parents buried her in a cemetery outside the city that quickly became a pilgrimage site. Hundreds of pilgrims visited her grave, depositing gifts and flowers, especially the emblematic flower of Shining Path insurgents, Flor de Retama, a fragrant member of the broom, Genista, family that blooms in the late spring in the countryside. Groups of young girls would bring bouquets of Flor de Retama to Edith Lagos's graveside and sing the song with the same name:

Flor de Retama

Wild herb, pure perfume
I beg of you follow my path
You will be my balsam and my tragedy,
my perfume and my glory.
You will be the friend that flowers over my tomb.
There, let the mountain cover me,
let the heavens answer me.
All will be engraved in stone.
Where the blood of the pueblo
pours out, that is where
the yellow flower of the Retama blooms.

When the supplicants departed, they would take small stones and dirt from Lagos's grave as mementos. The military responded by blowing up her grave three times. Her father rebuilt it each time and pilgrims continued to seek out her mystical power. For about a year, clay figures of Edith Lagos dressed in her Maoist uniform but with the body posture of the Madonna, her head inclined to one side, could be purchased in local markets. Instead of a baby in her arms, a rifle was nestled tenderly. The mythology continued to grow around this romantic figure, and stories circulated that Edith Lagos had a baby with Guzmán, Presidente Gonzalo. The new myth said that after Edith was tortured to death, her father spirited the baby away to Denmark, where she lives today. The baby's name, it is said, is Illa, or Messenger in Quechua, but her name has another meaning: ILA is the acronym that Shining Path used for El Inicio de la Lucha Armada, the Initiation of the Armed Struggle, in 1980.

When I entered the prisons in 1986, Shining Path inmates were held in separate pavilions: 250 males in El Frontón, 125 males in Lurigancho, and around 150 women in Canto Grande, a distribution that reflects the sexual division in the organization from the central committee to the rank and file. I observed that in all three prisons, Shining Path controlled who entered their pavilions; they even had the keys to their cells. Messages and goods flowed freely. The team of filmmakers and I were met at the gate of El Frontón not by a prison official, but by a Sendero leader. The rebels thought that a European film would serve their propaganda purposes. García's government had quickly rehabilitated El Frontón, an old abandoned prison in Lima, to house the increasing numbers of insurgents. Rather than an inaccessible prison for Shining Path, the government had provided a centralized location for the movements' leaders to coordinate the actions of the war. The Republican guards in charge of prisons seldom entered the Shining Path pavilions, partly because they were afraid but mostly because they were bribed.

In all three of the prisons, Sendero prisoners wore their own Maoist uniforms consisting of brown shirts, black pants or skirts, and Maoist caps. They marched and drilled regularly; they maintained a disciplined schedule of meetings and study of the ideology and science of Marxism, Leninism, Maoism, and Presidente Gonzalo thought. In the Blue Pavilion of El Frontón, the Shining Path prisoners had painted murals showing three standing figures: Marx, Lenin, and Mao as the three swords of communism. Presidente Gonzalo, the fourth sword, was given a wall of his own. He was depicted in his usual pose, a smiling face with horn-rimmed glasses, the red book of Mao in one hand and a red flag with hammer and sickle in the other to signify the struggle. I noticed that he was painted with a hard square jaw and firm muscles showing through his short-sleeved shirt. I distinctly remember Guzmán from my brief time at the University of Huamanga in Ayacucho in the 1960s. Guzmán, a professor of philosophy, had heavy jowls and a pot belly. Presidente Gonzalo, Guzmán's revolutionary alter ego depicted in the painting, had a chiseled chin and the arms and torso of a weight lifter. Edith

Lagos is not the only myth that had emerged from this war, I concluded as I entered the pavilion.

In the Blue Pavilion, the film crew shot footage of the prisoners marching in formation, waving the red flag of communism, and shouting slogans. Long Live the Popular War! Construct the Conquest of Power! Long Live Presidente Gonzalo!

The Belgian film crew and I arrived at Canto Grande in the early afternoon after filming in Lurigancho and El Frontón. First we were led into a long narrow room that seemed to be a chapel; an altar with burning candles stood at one end with benches in orderly rows facing the altar. But the iconography on the wall behind the altar was not of Jesus, Mary, nor any of the Catholic saints prisoners might pray to, but rather a large painting of Presidente Gonzalo. And like the painting in El Frontón, he was shown with the same symbols of the revolution and the same muscular physique. We were led into a courtyard where fifty uniformed women performed what could be called a revolutionary opera, with choreographed flag-waving, chanting, and singing directed to their glorious leader, Presidente Gonzalo, whose fifteen-foot-high face beamed from above with a sea of gun-toting peasants streaming off into infinity below him. Letters along one wall with ten-foot high letters read "Nothing Is Impossible!" I thought I was watching a scene from the Chinese Cultural Revolution.

One month later, on June 18 and 19, 1986, a coordinated uprising in all three prisons was met with crushing force from García's government. Three hundred prisoners were killed, most of them after they had surrendered and were lying face down on the floor. After that, Shining Path prisoners were no longer held together, but rather dispersed through the country's prison system.

No such display of revolutionary fervor was visible on the sunny December morning in 2005 when I finally gained entrance into the Santa Monica Prison for women. What a contrast with my earlier experience! A prison official reviewed my passport and papers from the Ministry of Justice at the front entry of Santa Monica and then led me into a guarded visiting room where fifteen inmates were seated with their visitors. Most visitors looked like family members wearing the signs of extreme poverty—haggard faces, frayed clothing, and run-down shoes. It was impossible to tell Shining Path prisoners from the "regular" prisoners. I looked around and saw no Shining Path artwork or slogans, only a lone crucifix and a large picture of President Toledo.

No Presidente Gonzalo was glorified on these walls, and there were no middle-class mestiza prisoners either. A woman guard interrupted my thoughts and informed me that Teresa Quispe was being escorted from her cell. *And I'll bet that Shining Path prisoners don't have the keys to their cells,* I thought.

A moment later a young woman was escorted into the room. She looked older that her thirty-four years, with hard lines around her mouth and eyes. About my height, thin, with very short black hair and hard, brown eyes, she was dressed in a blue prison uniform, not the Maoist uniform that I had seen before.

I rose and extended my hand, asking, "Teresa Quispe Huamán? I am Alicia Woodsley. I have worked for many years in Pumapunku. Do you remember me?" With that, I pulled out photos of Teresa's parents standing with me in the plaza of Pumapunku and placed them on the table. Then I took out another photo of Teresa and Cholita standing with me in Gregorio's patio, saying, "I took this is 1980 just before you and Cholita left. I also have a tape-recorded letter from your parents. May I play it for you?"

Teresa picked up the photos and looked at them but did not say a word. She placed the photos on the table and walked out of the room.

Well, I guess that's that, I thought. But when I picked up the photos, I found a very small folded note tucked between them. I slipped the photos and the note into my briefcase and called the guard.

I didn't dare open the note until I was in the taxi on my way to Carlos's house. I opened the note and in very small neat handwriting it said:

Come back tomorrow at two o'clock,
I'm being watched. I can't talk to you now.
Ask the administration for a private room.
The one lawyers use.

She wants to talk to me, thank God. I thought I had failed again. I have to think very carefully how to proceed. Maybe I shouldn't ask about Cholita at all. But I've got to. I'll wait until I think she's ready. I'll play the message from her parents first and see what happens.

I called the prison administration and made arrangements to see Teresa in the lawyers' interview room. The next day I could hardly wait for two o'clock to arrive. I rehearsed over and over what I might say to Teresa, playing one or another "what if" scenarios over and over again in my mind. Arriving at the prison fifteen minutes early, I had to wait for the room to be readied and for an available guard to escort Teresa from her cell. I entered the sparse, small room and sat down in one of the two chairs at the table. Ten minutes later

Teresa came in, accompanied by a woman guard who waited just outside the door after locking it.

"I do remember you," Teresa said as she shook my hand. "You're Cholita's godmother. She talked about you a lot after we left Pumapunku." She looked less stern; the lines around her mouth and eyes were softer. "I'd like to hear the tape from my parents."

I took the tape recorder out of my bag, put the tape in, and pressed Play. A long formal greeting in Quechua from both Teresa's mother and father was followed by a story of the ghastly events that had taken place in Pumapunku since Teresa left in 1980. First her father narrated how forty hooded Shining Path insurgents arrived the year after Teresa left and held a meeting. The guerrillas brought two prisoners into the village plaza, men who were known cattle thieves. They tied ropes around their necks, bound their hands behind their backs, and forced the men onto their knees. The Shining Path leader asked the assembly, "How many of you've lost animals to these cowardly thieves who would rather steal your animals rather than work for their own?" A roar went up from the crowd because at least twenty families had lost animals in the previous six months. "Let this be a lesson to all thieves," the leader shouted as he aimed his rifle at the older man's head and shot him in the forehead. The younger man, his son, began to cry and plead. "Please, I'll leave the district and never come back! I'll never steal again."

The hooded leader looked at him as if he were a bug, took aim, and shot the son as well. Next, the Senderistas tied signs around their necks that read "THE PEOPLE'S WAR WILL NOT TOLERATE THIEVERY." After their initial shock, the frightened assembled villagers nervously joined in as Sendero applauded.

For six months, recounted Teresa's father, Shining Path and the villagers coexisted in an uneasy truce. Shining Path held a court once a week where complaints were heard and the guilty punished. Women began to complain of abuse by husbands, who were subsequently whipped publicly. Drunkenness, lying, and cheating customers during market day were offenses worthy of public punishment. Teresa's father also explained that schoolteachers were carefully monitored by the guerrillas and new curricula were established. Mao's little red book became a bible, along with the book of Gonzalo thought.

Six months after Shining Path had established themselves in the community, a leader arrived demanding that all the authorities of the community renounce their offices and allow Sendero to install their own members of the movement in positions of authority; the departmental and state officials wouldn't even know they had taken power. Not realizing the potential brutality of the insurgents, the community refused to have their elected authorities thrown out of office. Shining Path's answer was swift: The leader lined up the eight village officials in front of the assembled community, tied their hands behind their backs, and shot them. Then he calmly took the keys to the town hall out of the mayor's pocket and gave them to one of his men. The transfer of power was complete.

Pumapunku gathered their dead and buried them in stunned silence. They had never dealt with such authoritarian rule because their region of Ayacucho was an island of self-rule that lived in a sea of hacienda domination; Pumapunku and surrounding villages had maintained control of their lands and villages since the sixteenth century. Other communities soon heard of Pumapunku's fate and concluded that there could be no discussions nor negotiations with Shining Path.

The next few years were extremely difficult, Teresa's father confided. They were required to welcome Shining Path combatants and to feed and house all of them, which made the community Communist sympathizers in the eyes of the military. They were caught between the sword and the flame. The military made numerous raids on Pumapunku and other villages in the region. Fatalities climbed.

In the third year a military post was set up in the school to patrol the surrounding mountain communities. News of Shining Path's operations in the region had reached the commander of forces in Ayacucho. Little did the military realize that the officials who welcomed them into the community were actually insurgents. In 1983 Shining Path attacked the military post in Pumapunku, but they were repelled when the military called for reinforcements that arrived by helicopters. Shining Path escaped over the mountain to the south and Pumapunku was now viewed as a village loyal to Shining Path. Men and boys fled over the mountain to the south, not to follow the insurgents, but to escape military repression, which was reaching extreme proportions. Ten men disappeared in the months that followed. Pumapunku became a village of elderly women and children.

After a long communal discussion, the villagers decided to request a permanent guardia, National Guard, or army post for protection before they chose new officials. A contingent of ten soldiers was ordered to remain in Pumapunku and patrol the region from there. Villagers thought that they would now be safe.

Teresa's mother's voice took over with the next installment of Puma-punku's saga. She began her story with the high-pitched keening of a funeral dirge and asked, "Do you remember María Conde? Well it was at her wedding to Juan Pacotaype. That was when it happened." She went on to report that the soldiers had been in the community for two months when two soldiers tried to crash the wedding party but were thrown out because they were drunk and abusive. In a vengeful fit, the two soldiers reported to their commanding officer that they had seen a suspicious gathering in one of the compounds and heard shouts of Long Live Presidente Gonzalo! Long Live the Revolution! They insisted that when they entered the compound, the villagers threw stones at them. "Those cholos de mierda were so riled up that we had to flee," they insisted. The young captain sent a small contingent of soldiers, none of whom spoke Quechua, to investigate. The gathered wedding party of twenty celebrants tried to explain, but the soldiers were convinced that Shining Path insurgents were hiding in the interior of the house. They turned the house upside-down stealing radios, ponchos, almost anything they could put their hands on. But they found no incriminating pamphlets or evidence of Shining Path. They swore that they would return.

And return they did, but this time with their captain and the full contingent of ten soldiers. The two soldiers who had initially attempted to crash the party swore over and over that they had heard revolutionary chants and songs. Perhaps the Shining Path bastards had gotten away, they suggested. The captain took all of the wedding party into custody and marched them outside the village on the path toward Pomabamba. Teresa's mother recounted that they were never seen again, but now twenty years later the excavation team from the Truth and Reconciliation Commission had uncovered a mass grave that people called "the place where souls rise up from the earth when a strong wind is blowing" on the same path. The bodies were identified as the long-lost wedding party. Teresa's mother's voice faded to soft whispers as she said, "My lil' dove . . . no matter what you've done, we want you home."

Teresa's father's voice shook with emotion as he declared. "Yes, we want you to come home. I know that Pumapunku is ready to forgive you, Terecita. Please come home and confess. Our grief has filled our hearts and stomachs and only you can make us well by confessing. Come home lil' dove." The tape ended with Teresa's father singing Palomitay, Little Dove, Teresa's favorite as a child.

After the tape ended, Teresa put her head in her hands and began to sob. "I really wanna go home! I've been in prison for three years. But I can't be

released under the law of repentance unless I name at least five comrades. I can't do that. I'd be killed if I give up names. Other Senderistas who have not been caught have gotten new identity papers and moved far away from anyone who knows them and started new lives. I can't do that. I wanna go home! I'll probably hav'ta serve my whole sentence of ten years."

"What if Pumapunku submitted a document saying they would be willing to forgive you and have you move back into the village?" I asked, "Would that work?"

"Maybe under the new rules of reconciliation. It might work," Teresa said thoughtfully, wiping her eyes on her sleeve.

"I'm going to Pumapunku now. I'd be willing to tape-record a message from you to your parents. You could propose such a plan. What do you think?" I asked while digging out a new tape and loading it into the tape recorder.

"It just might work," responded Teresa hopefully.

"Teresa, I have a couple of questions for you. Is Cholita alive? If so, where is she?" I waited and held my breath.

Teresa looked at me for several moments, pursed her lips, and bit her lower lip nervously. She said, "Yes, Cholita's alive. She's using our surname, Quispe, and her mother's name Juana. She's called Juana Quispe. But I don't know where she is."

THE ROSETTI NOSE

That evening after a leisurely dinner with Carlos, I hurriedly made reserva-
tions to fly to Ayacucho the next day. Carlos again tried to convince me to
abandon my quest, but I now felt certain I would find Cholita. He embraced
me after dinner and bid me good luck, saying, "You always have been such a
determined wench. I'll see you when you return. I won't get up at 4 A.M. to
say good-bye, so let me show how to turn off the alarm system."

After a fitful night dreaming of constructing my memorial wall, I rose
at 3 A.M. to make the 6 A.M. flight. Dressing quickly and slipping out of the
quiet house into the waiting cab, I got into the back seat and closed my eyes,
pretending to sleep on the way to the airport, afraid of another horror story.
The hour-and-a-half flight to the colonial city in southern Peru, known for its
thirty-three colonial churches and Holy Week celebrations, was breathtaking.
Small lakes sparkled and trails and paths formed intricate zigzag patterns on
the steep mountain slopes. Peering out the window of the plane, I tried to
concentrate on the terraced fields that clung to the vertical terrain. As the
plane banked to make its approach to Ayacucho's airport, large expanses of
high, dry puna became visible with snow-capped mountains rising jaggedly
above them. This approach allowed a view of the Pampa de Quinua, thirty-
seven kilometers (twenty-three miles) to the north of the city, where the
battle that sealed South American independence was fought in 1824.

Today the city of Ayacucho is better known as the home of the University
of San Cristobal de Huamanga, the birthplace of Shining Path. The university
was founded in 1677 as the second oldest university in the viceroyalty. It was
closed in 1855 in the aftermath of the War of the Pacific and reopened in 1959.
Guzmán accepted a post as professor of philosophy in 1962. The decade of the
1960s found the university swimming in a sea of revolutionary rhetoric. The
debates concerned which revolutionary model to follow: China's, Russia's, or
Cuba's. By 1965 Guzmán and his followers in Shining Path were advocating

armed conflict at the Fifth National Conference of Communism, and they prepared the way for that war over the next fifteen years. Guzmán and several other leaders of Shining Path traveled to China to take part in the Cultural Revolution and to receive explicit training for war.

As soon as I stepped off the plane, dirt devils swirled around my legs and I was overpowered by the particular odor of Ayacucho—the musty, earthy smell of dust, the smell that I had identified years ago as the dust of the ancestors. I collected my bag and made my way to the front of the airport, hailed a taxi, and gave the address of the Rosetti house facing the barranco before crossing the bridge to the Convent of Santa Teresa. All memories pass through the olfactory organ, and as I descended from the cab into the dusty road in front of the Rosetti house, the dirt devils engulfed me again and the dust of the ancestors carried me on a swirl back to that fateful day in the Rosetti household in 1975 when I had first met the snotty-nosed, filthy child sitting under the dining table who had not been given a Christian name but rather was simply known as Cholita.

Toilet paper from the barranco swirled upward in the dirt devils, reminding me that the unwashed, unbaptized child was never allowed to use it. It seemed to me the ultimate degradation.

Standing in front of the door, I remembered how the old house had impressed me as a metaphor for collapsing colonialism when I entered the compound for the first time years ago as a naïve graduate student. The Rosetti house had been built in the late seventeenth century; the courtyard formed a gracious entrance with a circular carriage path around a baroque fountain that featured tropical forest motifs, with the master of the jungle, a crouching jaguar, on a pedestal in the center. Out of his mouth gushed water into the marble bowl below. On the outer wall of the fountain, brass monkeys in various playful poses held large brass hitching rings for horses. The fountain, fed by gravity from a small stream to the northeast of the house, had silted in long ago and the top of the jaguar's head was broken off for the installation of a water pipe. He now looked somewhat grotesque, not at all the noble master of the jungle. Only two of the monkeys remained; one still dipped a hand in the water and the other seemed to be splashing water onto his own head. Their brass rings held laundry left to dry. As the washing place for most of the residents, the dilapidated fountain had become the social center of the crumbling house. Young people gathered to flirt and women congregated to gossip. All that remained of the twenty or so trees that had once shaded the carriage path around the fountain was the stump of one large molle tree, heavy with clusters of red peppercorns. In their place stood two rows of cement-block structures with tin roofs, small cubicles rented to students from peasant families who flocked to the city of Ayacucho to attend the university. The beginnings of construction for a Turkish-style toilet with brass footpads that indicated where and how to squat, a single showerhead, and a bathroom sink littered the end of the yard.

Surrounding the courtyard were the old hacienda buildings, with the opening to the street protected by the great colonial door, designed to be wide enough for a carriage to enter. I stood in front of the four-foot-high step-through door cut into one side of the great door. I wondered if the great doors were opened wide any more now that Ramón, Romulo's older brother, was dead. He used to make the market rounds to the villages along the River Pampas. Then, thirty-one years ago, the doors had been pushed open wide for the family's battered dump truck loaded with aluminum pots and pans, plastic water jugs, and ready-made clothing purchased by another Rosetti in Lima. It always returned carrying hard goat cheese, animal hides, and alpaca yarn. I noticed that the great door's sliding hasp and bolt were hopelessly corroded and the ornate colonial padlock had rusted in place. The carving on the door depicting gargoyles licking a block of salt recalled more prosperous times.

The architectural style of the hacienda house had been designed for the temperate climate of southern Spain and not for the harsh extremes of the southern Andes. The three-foot-thick adobe walls provided relief from the intense sun and dust during the dry season from June through October, but during the peak of the rainy season, a damp, cold wind blew from the inside of the house as if some sort of temperature inversion originated there. Feeble rays of light tried to warm the rooms from the small windows eight feet above the floor. The pattern cast on the tied cane ceilings reminded me of the light in a Romanesque cathedral.

Members of the Rosetti family and their boarders used to flee the clammy rooms to seek warmth on the veranda-like porch that encircled the inside walls of the building facing the courtyard. Many of the red tiles of the colonial roof were missing even then, exposing the cane and straw ceiling that gave shelter to numerous species of vermin. Rain seeped into almost all the rooms of the old house, but as the first gringa boarder to ever seek a room, I had been given one of the driest, next to the dining room. At night I could look up into the bright eyes of a family of weasels that shared my dry abode. *They seem to reside with me wherever I go*, I mused, remembering the weasels

in Gregorio's house in Pumapunku and earlier here in Mama Jesús's house. Their beady eyes no longer frightened me.

The hacienda structure had been originally built in the shape of a U with the closed end facing east framing the great double doors with six rooms on each arm. The western end, giving access to the animal yard and cooking hut where Juana and Cholita lived, originally had a low wall and gate to separate it from the house and courtyard. The wall fell during an earthquake and had never been repaired, leaving the gate standing precariously alone. Romulo and his wife, Beatriz, occupied the two rooms adjacent to the gate on the northern side of the courtyard. Their rooms were either in constant repair or in exquisite disrepair. I could never tell for sure. Part of the wall was missing from Romulo's bedroom, and a plastic curtain hung over the hole. Romulo joked to his buddies that he made the hole in the wall so he could get to Juana quickly when passion overtook him.

Romulo's mother, Mama Jesús, lived in two rooms at the northeast end of the U adjacent to the front portal. The dining room and my room were in between Mama Jesús's quarters and Romulo's. If there had been windows onto the street side, Mama Jesús would have had a commanding view of the sunrise on the eastern horizon, but there were none; only two small doors gave access from the street to the rooms to either side of the portal. These rooms were originally used for receiving guests, but Mama Jesús never used the door from her bedroom to the street. Long ago she had it nailed shut. The other door, to the south of the great door, saw a lot of traffic that Mama Jesús chose to ignore. It opened onto the three-room apartment of Rodrigo, the youngest Rosetti, who was one of the few maricónes in Ayacucho. The men who visited his apartment filled with the family's colonial paintings and antiques, massive stuffed furniture covered with handmade doilies, were not considered homosexuals because they played male roles to Rodrigo's caricature of a drag queen. His visitors were tolerated because he was the financial wizard of the family. He advised, bought, sold, and invisibly ran the family's various businesses. Sometimes when she was in her cups, Mama Jesús allowed that Rodrigo was like the daughter she never had.

The remaining three rooms of the southwest arm of the U had been occupied by poor Ramón, the dimwit of an eldest son, who had remained under the matriarchal thumb of Mama Jesús. When not peddling pots and pans in the surrounding villages, he was hauling gravel in the only vehicle the family owned, a battered, 1950 Ford dump truck kept running by sheer mechanical ingenuity on the part of the young ayudante who accompanied Ramón on his trips. Ramón shared his half of the colonial house with his taciturn wife, four or five of his seven children, and an occasional chiquita from one of the Quechua villages. He brought these young girls into town to prove to his brother, Romulo, that he too was living up to family expectations. I wonder if Ramón's family still lives here. I stood thinking about the day when Romulo had said prophetically, "Cholita is the real revolutionary of Peru." *Did Cholita kill him? I'm becoming more and more convinced that she was a member of that all-female hit squad that killed him in 1980.* I didn't knock on the ancient, battered door. Rather, I stood transfixed while the dust of the ancestors carried me back to the beginning of this obsessive search for Cholita.

• • •

On that Sunday in 1975, my compadre Gregorio had come to divine the future of his sister, Juana, the mother of Cholita. Gregorio had feared for Juana's safety and had wanted her to return to Pumapunku, but she had scoffed at him.

My compadre, Romulo, the director of schools in Pumapunku, had come into Ayacucho to spend his vacation in his mother's home. I remember that during that memorable lunch with Romulo when I first laid eyes on Cholita, he had been called away to speak to a visitor. The visitor must have been standing right here where I am now—at the great door of the hacienda. From the dining room, we anxiously watched the scene at the door when Gregorio suddenly appeared. After he had performed the divination for his sister, he had retreated to the racially neutral space of the courtyard and squatted outside the dining room. He, too, had watched Romulo's conversation. He had surprised me when he had stepped inside to speak to us. The dining room was a space reserved for mestizos that he would have never been allowed to enter. I remember that we were anxious for him to return to the courtyard before Romulo's return. Even though his niece, Cholita, was being fed under the table and his sister was the maid serving the lunch, Gregorio was out of place. I was relieved when he turned and moved toward the door, but then he suddenly hesitated, turned, and stepped back over the threshold into the dining room. I can still picture the mischievous grin on his face and I had wondered, *Oh my God, what now?*

Between his gnarled hands, he had twirled his old, worn, black felt hat, careful not to damage the peacock feather in front. Suddenly inspired, he had turned toward me, bowed with great ceremony, and offered me coca leaves and lime, which I accepted. I carefully wrapped the coca leaves around the lime and deposited the wad in my cheek. Gregorio adjusted his poncho

while he delicately removed his wad of coca from his cheek. Tucking the green, masticated mass into his coca bag, he marched across the dining room and, to my amazement, sat down at Romulo's place at the head of the table. Then, placing his hat in the middle of the table, he picked up the fork as if it were a religious relic. While waving the fork over the food in the shape of a cross, he had intoned a special incantation in a low voice that sounded to me like obscene references to Romulo's anatomy, but my Quechua was not good enough to catch everything. Whatever he was saying caused Juana and Cholita to burst into laughter. Gregorio had then proceeded to eat Romulo's plate of food, eating ever so slowly and with great deliberation, manipulating the fork and knife as if he had used them all his life.

"Comadre Alicia, our compadre Romulo treats us so very well. Don't you think so, comadrita? Our compadre Romulo doesn't know how lucky he is to have such a fine cook as my sister, Juana. Don't you agree?"

Before I could respond, I realized that Romulo had been standing near the doorway, watching. We had been so engrossed in Gregorio's antics that none of us had heard Romulo's footsteps. Cholita looked frightened and she took refuge under the table. Romulo's eyes shot fire first at me and then at Gregorio. He advanced toward me, marching with his best military bearing, and I expected El Capitán to call out the firing squad, but Gregorio took matters into his own hands and said, "Thank you, compadre. May God repay you with the same boundless generosity that you have shown our comadre Alicia . . ."

Romulo stopped short in his headlong advance. He was temporarily immobilized by Gregorio's ritualized expression of gratitude. He even responded with the appropriate phrase in Quechua. For several moments, an impasse of gigantic proportions froze all of us in our tracks. Gregorio leaned back in Romulo's chair and a green-stained grin spread mischievously across his broad face. *My God, Gregorio has won! Because I am comadre to both of them, Gregorio can demand Romulo's generosity. Yes, but Romulo can wait a long time to get even.*

"Juana, get these dirty plates out of my sight! This place looks like that pigsty you live in. And get that snotty brat of yours out of my dining room!"

Cholita whimpered, "Papá."

I could think of nothing to say, so I just sucked nervously on my coca wad. I was aware that my cheek and mouth were becoming slightly numb and the coca was giving me a momentary boost—like a cup of strong espresso coffee. Is Romulo going to kick Gregorio out of his chair? Or defer to my presence? We watched the two men nervously, waiting for the next move. Just as Gregorio picked up his hat from the table, José, Romulo's favorite bastard son, burst into the room. He was so excited he didn't notice that the social order was out of whack in his father's dining room.

"Papá, I found these gringos on the plaza and invited them home to meet our comadre, Alicia! I tried to tell them that our ancestors were Italian. Alicia, explain to them. I don't think that they understand me. She speaks French!" he babbled, pointing to an attractive woman in her thirties. "Papá, isn't she beautiful!" José took the woman's arm and pulled her toward his father.

The prize that José had brought home to show his father had been talking incessantly in the low, melodic tones of Parisian French. We could hear her as the group entered the front portal. She didn't miss a beat in her rapid-fire commentary as she bowed slightly to Romulo. She continued in French, "This must be the boy's father. They look just alike. At least they have the same nose. And they do look Italian, don't they? Isn't that what he said? That they were Italian?"

Another of the gringos responded in English, "Yes, their noses could be on Roman portrait vases. I wonder who these other people are." He turned and said something to another man in what sounded like Danish.

"At your service, madame," Romulo said as he bowed and kissed her hand. "Please sit down and join us. My house, of course, is at your service."

José held onto the French woman's arm, keeping her as close to his side as possible. Romulo pulled her by the other arm toward one of the dining room chairs.

She prattled on in French. "How lucky we are! Right through those big doors into the private quarters of an Ayacuchano family! Who is that man at the head of the table? He has some sort of staff next to him. He looks Indian. And that woman? She's got to be a foreigner or maybe upper-class Peruvian. But what is she chewing? She looks a bit ragged, doesn't she? I don't believe our luck!"

"Please, Claude, do stop talking!" another woman said laughingly in French.

But Claude only giggled and the words kept tumbling out of her pert, fire-engine red mouth. "Wait until we tell our friends! They will never believe it! What a bargain! Only $350.00 round-trip from Paris with a whole month to travel on our own! And to think that I was against coming to Ayacucho! I wanted to go straight to Cuzco. But, here we are—right in José's home. What was he saying about his ancestors?"

She was beautiful, tall and rounded in just the right places that are appreciated by Latinos. Her short, dark auburn hair, styled in the unkempt manner popular in Paris, seemed to say, "I have just gotten out of bed and I'm ready to get back in again, and if you're lucky it might be with you, mon cher." Her newly purchased Ayacuchano sweater, two sizes too small, barely restrained full, round breasts above a small waist cinched in by a wide leather belt. Her tight jeans were shiny and slightly worn in just the right places. And she had green eyes. Romulo pulled her gently toward the chair beside me. José was still attached to her arm.

"José, mon cher, thank you for inviting us into your home. This must be your father. You look just alike. You both have the profiles of Roman patricians. Are you Italian?"

As she talked, she ran her index finger down her own profile. I noticed a massive diamond ring that probably dated from the thirteenth or fourteenth century when roughly cut stones were mounted in thick gold settings. She was evidently a novice traveler to wear such a ring on a trip to Peru.

Romulo noticed the ring as well. Comprehending the word "Italian," he replied, "Yes, we're Italian." He propelled her into the chair beside me and stood in front of her for a moment. Pulling himself up and sucking in his gut, Romulo gave a slight bow and excused himself to make preparations, he said, for a fiesta they would never forget.

When José had to let go of Claude's arm so she could sit down, he stared resentfully at the tops of his shoes and muttered, "This is our comadre, Alicia. She's a doctora, a university professor, an anthropologist from the United States."

Damn! How did Gregorio get his coca wad out of his mouth so delicately? For a moment, I couldn't decide whether to keep the damn thing in my cheek or to remove it. Looking at our five gringo tourists, I decided I had better remove the green sticky wad because I hadn't mastered the art of keeping it tucked above my back upper molars while talking. I tried to look as nonchalant as possible as I rolled the coca wad out onto the palm of my hand and tucked it into my pocket. Being exceedingly aware that my lips had that telltale line of dark green and my teeth looked like I had brushed them with grass, I smiled thinly at our guests and offered my hand to all of them in turn: Three men and two women. But obviously they were not all French. The two women gave me limp Parisian handshakes, but the three men grasped my hand firmly in both of theirs and shook it enthusiastically.

"Parlez-vous anglais ou español? Je ne parle pas français," I asked the woman as I took her hand. She is about thirty-five, I thought.

"Oh, yes, a little English. I am Claude. My friend is Evette. She, she—"

"She doesn't speak English well, but we do. My name is Niels, this is Carsten and Jurgen, indicating his two smiling companions. We're Danish. None of us speaks Spanish but we've been learning enough to get along. We're pleased to meet you."

"I'm Alice Woodsley. This is my compadre Gregorio and his sister, Juana, and her daughter, Cholita."

Gregorio retreated to the doorway with a bow to the gringos and Juana scurried out with the plates, nodding as she passed. Cholita took up an advantageous position in the corner, determined not to miss a thing.

"Didn't José say you were an anthropologist from the United States? I've heard so much about this part of Peru from an anthropologist who came to Copenhagen to teach in the university. He is from Ayacucho and that is why we decided to take this trip. His name was Eduardo Wamani. Do you know him?"

"Well, such a small world, yes, I know him well. We did fieldwork together in the River Pampas region two years ago and we have stayed friends ever since."

Niels continued. "He married a Danish woman, a friend of mine who was a ceramic engineer sent here to improve pottery production. Eduardo looks very Indian and Danish women find him attractive."

"Yes, I know. Eduardo wrote me letters from Copenhagen saying he hated the cheeses in Denmark but the women were wonderful."

"In Copenhagen, Eduardo and Kirstin told stories about how much trouble they had here in Peru getting hotel rooms together, even after they were married. Also, they said that after their son was born, people said 'Well, that woman ceramic engineer didn't improve pottery too much, but she sure did improve la raza!' But I don't see much racism here. Some of these people are obviously Indian."

"Well—"

Another of the Danes cut in. "Eduardo sang such beautiful, sad songs about Ayacucho and told us such wonderful stories that we had to come to visit and see for ourselves. We plan to go to the small village where he's from. We invited the two French ladies to accompany us. We met in a small pension in Lima."

"Yes, Eduardo sings huaynos beautifully. He even wrote me one, in Quechua and Spanish, an especially moving poem about Ayacucho that he says he has set to music. Has he learned to eat Danish cheeses? He used to hold his nose every time Kirstin got a cheese through the diplomatic pouch. He would proclaim loudly, 'How can you eat anything that smells like dirty socks?' Once Kirstin and I were eating a wonderful cheese that had just arrived and Eduardo came into the house, stopped, and looked at the soles of his shoes. He was sure that he had stepped in abomination! He writes letters from Copenhagen saying that he misses the hearty soups, Peruvian potatoes, and toasted corn, cancha."

"Yes, he complains a lot about Danish food," responded Niels. "He even grows his own chili peppers on his windowsill and puts them on everything—even pickled herring. Tell us about this family. We're not sure, but José seems to be telling us that his ancestors came from Italy. Is that true?"

"Probably the first Rosetti was Italian but he arrived from Spain sometime during the first half of the sixteenth century. I have no idea how he got from Italy to Spain, but his luck was extremely good in the New World. He gained so much favor with Viceroy Toledo that he was awarded an encomienda of one hundred Indians in the region of Pumapunku to Christianize them as they worked in the salt mine that he was given. I was first introduced to this illustrious ancestor of the Rosetti family in a document dated 1653 in which one Don Diego Rosetti Flores was accused of beating his Indian charges who were obliged to work in the salt mine. The accusations were brought against him by the two caciques, or chiefs, from Pumapunku—Juan Asto Cabana and Julio Carhua Poma. Don Diego declared that he beat the Indians because they refused to attend their catechism classes. He was mildly rebuked by the visitador real."

"Where did you find such information?" remarked Jurgen.

"Village church archives are gold mines; they contain marriage, birth, and death records and land and inheritance disputes, as well as evidence for official inspections from the Spanish government. The earliest document I found dates 1593. The later birth records testify to the multitude of bastard children that Don Diego Rosetti sired during his lifetime. However, this Rosetti family is legitimate and Romulo is a direct descendant of that first Italian who somehow ended up in Ayacucho, Peru. This is the branch of the family that continued over the centuries to administer the salt mine in Pumapunku. If you look at the carved detail on the great door to the street, you will see how the first Rosetti had a coat of arms related to the mining and marketing of salt."

"How fascinating! Please wait, let me briefly translate for my French companions," pleaded Niels.

Romulo solemnly entered the room, holding his guitar. He sent one of the ever-present bastard children out to buy beer. He raised his guitar. "I will sing you the songs of Ayacucho. In Quechua, the language of music and of love."

I translated.

Romulo planted himself in front of Claude, with his foot on the edge of her chair seat. He swung around toward the door and shouted to Cholita, who was seated on the stoop, not quite in and not quite out of the dining room. "Anda, Cholita. Go tell my compadres, Don Pedro and Don Julio, to bring their guitars. Juana, prepare a banquet. Only the best for our visitors! We are going to show these gringos the heart and soul of Ayacucho! Ai—i carajo." He strummed several chords. He was a magnificent guitarist.

Gregorio quietly reappeared and squatted on his haunches just outside the doorway.

Juana left, muttering, "Now, where in the world am I going to find someone to give me credit to prepare only 'the best' for our visitors?"

Cholita ran for the great door and collided with Beatriz, Mama Jesús, and Ramón, who were returning from Cangallo. Mama Jesús had ostensibly retired from her market business and Ramón had assumed the job as manager, but it was clear that she was still the boss. Ramón drove the truck for his mother for fifteen years before she let him have a share in the business. Shrewd, tough, and almost illiterate, Mama Jesús could add and multiply faster in her head than I could with my pocket calculator. Her unvarying costume included a stiff, broad-brimmed, white hat, numerous floor-length skirts around her ample girth, a ruffled polyester blouse, a small square shawl fastened in front with an ornate pin, large gold earrings, and black lace-up shoes. The costume of an Ayacuchano market woman derived from eighteenth-century Spanish dress.

Hushed family rumors had it that Mama Jesús was pregnant with Ramón, the eldest of the Rosetti sons, when she married Cesar, who had just inherited the position of manager of the salt mine. She was fourteen when she met her future husband. As the daughter of mestizo merchants and with a market stall of her own in Ayacucho, she was decidedly of lower class than the Rosettis. But her father owned a gun and bullets, as well as a market stall, so Cesar married his young bride. Doubt probably would have been cast on Ramón's paternity if it had not been for his nose—that promontory prominence left

no doubt of his paternity in anyone's mind. Mama Jesús had eight births in all. Providence saw fit to spare only three males to carry on the Rosetti nose, name, and heritage. Mama Jesús's fecundity not only purged her reputation, but it also gave her a higher social status in the class hierarchy of Ayacucho. Now in her old age, she was the revered madre and she ruled over the extended household like a benign despot.

Unfortunately, Romulo's wife, Beatriz, was condemned to purgatory in the Rosetti household. The child she had been carrying when she was marched down the aisle aborted during a trip to Pumapunku. She never redeemed herself in the eyes of Mama Jesús because she was not able to give the Rosetti family a son. She never got pregnant again after her early miscarriage. Had she given birth to numerous sons, she would have inherited Mama Jesús's position as matriarch of the family. But without children, she languished in that ambiguous status of a woman who had succumbed to seduction, but who unfortunately had not been able to redeem herself through fecundity.

Mama Jesús came toward the dining room calling out, "Comadre Alicia, how wonderful that you're here!" I rushed out to meet her and she gave me a bear hug, kissing me on both cheeks as she proclaimed, "Maybe I can convince you to come on the next market trip with me. You'd be good for business. Carajo, my head hurts. I'm too old for this, but Ramón is too stupid to handle it by himself. Comadre Alicia, give Ramón your little adding machine so that he won't make so many mistakes! The rest of my children think they are too good to sell in the market. I need a daughter or granddaughter to work with me." Mama Jesús firmly believed that women made better vendors than men.

Suddenly, Mama Jesús turned and marched out into the narrow street. She raised her skirts over the raised step of the portal and stooped. With surprising agility for a woman her size and age, she picked up a couple of small stones and hurled them at a six- or seven-year-old boy backed up against the adobe wall that enclosed the Rosetti compound.

"Carajo, cochino! Go shit on someone else's doorstep!" she shouted at the child who had just hurled his own stones at pigs eagerly waiting for his waste. The child had difficulty avoiding the stones, the pursuing pigs, Mama Jesús' wrath, and pulling up his pants at the same time.

When I heard the commotion at the gate, I followed Cholita to see what was going on. Romulo, then José with his invited guests trailing close behind, arrived just as Mama Jesús was chiding us for laughing. Niels, the Dane, asked me, "What is going on? Why are you all standing here laughing?"

"Mama Jesús, Romulo's mother, chucked some stones at a kid who was trying to—"

Romulo stepped between us and took Niels's arm and pointed to the door. He began his familiar discourse on the great colonial door, disregarding the fact that Niels couldn't understand a word he said.

I whispered to Niels, "I'll tell you later . . . about . . ."

"My ancestor, Diego Rosetti, designed this door to commemorate the opening of his business as the royal salt distributor for the department. He commissioned a local wood carver to make a door in the baroque style but with animals from the New World. Look, you see the gargoyles have the faces of pumas with snake tongues that have tiny faces of pumas at the end. Do you see? The two large cats facing each other are licking a block of salt and even the miniature pumas at the end of the snake tongues are licking tiny blocks of salt. The two pumas facing each other licking a single block of salt became my ancestor's coat of arms. The salt mine is located in Pumapunku, which translates as Door of the Puma. He had it engraved in silver, carved on furniture, and painted on his carts and carriages. The same motifs from the jungle were executed on the fountain in the patio . . . come . . . I will show you. Translate, comadrita."

"Con mucho gusto, compadre. His ancestor, Diego Rosetti, the guy I told you about who was charged with beating his Indians in the 1653 document, made enough money off of his salt mine to build this house and a warehouse next door that has since been converted into private housing. He used Indian labor from Pumapunku to build all of it. One of his encomienda Indians carved this door. Rosetti designed it as a typical baroque door like those he remembered as a young man in Spain or Italy. However, he must have added the motif of the salt blocks here. But I wonder whose idea it was to depict the tiny cats at the end of the snakes' tongues also licking tiny blocks of salt? The Indian craftsmen probably interpreted the design in terms of symbolically significant animals. The puma is the door—in Quechua, punku—to the underworld, as well as the door to the inside of the world, which is thought of as the jungle. The large cats are jaguars. They have spots, but the coat of arms and other emblems show pumas, a cat that ranges higher than the jungle. The village where the salt mine is located is also called Pumapunku. The snake is the amaru, the mythical, two-headed, cat-dragon-snake of the underworld. It is a symbol of both disruption and renewal. The Indian artist depicted the cat crouching as cats do before they attack. I've looked at this

door for hours and wondered if Diego Rosetti ever knew how subversive the artist's rendition was. I doubt whether—"

"Comadre, are you translating?"

"Certainly, compadre. It just takes longer in English."

We walked back to the fountain and Romulo continued his mythical musing about his ancestors and I continued giving my own mythical version of his family history. I smiled and nodded at him, feeling wonderfully wicked. Finally Romulo pulled his shoulders back and led the group back to the dining room just as the case of beer arrived. He looked every bit like his nickname: El Capitán!

Romulo sent for the blind harpist. He ordered Juana to prepare more food. José bought case after case of Cristal beer—on credit. The gringos looked pleased. The other musicians arrived and the party got into full swing. The Rosettis gathered in the dining room and spilled out into the courtyard. The legitimate Rosettis were seated along the walls of the dining room. The married women sat next to the plastic Jesus, whose little red heart now glowed from the concealed bulb behind the picture. The men were lined up against the opposite wall. The illegitimate Rosettis and the boarders gathered in the courtyard to peer in at the fiesta. Cholita sat next to Gregorio on the stoop where they could respond to Romulo's demands and fetch things from the kitchen. We were all in our proper places.

Passionate songs in Quechua. Huaynos, Harawis. Competitive displays of musical virtuosity. Sometimes the blind harpist led the musical dialogue, sometimes he answered the guitarists. Frenzied dancing to huaynos reached a high pitch. Everyone drinking and pissing. Singing and dancing. Drinking and pissing. The gringos tape-recorded the music, took pictures. El Capitán had won a major victory. The foreigners would never forget that evening. They were experiencing the heart and soul of Ayacucho. Singing and dancing. Drinking and pissing. Juana, Cholita, and Gregorio served bowls of quinua and chuñu soup, followed by two main dishes: potatoes, papas a la huancayina, followed by aji de gallina, a spicy chicken dish. Beer continued to flow. Eating, singing, dancing, pissing.

"Voy a dormir," announced Mama Jesús. Children squealed and ran for the patio. They appeared to be embarking on a race.

"What's happening now?" asked Niels.

"Mama Jesús suffers from headaches and the children are running to get the toads they have collected today in the arroyo. She gives the child who finds the fattest toads candies. Then she takes the fat toads and ties them to her forehead as a cure. In the morning the toads are dead because they have 'eaten' her headache. Excuse me I have to go kiss her good night along with all of the other women in the family."

"My God, she ties toads to her forehead! Ella attache les crapauds . . . a vielle . . ."

When I entered Mama Jesús's room, she was already in bed with six or eight wriggling toads tied to her forehead with a red bandana. The toads were visible under the brim of her white hat. I felt the damp cold of the squirming toads against her hot, fleshy face as I kissed her. One of the toads had pissed on her forehead. Pissing and eating, pissing and eating. The toads were dancing. "Buenas noches, mamita, duerme con los angelitos. Your toads are especially lively and fat tonight. Maybe you'll feel better tomorrow."

"If God wishes it. Goodnight, comadrita Alicia."

I returned to the dining room where the fiesta was going full swing. The old record player was cranking out scratchy music by the same musicians who had just been playing. The visitors seemed very impressed. The popular huayno, Ayrampito, began to play. As people searched for their next partner, the blind harpist recognized my voice, stood up, and took my hands. "Takisunchik mamacita," he said.

I led him to a clear spot on the dance floor where we began the intricate steps of the dance. As first, I initiated the moves and steps and he did remarkably well in sensing where I was, answering every move with the more complicated ones that I had to answer.

Rapid, pounding steps, staccato beat, the lyrics' mournful histories:

I am very sad in my life.
My destiny is wrong.
Your thorns, arampito, give me pain
without the comfort of love.
So many lies,
so many deceits have made me lose my way.

Our dance turned into a competition of skill. We were two birds, one blind and one dumb, doing a ritualized dance. At the end, I was drenched in sweat. The blind harpist always won the competition.

"Incredible. Why does the harpist play the harp upside down?"

"Because we are south of the equator. Everything here is upside down. Haven't you noticed?"

"How did you learn that dance? It looks difficult. Can you teach me?" asked Niels.

"Here, I'll show you. The steps have a double rhythm . . . da da, da da, like that." The clumsy chorus line of the gringos and my improvised rhythm section were joined by several musicians with an erratic tune that matched their awkward steps.

The music stopped and José appeared with another case of beer. "You dance so badly that each of you must drink a multa!"

José opened a quart bottle for each of the foreigners. To a round of applause, they were forced to drink every drop as a fine for their inept skills at dancing.

"Madrina Alicia, help me. I am going to put on the song 'Impossible,' and you've got to translate the words for me to Claude. I'm in love!"

"José, I don't speak French or Italian!"

"No matter, get one of the other gringos to help you."

The music started. A slow Hawari. Young José led Claude onto the floor and I grabbed Niels. "Come on, Niels, this is called collective wooing." Niels and I danced close to José and Claude. I translated in English to Niels and he gave some sort of rendition in French to Claude, who whispered sweet nothings in who knows what language in José's ear.

> The impossible is what I want.
> Your eyes looked at me.
> For those eyes I would die.
> "Damn, I missed a line in the translation lag," I complained.
> Ayi, Ayi, white dove,
> you have robbed my soul.
> Robbed my soul.

"My God, it's working," proclaimed Niels as José pulled Claude out of the room. We heard the stairs squeak as they ascended to the roof where extra beds, under a makeshift plastic canopy, had been set up.

"I hope Mama Jesús doesn't charge Claude rent—that's her new overflow area for the university students."

Several other people also noticed their departure. As Romulo slapped one of his compadres on the back, I heard him say "mi hijo, my son. He's a real Rosetti, by God!"

An hour passed before Romulo's wife, Beatriz, seated next to the plastic Jesus, called to the group of children playing and dancing in the courtyard, "Chicos, run upstairs and see what your uncle José is doing!"

A dozen children, giggling and shouting, scampered up the stairs. Only two minutes passed and then a cascade of giggles descended rapidly just ahead of the children.

"Well?" Beatriz demanded.

"Quien sabe que pasa. They're on top of each other like this," Cholita explained with the palms of her hands together, wiggling her index fingers to represent two sets of feet.

As the Rosetti household broke into laughter, El Capitán rose to his feet, lifted his beer bottle and shouted, "Ayi, un Rosetti!" Grabbing his guitar, he set to music the refrain. "Ayi, ayi ayi un Rosetti! Verdadero un Rosetti ! CARAJO, HOMBRES!" The band followed suit and we witnessed the birth of a new song.

"Does this happen often at these fiestas?" asked Niels innocently.

"Only to somebody else's women," I responded.

Ahh, perhaps the great Italian Rosetti nose would transmigrate back across the ocean to begin a conquest of France!

Laughing, sharing with the other foreigners the sense of the overall ridiculousness of our improvised fiesta, I turned to take in the scene and caught a glimpse of Cholita. She was sitting near her uncle Gregorio on the stoop to the dining room where they awaited orders from Romulo.

. . .

Staring at the battered door, a chill of foreboding gripped me as I remembered Cholita, crouching underneath the dining table earlier that day, grabbing whatever food her father, Romulo Rosetti Martinez, threw to her. Cholita, his daughter, ragged and unkempt, cracking open chicken bones to suck the marrow. Treated like a filthy stray dog. *Cholita, where are you?*

CHAPTER 9

ROMULO'S LETTER

As I stood in front of the battered door to the Rosetti hacienda, echoes of that fiesta so many years ago sounded in my head. My reverie was broken when a group of musicians, a harpist and several violinists, passed by on their way to early Mass and Christmas rehearsal. I turned to knock on the great double doors, which looked as if the twenty years of warfare waged in Ayacucho had been directed at their ancient iconography. The doors had gouges and slashes that almost destroyed the original figures. The puma motifs were almost entirely obliterated and the blocks of salt that signified the family's colonial power could not be distinguished at all. How prophetic, I thought. The ravine, however, was still filled with garbage and human and animal waste. Plastic bags had multiplied and instead of water the gully was awash with hundreds of multicolored plastic bags that wafted upward with every gust of wind. The smell of the ancestors was replaced by the pungent order of garbage and excrement. The rains were late this year and the ravine had not received its seasonal bath from the onset of daily showers. I pounded on the side of the ancient double door where the small six-inch hinged panel was cut into the right side at eye level. The panel opened and an eye appeared. "Quien es?" the eye asked.

"Comadre Alicia, está Mama Jesús?" Is Mama Jesús here?

"Yes, come in Comadre Alicia, Mama Jesús is waiting for you. She's lying down in her room with one of her headaches."

"Have you applied the toads yet?" I asked, laughing while I remembered the wiggling toads that were sacrificed every night on Mama Jesús's forehead.

"Yes, but we could catch only a few. The rains are late and toads are hard to find. Here, let me take your bag."

As we walked to my old room, I learned that her name was Julia and that she was from Pumapunku. She had come to Ayacucho to go to night school.

She was a bright-eyed fifteen-year-old who could be a younger Juana. But her fate will be different now that Romulo is dead.

"What are you studying?" I asked as I followed Julia into the courtyard.

"I'm in secondary school now and I plan to apply to the university to study to be a pharmacist," Julia announced as she led me through the courtyard. A lot had changed since 1975. The old colonial fountain was gone and the space was filled with one-room cinder block rentals. A communal bathroom with shower stalls and toilets faced the row of cinder block rooms. Mama Jesús was still a landlady. As we passed the living room and dining room, I peeked inside and noticed that Sr. Philco still ruled supreme over the same plastic covered furniture and the plastic Jesus with the glowing heart.

"Are these rooms occupied by university students?" I asked, pointing to the row of rooms where the fountain had been.

"Yes, mostly, but a few secondary students too," answered Julia.

I wondered how many Shining Path guerrillas had used this place as their quarters. They could have observed Romulo and reported on his activities. How much does Mama Jesús know about Romulo's assassination? Probably much more than she will tell me.

I deposited my bag in the room and noticed that the high front window that looked onto the path along the ravine had been uncovered, and a stream of light was cast on the worn furniture and the bed against the wall. A single light bulb hung from the sixteen-foot-high ceiling. Nothing had changed. I instinctively looked up into the tile and thatch ceiling, wondering if my old companions, the resident weasels, still scampered around at night.

"Shall we peek into Mama Jesús's room and see if she's asleep?" I asked.

"Sure, she told me to wake her when you arrived." Julia led the way to Mama Jesús's room and tapped softly on the door.

"Imata. Who is it?" Mama Jesús called out in Quechua.

"Your comadre Alicia has arrived."

"Come in, come in, comadre. What a miracle to see you."

Mama Jesús was lying propped up on several pillows on her bed with her clothes on, including her broad-brimmed hat and the scarf to hold the three toads that hung on her forehead. As she sat up, the toads wiggled energetically.

I embraced Mama Jesús and kissed her on each cheek. Poor old dear, she has outlived two of her sons, Ramón and Romulo. I wondered if Rodrigo still lives here? I'm sure he does. He's the daughter that Mama Jesús never had.

"How are you, comadre?" I inquired as I helped Mama Jesús sit up. "I see you still have your headaches. But you look well. You haven't aged a bit."

"Oh yes, I have," Mama Jesús responded. "I've stopped traveling to communities to sell, and with Ramón gone there's no one who can do that. But I'm surviving and Julia is a great help. She pulled her knitting from one of the large pockets in her apron, arranged her five skirts to cover her legs, and started to work. She stopped and gazed at me and said, "Dios Mío, your hair is whiter than mine."

"Yes, and I have two mechanical knees now."

"God forbid! What will they think of next?" Mama Jesús crossed herself and went back to work.

"What are you making?" I asked, realizing that Mama Jesús typified the industrious market women I so admired. Always busy producing something.

"These knitted hats," responded Mama Jesús as she pulled a black hat with red llamas on it out of the other pocket. "We've found that tourists like them. Thank God, the tourists are back, but mostly Europeans, not many from your country."

"This is attractive," I said as I put the hat on and looked into the ornate mirror that hung on the opposite wall above an equally ornate chest of drawers. "Didn't this mirror and chest of drawers used to be in Rodrigo's room? How is he?"

"He's fine. He has a young fella living with him now. You'll meet him. Rodrigo's a maricón you know. Strange how life turned out. Two of my sons are dead and the only surviving one who lives here with me will never give me grandchildren. But he does seem happy and he knows how to make money. He found someone to teach the market women designs and he's trying to market our artesasnia in Europe."

"That's good. I always knew that Rodrigo had a talent for marketing and I'm very glad he's happy. You have several grandchildren. How many children did Ramón have?"

"Too many, but none of them want to work with me. I have only Rodrigo and I'll leave my businesses to him. He's good at most things but not at selling in the market." Mama Jesús loved selling in the market, where women are the communication system for the region. Whatever happens in the city or the countryside is transmitted through seller-customer relationships.

"But you're still selling in the market aren't you?" I inquired.

"Yes, but only three days a week, Friday through Sunday," answered Mama

Jesús as she reached into her large apron pocket once more and pulled out an envelope that was folded in half. "This is for you. Romulo wrote it before he was killed and never got a chance to mail it. I found it among his things and I didn't know how to mail it to you," she explained as she handed me a letter.

I slowly took it and noticed that it was not worn, stained, nor torn, unlike the portfolio of horrors that I carried around with me. Mama Jesús must have put it away for these last eleven years and only put it into her pocket for today's encounter. I tore the envelope open and unfolded the letter with trembling hands.

I felt a cold chill. Within a week after writing this letter, the female hit squad cut him down in the plaza of Pumapunku. *I wonder if they gave him a public trial first. I'll bet they did.*

Dear Comadre Alicia   5th of Feb. 1985
Saludos from Pumapunku.

How are you? Teaching in Washington I presume. We received your Christmas greetings and long letter. Mama Jesús, Beatriz, Ramón and Rodrigo send their greetings and they hope you are healthy and happy in your work. Beatriz is visiting her sister in Lima. I am no longer director of schools in Pumapunku. I work in the central administration of the Ayacucho department of education. I'm in Pumapunku to conduct an inspection of the schools. It's strange to be back.

These last five years have been extremely difficult. After the burning of the ballots in the neighboring village of Chuschi in 1980, Sendero moved into several communities, including Pumapunku, kicking out officials and controlling the municipalities. They arrived in December of 1980 in Pumapunku and publicly shot two cattle thieves. Then a few months later they shot the mayor. They set up a court system to try offenders of stealing, drunkenness, and wife abuses. When the thieves were shot in the plaza, I fled to Ayacucho and refused to return because it was too dangerous. Most of the teachers were in sympathy with Sendero and those who were not fled as I did.

Sendero has retreated from Pumapunku and a guardia station has been established. But it is very difficult to determine which of the schoolteachers are actually Sendero members or sympathizers. I am going to spend only a week here and I've been asked to make a full report to the military commander in Ayacucho. I tried to get out of conducting this inspection. They want me to go to ten communities. I have been meaning to write to you but I find it difficult to ask the great favor I want to ask, Comadre Alicia, I am pleading with you to help your comadre Beatriz and I come to the United States. Our lives are in constant danger. I suspect everyone. Even people who live in our household and people in Pumapunku I have known all of my life. You never know who is sympathetic to Sendero. Who would have guessed that Cholita would join them? I saw her place the red flag on the coffin of Edith Lagos during the procession of her funeral. The way Cholita marched alongside the coffin in such defiance scared me.

I am sorry for my role in getting you arrested in 1980. I ask your forgiveness and I beg you to help us. I've been thinking about Cholita. Perhaps I am responsible for the revolutionary that she became. The way I treated her mother was a drunken mistake that never should have happened. I have made so many mistakes in my life, but I am ready to start all over in the United States. I hope you can help us.

Your compadre, Romulo Rosetti Martinez

I folded the letter carefully and put it in my portfolio. I went to Mama Jesús's bedside and kissed her on both cheeks. My tears dropped onto Mama Jesús's large apron. The old woman clung to me for several minutes as we sobbed.

Am I crying for Romulo, whom I hated? For Juana? For Mama Jesús? For myself? For Cholita? For all of us? Romulo probably could not escape his own circumstances. He was captive to the macho culture that drove him to father bastard children, to rape Juana, and to perform that horrendous autopsy, just as I am captive to all these damn stories that are my burden. These stories have eroded my bones and rotted my cartilage. They're the cause of my arthritis. This letter will probably give me a new ache in my back or knees. Can I ever forgive him? I wonder what Cholita's cross is? That she assassinated her father? Is she repentant? Does the image of his face haunt her? I've got to find her.

After dinner that evening, Rodrigo and his lover Eduardo brought me into Rodrigo's quarters for a glass of sherry. I had to conceal my amazement as I looked around the elegantly furnished sitting room with its velvet drapes and couch and ornate antique tables and chairs. I felt as though we had been transported back two, maybe three centuries. Rodrigo was even dressed for the part. He had on an ankle-length velvet burgundy dressing gown over his black turtleneck sweater and black slacks. He was a handsome man in his early fifties. Tall, lean, with a full head of black wavy hair, he cut a fine movie star figure in his dressing gown. The image was so perfect that I expected a servant to enter the room, candelabra in hand, and announce that the master's carriage was waiting at the front gate. What bizarre film was this? Rodrigo's facial features resembled Romulo's except that his nose was a much smaller version of the Rosetti nose and his eyes lacked the puffiness and circles that years of debauchery had proclaimed around Romulo's eyes.

Rodrigo's face was firm; his eyes were clear. His mouth was full and pleasant. Only a slight double chin betrayed his age. But the letter in my bag from his assassinated brother reminded me that the real movie we were in was taking place in the ravaged past.

His lover, Eduardo, was perhaps twenty years Rodrigo's junior. He was in his thirties and also lean and tall but with traces of a Quechua heritage in his facial features—the characteristic high cheekbones, almond eyes, and "Inca nose" with its arch at the bridge. His hair was also characteristically jet black and straight. Both men were attractive and I imagined the wails of mothers and daughters bemoaning that they were gay. I enjoyed watching the easy affection between them that consisted of light touches. Both of them had slender, delicate, beautiful hands, and their caresses of each other were like light feathers. How long had they been together? At least ten years, if my calculations were correct.

As we settled down with our sherry served in antique silver and crystal glasses, I wondered how to approach the matter of Romulo's death. But I didn't have to introduce the subject because Rodrigo said, "Mama told me that she gave Romulo's last letter to you. He must have written it just before he was assassinated."

I told them that yes, it was only a week before he was killed in the plaza. I related that I had heard rumors that Cholita had killed him, and I asked them whether they thought she could have been a trained assassin at fifteen. Rodrigo's answer was yes, several witnesses in Pumapunku said that Cholita was the leader of the assassination squad. Rodrigo went on to tell me that Sendero held a swift trial and charged him with rape and theft.

"What was the attitude of the people of Pumapunku? I know they stopped the assassination of one of their officials in 1983 or 84. Did they try to stop Romulo's?" I asked.

"Evidently not," Rodrigo answered as he poured us more sherry.

"I have hated Romulo for all these years," I said, "even though I know he was a product of his history. We all are. I wonder at what age his band of boozers began their macho marauding. He was literally undone by his own sexuality, wasn't he?"

"Yes," replied Rodrigo. "I used to listen in on some of their exploits. Do you know that our father got Romulo drunk at the age of thirteen and told him to screw our fifteen-year-old maid. Afterwards, father and his cronies had a party for Romulo. When it came my turn to be initiated, I refused, and that was the first time my father called me a maricón."

"I wonder if your grandfather initiated your father in the same way," I commented sadly. "Romulo's letter indicates that he was becoming reflective about the consequences of his actions. Do you think he might have changed if he had lived? Do you want to read the letter?"

"Please, could I see it?" replied Rodrigo.

I pulled the letter out of my portfolio and several articles spilled out onto the floor.

Rodrigo helped pick them up and noticed the article about his brother's assassination. He commented, "He was a bastard, wasn't he?" He handed me the articles.

"Yes, but so were most of his cronies. Fathering illegitimate children seemed to be their principal sport," I responded.

Eduardo cut in. "And they competed over how many virgins they could deflower."

We laughed nervously. A sad calm filled the room.

As I replaced the articles into my portfolio, I asked, "That reminds me, what was Romulo's funeral like?"

"Oh my God!" responded Rodrigo as he covered his mouth in a stereotypically gay gesture. "A hundred women attended with their lil' bastards al'tryin' to claim inheritance. I thought Beatriz was going to have a stroke! Mama Jesús was elated. She said that Romulo had finally given her grandchildren. Did you meet Julia, the young woman who takes care of Mama Jesús?"

I nodded affirmatively.

Rodrigo explained that Julia was one of Romulo's bastard grandchildren. She was at the funeral with her mother and her grandmother. They approached Mama Jesús and asked if Julia could live here and go to school. Mama Jesús thought she had found her potential heir apparent. But Julia doesn't want to be a market woman. She wants to be a pharmacist.

"Yes, she told me." I responded. "I had a feeling that she was somehow related, but she doesn't have Romulo's nose."

Both men laughed. Rodrigo said, "None of the girls do. But it was something to see at the funeral—most of his male progeny had Romulo's nose!"

I laughed with them and retorted, "I'm not surprised. Your brothers and even you have the famous Rosetti nose."

"But mine is less pronounced; that's why I'm gay. You know, all the 'great noses' in the family are dead. I hadn't thought of that until now."

"I've always associated that nose with machismo; maybe their machismo killed them as it did Romulo."

Eduardo chimed in. "Don't forget the whole new generation of Rosettis who are coming into their own now. Will they continue the macho tradition?"

I asked Rodrigo if he remembered the party with the Danes and the two French women when José took one of the French women upstairs to bed her. We laughed at how Romulo crowed like an old rooster and composed an impromptu song and bellowed out, "He's a real Rosetti, by God, a Rosetti." Rodrigo related that José married another French tourist and lives in Paris, handling the family's marketing of crafts in Europe.

"I wonder if he is repeating his father's history. The Latin lover is greatly appreciated in Paris," I replied, "until women figure out that they're all about the chase and not about giving women pleasure."

The two men gave each other knowing looks and Eduardo gently touched Rodrigo's hand.

I continued. "The funeral must have caused quite a stir here in Ayacucho. Such a scene is every mestiza wife's nightmare."

They described the funeral in great detail and said that the women were horrified over how Romulo died. Of course Cholita came up as the prime suspect for Romulo's murder. His old cronies, El Capitán's soldiers, got drunk at the wake and sang songs to his glory all night. They ended up weeping and singing sad songs in Quechua. Meanwhile, the women of the family sat in their long disapproving line against the wall and gossiped about the women who had brought paternity claims after the funeral.

I handed Romulo's letter to Rodrigo, and Eduardo moved over closer to him so they could read it together. I waited in silence, fingering the collected papers in my portfolio. I waited a few more moments and then asked, "Do you think he had really changed after all those years?"

Rodrigo thought for a moment and then replied slowly. "Yes, I do; he was kinder to Beatriz and he stopped screwing around. I think that when Cholita joined Sendero he began to think about his life."

"Did he plead with them before they shot him?"

"Yes, people say he kept repeating, 'I'm a different man now. Please, don't kill me. I'll do anything you say to show I've repented.' But the village did not come to his aid and the hit squad filled his body with bullets—and then they cut off his penis and balls."

"My God, the paper didn't report that!" I said, alarmed.

"No, but everyone in Pumapunku was witness to the mutilation. They say that the three women left his body in the plaza but they took his penis and balls with them."

Holy Jesús, what did they do with them, I wondered? The newspaper reported that one woman turned to the others and said, "Well, Cholita, we've finally killed the old bastard haven't we." I've always wondered if she was "our" Cholita.

Rodrigo seemed to read my thoughts, and he answered, "We're quite sure that the leader was our Cholita." He handed his brother's letter back to me.

Eduardo asked, "What are your plans now?"

"I'm going to Pumapunku tomorrow."

"We wish you the best of luck," replied Rodrigo. "You're going to need it." Both men rose and embraced me as I left the eighteenth-century drawing room. And a few steps brought me back into the twenty-first-century patio in all its devastated neglect. Several students were lounging about studying and talking. They glanced up and greeted me as I made my way to my old room.

Could any of these students be ex-Shining Path?

I crossed the patio, taking special notice of the knots of students, perhaps fifteen in all, sitting in the courtyard. I wondered what I would find the next day in Pumapunku as I opened the door to my old room and peered into the rafters to see if the descendants of my former roommates, the weasels, were in residence. Yes, at least thirty pairs of beady eyes glowed in the beam of my flashlight.

CHAPTER 10

THE DUST OF THE ANCESTORS

That night in my dream, my wall-constructing project advanced further than it ever had before. I felt exhausted when I rose at five A.M. to pack my travel gear for the trip to Pumapunku. I rolled up my sleeping bag and thought that without this bag I would have frozen last night. This room had the same cold breeze gusting through as Gregorio's house. If the dust tastes and smells like the ancestors, did the ancestors inhabit the interior of houses in the form of cold wind? I had slept in my aqua silk underwear and wool socks. I'd probably keep these underwear on for my entire stay in Pumapunku. I can't stand being cold. My silk long johns seem to collect more warmth as they get dirty. I remember when Gregorio's children gave me the nickname of gringa sucia, the dirty gringa, because I refused to plunge my hands into a bucket of ice-cold water to wash my face. They would break the ice on the top in the morning and just plunge their hands into the icy depths and splash their faces, but I'd wait until water was heated for our morning soup or bowl of quinua. When it was warm, I'd dip a cup out before the ingredients were added and, wetting two fingers, I would gingerly wipe my eyes. I've never gotten used to the cold and my hands and feet have never developed the capacity to hold heat like theirs can.

I dressed in jeans, a cotton turtleneck shirt, and down vest over an alpaca cardigan sweater. Peelable layers. You have to peel off layers when the sun is in the zenith at noon and put them all back on when the sun goes behind the mountains at four in the afternoon. Before I put on my silk socks with heavy wool socks over them, I examined my arthritic toes and gave them a massage. After lacing my Avia shoes, I searched for my Gortex parka with a hood just in case the rains came. The rains should have started last month. What does it mean? Are the mountain gods, the Wamanis, angry? Is Pachamama punishing us? I'll have to wait and see what people say in Pumapunku. They must be frantic. If the rains don't start soon, they won't have a harvest.

Now my identity as a fieldworker was complete. I was dressed for the part. As I stepped into the courtyard I heard the song of the bread seller, then the melody of the fruit vendor. Who needs supermarkets. The sounds of the street made me feel at peace. No curfews, no military on the streets. I thought of the taxi driver searching out the two children at about this time in the morning and waiting all day for them and their mother. No wonder he has gone almost mad, poor man. I shuddered. Now it was six o'clock and the mournful whistle of the knife sharpener pierced the air. All was well . . . at least for now.

Today I'm playing the role of Alicia, the Quechua-Spanish-speaking anthropologist who became filled with rage over the years but now feels bone-weary. Quechua women are right, my body does feel like it's filling up and becoming heavy with sadness. Is my blood filling up with a thick viscous fluid that can't be spun out of my heart to reach my organs? Is my heart turning to stone like my comadre Clotilda claims? I touched my heart and wondered, is my blood not spinning outward into my arteries but rather seeping sluggishly and not sending sonic messages to my brain? Certainly, when I was full of rage, my heart and head were in unison. I could feel it pounding when I asked: Could I have killed Romulo? How about when I escaped being raped in Cangallo? What would have happened if Gregorio had not saved me? Perhaps if I had experienced repeated abuse and neglect, I could have become a member of Cholita's hit squad.

What if I had lived in these conditions of war for twenty years like so many people here have? I fell from the ivory tower into a messy world of war and human rights abuses, but I have always been able to escape to the safety of Washington, D.C., and my role of professor, the rational intellectual. In my fall into the real world, I amassed five large boxes of clandestine interviews and became, against my will, a "Senderologa"—an expert on Shining Path, giving lectures in Paris, London, New York City. In these cities, Senderistas attended the lectures and shouted slogans from the audience. Shining Path supporters even attended a lecture I gave at the University of Syracuse in upstate New York. At a conference at Cornell University to compare Maoism in Peru and Nepal, where Sendero had become a model for revolution, a group of young, naïve armchair revolutionaries repeatedly intervened and attempted to distribute *The Red Flag*, a magazine published in New York City. I can understand their motivations. They identify with the impoverished, repressed peoples of Peru and Nepal, but they misunderstood Shining Path's development into a death cult with a maniacal leadership that would have imposed themselves as an upper class had they gained power.

Could I have become such a supporter? Or would I have gone even further and joined the revolution if I had been born here? Would I have been driven to violence? What a frightening thought. What turns an intellectual like Guzmán into a revolutionary? He may have started with rage over the social conditions that he saw, but the thirst for power made him into a god-like figure when he became Presidente Gonzalo, with whom no one could argue. Does it all go back to his father? He was the bastard child, one of many, of a very prominent man.

During the 1980s I gave no lectures in Lima. My focus on peasants' responses and interpretations of the war did not attract an audience in the universities in Lima. Limeños denied that a war was ravaging the "other Peru—the Indian Peru"—until Sendero, under the command of Camarde Karina, a nineteen-year-old woman, bombed the Bayer chemical plant in Ventanilla outside of Lima in May of 1983. Meanwhile the war intensified in the highlands, with the highest number of deaths and disappearances occurring in 1984. On the 22nd of August, 1984, fifty cadavers (forty-nine men and one woman) were found in a common grave one kilometer from Huanta. I reflected that 1984 was also the year that María, the woman I interviewed in the mental hospital, was taken prisoner and tortured in Huanta. Were any of the dead in that mass grave the other captives that she described?

Massive car bombings in Lima finally woke the slumbering city to the seriousness of the war in 1985, the eve of Alán García's election. His government responded with coordinated attacks in three prisons in June of 1986. At least three hundred Shining Path were killed after they had surrendered. García also expanded the state of emergency that suspended civil liberties. Congress cooperated with García and passed a law to form Peasant Patrols that same year, but they were not armed until 1989.

The U.S. embassy took a different course of action. I remember interviewing members of the embassy staff in 1986. The most bizarre encounter I had was with the head of the U.S. Information Service (USIS) who had served in Afghanistan as a counterterrorism specialist. He had also served in Central America. He ushered me into his office, indicated that I should be seated at a table, then left the room. Strange, I had thought, why did he leave like that? After a few minutes, I began to read through telegrams piled on the table that were communications between the major human rights organizations of Peru and international ones, such as Amnesty International, reporting human rights abuses in the highlands.

The USIS officer came back into his office, smiled condescendingly at me, and announced, "We monitor these messages through our satellite installation at our Southern Command station. I have to decide which to block. We suspect that certain human rights organizations are sympathetic to Shining Path."

"That's absurd," I had responded. "Announcing such an opinion in certain circles would be an invitation to one of the right-wing death squads to assassinate human rights activists. Is that your intent?"

"We're just monitoring the situation," he answered.

Alarmed and shaken, I recounted the conversation to the human rights organizations in a meeting of directors who voiced the widely held opinion that the USIS officer was a CIA operative. The directors increased their security and put a courier system into place to get reports in and out of the country. Nevertheless, a month later, one of the directors was shot dead near his home. Tragic, and we were so helpless.

I looked out the door to see Julia hurrying to my room to help me with my travel gear, but in my mind's eye an image of Juana coming toward me materialized—Juana's small frame, sad eyes, features aged beyond her years, and most of all her worried glances to and fro. I was transported again to 1980, and I shuddered as I remembered the autopsy. Perhaps Romulo had truly grown to regret that ghoulish charade he had performed. Did he also regret raping Juana? How many other girls had he violated? What was his socialization of evil? Was El Capitán created by his family, especially his father, his culture, or by his army of hard-drinking, womanizing cronies? Were their exploits similar to the gang rapes committed by the military? Both types of violation are rites of passage into a male world of power. How could a reasonable human being commit such acts? The only explanation that seemed applicable was that of Robert Jay Lifton, who thinks that the socialization of evil involves a psychological process of doubling, or allowing another persona to take over in situations of torture, rape, or genocide. Something that he wrote has become my mantra: "One looks into the abyss in order to see beyond it."

What about Romulo and his buddies? Did they consider the girls they raped less than human? Perhaps. Certainly their targets were always of lower social status than themselves. To perform the horrific autopsy on Juana, Romulo's other self must have seen her as less than human. Are men more prone to engage in such acts? Especially in groups? But if women are given the same kind of power and the same socialization of evil, they commit similar acts.

Abu Ghraib comes to mind. It's all so worrisome and I have no real answers. When will I get a glimpse beyond the abyss?

In spite of their conquests, El Capitán and his band of marauders composed and sang braggadocio ballads about unfulfilled love and longing. Obviously none of their exploits gave them fulfillment. And Carlos? He is macho also. But he's different somehow. I can't imagine him raping a woman. He loves and admires women even though he doesn't know how to give them pleasure. But he thinks that he and his little brother, Juan, his penis, give every woman he notices shivers of joy. I laughed out loud. Carlos is upperclass, educated, and well-traveled. He spent twenty years in exile in Europe. The bottom line is that he just doesn't equate sex and power. He relies on the power of his words to seduce. Perhaps the least powerful commit the most heinous sexual abuses. On the other hand, the navy personnel like those who raped María are the most educated of all the branches of the Peruvian armed forces, and in Ayacucho they committed the worst offenses. What about the Indian population? Do they rape women? Civil patrols have. But I haven't seen rape in Pumapunku. Sex and power are not connected in the same way. I sighed heavily and returned to the tasks at hand.

Julia asked, "Are you all right? You seem so sad."

"This house holds too many memories for me, Julia, that's all," I replied as I reached for my cane. "The terrain is difficult in Pumapunku and I will have to walk up the almost vertical stone paths to reach Gregorio and Clotilda's house. Last year when I was there observing the activities of the Truth and Reconciliation Commission, Gregorio promised to carve a vara for me. He joked that he was making me a vara all my own and that I would be the gringa alcalde varayoq. How has he maintained his sense of humor?"

"It is remarkable that even though we have suffered so much we can still find things to laugh about," remarked Julia.

"Thank God, he and his family have survived. I wonder what scars the twenty years of warfare have left on them." I sighed heavily as we carried my gear to the front gate. A dirt devil engulfed me, and I imagined that I could see the ancestors swirling in the dawn's glow.

CHAPTER 11

THROUGH THE PUMA DOOR

The king-cab Toyota truck was waiting for me as I ducked through the small door cut in the ancient, battered portal and handed my gear to the driver, who tossed my bags into the back and fastened the canvas tight over the cargo. He introduced himself as Jorge Quispe and presented the two psychologists traveling to Pumapunku. Florencia Garces was in her fifties, a professor of psychology at Catholic University in Lima. She was small, about five feet tall, fair-skinned, with intelligent, kind brown eyes. Her shoulder-length brown hair showed signs of having been dyed to cover the gray. As we greeted each other cordially, I remembered that she was not a member of the elite Lima Freudian School of psychotherapy whose members published books on the Incas but knew very little about contemporary Quechua communities. In contrast, she was a Jungian psychologist, and we had met in 2002 when we both worked as consultants with the Truth and Reconciliation Commission's interviewing teams working with survivors to identify victims during the excavations of mass graves. I remembered that she was especially good at dealing with the teams of interviewers and excavations crews who showed the signs of psychological stress. I knew she was here to design a mental health plan to be implemented in the communities of the province of Cangallo. As I settled myself and my cane into the front seat, she introduced me to one of her graduate students, Margarita León, who was hoping to develop her thesis on posttraumatic stress syndrome in Pumapunku. I turned to look at them. Margarita looked to be close to thirty, slim and lean, with hazel eyes and short, black, stylishly cut hair. She looked athletic.

"It is so good to see you again, Dr. Woodsley," Florencia said as she shook my hand. "We're pleased that you'll be in Pumapunku with us. You have so many years of experience there."

Margarita added, "I'm hoping that you will be able to look over my survey questions and give me some advice."

"Please, call me Alicia." *Not another survey,* I thought. *Maybe I can get her to change her methodology.* I though about the stories I had heard that described memories of trauma as a liquid in the body such as breast milk or blood. She would do better with life histories with descriptions of events and symptoms.

"We've heard that you're the massaging anthropologist," commented Margarita with more than a little surprise in her voice.

"Yes, I've found that women describe their symptoms and experiences somatically. Their personal histories are manifest in their bodies, especially in their hearts, lungs, and wombs, which they consider their stomachs."

Florencia looked pensive and allowed that she thought that the most traumatized women are those who have been gang raped by the military. They can't tell anyone in their communities and often become outcasts and alcoholics. The worst cases are widows who have illegitimate children from rapes. Both mother and child are pariahs. If a woman is a widow or her husband has fled and she becomes pregnant after the military has gone from house to house gang raping every female they can find, she has nowhere to turn for support.

"Yes, that's right." I answered, "What's surprising is that these victims of systematic rape don't talk to each other nor to their families but suffer in silence with their pain and sadness filling up their bodies until they are totally immobilized, often lying in the streets in drunken heaps."

"What do you suggest that we do to reach them and get them to start talking?" asked Florencia. "We plan group therapy sessions."

"Well, group therapy will be good but you'll need the assistance of a native Quechua speaker because so many of the women are monolingual. But maybe we can create a ceremony, hampi—that's medicine in Quechua—to give them relief."

The two psychologists gave each other puzzled looks and Florencia asked, "When and why did you start massaging people?"

"I started massaging rape victims when a woman who had been gang raped by eight soldiers put my hand on her belly as she was describing how one after the other of the men jabbed into her while four men took turns holding her arms and legs." I explain that the woman related how one young recruit rebelled and said he wouldn't do it. The sergeant in charge said the men would rape him if he didn't act like a man. The boy only pretended to rape her when it was his turn. She was in the seventh month of pregnancy and lost the baby. When she reached the part of her story about losing the baby, her belly began to churn under my hand as if the miscarriage was occurring right in front of my eyes.

"My God," exclaimed Margarita, "she was having a sympathetic abortion!"

"Now women will stop me and whisper, 'Can you come to my house this afternoon when my children are in school and my husband is in the field?'"

I went on to tell them that when I arrived at their houses, invariably the women would bring me into their cooking huts and serve me something to drink or eat and tentatively begin their stories by telling where in their bodies their grief is located, usually in the heart, lungs, or uterus and stomach. Rarely do any of the women say that the past events are located in their heads or brains as we would. Their past resides in their hearts, which become heavy as their bodies fill up with sad memories; the only thing that dulls that sensation is drink. My massages seem to help. We also cry together.

"Isn't this having an adverse effect on your own mental health?" Florencia inquired.

"Yes, I seem to be absorbing their pain into my own body," I answered as I fingered my cane that was located beside me and thought of the incision on my tongue. "I often have an arthritis attack after one of the sessions with victims. And I feel the weight and sluggishness in my own heart. I seem to be carrying these stories like sacks suspended from tenterhooks that rip through my muscles. But there was one point in time where I developed lesions on my tongue that had to be operated on. I was left speechless."

"After the first excavation that I participated in," Margarita explained, "I had terrifying dreams that the bones of the victims rose and kept asking me when they would get justice."

Several minutes of tense silence went by and I decided to tell them about my recurring dream of trying to build a wall that continually disintegrates into a puddle of mud while a crowd of mute victims looks on from a distance. Perhaps talking to Florencia will help.

After I told them, Florencia touched my arm and said quietly, "If you would like to explore these issues, I'd be willing to work with you while we are together."

"Yes, good." I exhaled a sigh of relief, feeling the lump in my throat diminish. Florencia said that recurring dreams such as mine were common. She recounted how excavation and interview teams went through periods of depression or went on benders. She explained that she had to establish group sessions for interview teams when they returned to Lima so they could work through their own trauma. Excavation teams went through similar sessions and individual therapy was available as well. After thinking a moment, Florencia looked at me and asked:

"It sounds like you're absorbing your subjects' symptomatic pathologies. Did you have any psychotherapy before or after fieldwork?"

"No, and now I wish I had."

"We have to go through extensive therapy before completing our degree. Perhaps anthropologists who work on violence should be required to have psychotherapy as well."

"I agree with you, Florencia. Franz Boas, one of our founding fathers in anthropology, required his students to have psychotherapy before going into the field to do fieldwork. Perhaps we need to re-establish that practice."

We traveled in silence for a time, until Margarita looked up from her notebook and said, "Rape has different configurations in different cultures and I was taught that rape is rare in the indigenous culture here."

"Yes," I answered. "That's true."

She summarized her notes from one of her courses and declared that it's too simplistic to throw everything into the boiling caldron of machismo. She explained that she had worked with a task force in Lima with rape victims and she had learned that only 1 percent of rape cases ever make it to the courts. Moreover, she learned that Peru's prohibition against abortions as the result of rape, ironically called a sentimental abortion, is still on the books in spite of efforts to get it repealed.

"Yes, I know, and the truth commission has not really dealt with rape. My experience here in this region is that rape is rare because sex is not a form of power and domination. For the adolescents I studied years ago, sex was a form of physical and intellectual play."

"What do you mean?" asked Florencia.

I explained that when adults were engaged in ritual celebrations, teenage girls traded clothes, covered their faces with their shawls, and paraded in the village streets in small groups singing high-pitched falsetto songs to call young men out to "play" or "to put their lives out to pasture." The group of teenagers congregated outside their communities either in the cemetery or in the high herding lands, spaces considered "uncivilized," and engaged in competitions of riddles followed by sex. The girls initiated the riddles and each girl would challenge a boy she fancied with a riddle for him to solve. The riddles, created on the spot, were always sexual in nature and extremely funny. If a young man couldn't solve the riddle, he was metaphorically thrown off the mountainside in a song of defeat and landed at the bottom of the valley as a piece of shit.

"Well," Margarita laughed. "That certainly turns machismo on its head!"

"Yes, it does." I continued, "The competitions between couples culminated with sex, and the name of the game was to have sex with as many partners as possible. Of course the young women were always victorious because they had the sexual stamina to have sex with five, six, or even ten partners a night. The young men could not, literally, keep it up that long."

Florencia looked pensive and then asked, "But what about incest?"

I explained that as the nighttime play escalated, participants had to be careful not to have sex with anyone they were related to because then they would be turned into qarqachakuna or condenados, incestuous folks who were transformed into animals at night, usually llamas or sheep identifiable by the bells around their necks. Young women didn't win the competition by just screwing ten guys in one evening. They said that was easy. What was really hard was to create the ten cleverest riddles of the evening. During these sexual competitions, young men hung their heads in shame because they couldn't compete with the girls who strutted through the village streets decked out in their finery with their hats adorned with flowers to signify their victory in the competitions. Girls were proud not only of their sexual prowess but also of their intellectual and verbal skills.

"What about unwanted pregnancies?" Margarita queried.

I went on to relate that pregnancies were rare because the onset of menstruation is delayed due to lack of protein in the diet and high altitude. Moreover, if pregnancies did occur, the babies were readily incorporated into the girl's family. Half of all the children born died before five years of age, so children were highly valued. I anticipated their next question and asked if they were wondering what happened to children when a girl got married. They both nodded. Because marriages were arranged by the two sets of parents as an economic matter, usually to improve access to land, if a girl had a child before marriage her value as a marriage partner increased because she was fertile. The placement of the girl's child was negotiated. Say for example that the girl's mother was a widow who needed help, then the child might be assigned to look after her in her old age.

Florencia added, "And Quechua love songs are replete with stories of unrequited love as well as stories of couples who had to flee their communities to escape their families' disapproval. I love those melancholy songs."

"Yes," I observed, "and many of those impassioned stories involve teenagers whose liaisons during the games of 'putting your life out to pasture' ran afoul of parental control."

Margarita commented, "I wonder what one of our Limeño dandies would do during these sexual competitions."

I answered with relish, "I can tell you about one case." I recounted that a young male anthropology student from Catholic University worked with me as an assistant in Pumapunku when I discovered these games. He insisted on attending a night of celebration with the young people of Pumapunku, saying that he was up to the challenge. Not only was he not up to it, he couldn't perform sexually at all in such a public setting. Young women ridiculed him in public and that was impossible for him to endure. He left before the summer was over.

Florencia looked thoughtful and said, "Yes, machismo demands passivity on the part of women who are socialized to become sexual victims. I can understand why rape is rare here. Young women are empowered early. But rape is common in the U.S., isn't it, where women have a great deal of power."

"Yes, one in three women experiences some kind of sexual attack during her lifetime," I answered, and then I remembered something from my own youth and related the following story. When I was nine years old, I and my best friend, my next-door neighbor, were playing with paper dolls on my friend's bed. My friend's father came into the room and sent his daughter to the store. He sat down with me on the bed and knocked some of the paper dolls off the bed so that they fell to the floor on the wall side of the bed. He told me to crawl under the bed and retrieve them. When I crawled under the bed, he dropped his pants and undershorts, slid under the bed, and attempted to grab me. I was skinny enough to exhale all of my breath and escape under the end of the bed, scraping my legs on the bed frame as I did so.

"Oh my God, what did you do?" asked Margarita.

"I ran home and locked myself in my bedroom, afraid to tell my parents what had happened, sure that my father would kill the neighbor." I explained how I decided to take matters into my own hands. When nighttime came, I crept next door and stole a pair of the man's undershorts from their clothesline. I took them home and used them as the centerpiece of a ritual table that included two candles, my lucky rabbit's foot, a rattlesnake skin, and a small amount of my father's scotch. I sprinkled the shorts with the scotch and waved the snakeskin and the rabbit's foot over the shorts, while repeating over and over, "you will die, you dirty old man; you will die." I repeated this ritual every night for weeks after my parents had gone to bed. Of course, my friend was puzzled when I said I couldn't come over to play any more.

Florencia laughed and observed, "That was the beginning of your career as an anthropologist."

I finished my story by saying that my efforts were rewarded about a month later when the man died of a heart attack. Oh my God, I thought, breaking out in a cold sweat. I killed him. But then I said to myself, "He deserved it!" I remember attending the man's funeral feeling ambivalent and slightly guilty but also powerful. Maybe that's why I've never been afraid of being raped, even in Cangallo in 1980, which was a close call. My hands burned and tingled as I remembered Señor PIP, Mr. Hard-On's dick and gun.

"What happened?" inquired Margarita, leaning forward and touching my shoulder.

I told them the story about Señor PIP and asked if either of them had experienced sexual attacks. Both women looked at each other and finally Florencia answered. She was looking out of the window to avoid our gaze, but I could see tears welling up in her eyes. She related that when she was twelve years old, an older cousin raped her. They were at a fiesta together and her aunt told her cousin to drive her home even though she lived only three blocks from their house. Her aunt said she was afraid that Florencia wouldn't be safe walking home alone. Her parents had gone home early. She paused and we sat in silence for several minutes.

Margarita put her arm around her mentor's shoulder and Florencia whispered, "He drove to a wooded area several miles from our neighborhood and attacked me. I still hate the site of fig trees. Their gnarled branches . . ."

"Did you tell your parents?" I asked.

"No, I was too ashamed. I assumed that I had done something wrong. I didn't tell anyone until I was required to see a psychoanalyst as part of my training."

Margarita looked defiant and said, "If anyone touches me, I'd flatten 'im. I've taken self defense classes."

"Good for you," I said. "When I was very young and just starting research, I was seated on a crowded bus in Lima and a guy ejaculated on my shoulder! I was horrified but couldn't think of anything to say except, 'Señor, stop bothering me!' He answered, 'But chica, can't you see you're bothering me!'"

"Good grief," exclaimed Margarita. "Then what happened?"

"Everyone on the bus laughed and that made me furious. I started pounding on the bastard with my fists and he struggled to get to the back door with his dick hanging out. I chased 'im off the bus and up the divided parkway. I don't know what I woulda done if I'd caught him. We were quite a spectacle. My women friends taught me how to hurl insults at men to humiliate them if anything like that ever happened again."

"Do you think mestiza women are socialized as potential victims of rape?" I asked. "It seems that Quechua women are not."

Margarita answered vehemently, "Some women are socialized to be passive and mestiza women's virginity used to be guarded as a valuable commodity. Thank God that's changing."

We fell silent again and I thought to myself. Both Juana and María were raped, but not by members of their culture: María was gang raped by the navy officials to punish her and to demonstrate their power to each other. Likewise, Juana was raped to demonstrate Romulo's power to his cronies. I asked out loud, "Has Shining Path used rape as means of power?"

"No," answered Florencia. "Not in the systematic way the military did to instill fear in highland communities. Sendero has destroyed villages, cut people's throats, blown innocent people up with car bombs, and engaged in all kinds of atrocities against anyone defined as an enemy of 'The People's War.' But they have not used rape as a systematic weapon to instill terror or demonstrate their power."

I added, "In contrast, the military have used gang rape to initiate young recruits, requiring them to participate with the threat of being raped themselves if they refuse."

The diver climbed into the cab and we fell into an uncomfortable silence as he smiled and asked, "Ready doctoras?"

We just nodded affirmatively as we drove out of the city in silence.

Finally I pointed out the window and said, "Look, there's the Rio Cachi Irrigation Project. See the large canals leading down into the valley of Ayacucho? What a boondoggle! The World Bank loaned Peru millions to construct the damn thing, but 25 percent of the funding has disappeared and the lateral canals that were supposed to feed water to the communities in the upper reaches of the valley were never constructed. So instead, all the irrigation water that comes from the high springs and lakes is delivered to the commercial growers in the Ayacucho valley at the expense of the peasant communities, who feel like the city of Ayacucho is robbing their water. Which is true. Communities have always had their own system of sharing water, not always without conflict, but now they are left literally high and dry."

"Que terrible!" Margarita exclaimed. "What's being done?"

I informed them that peasant leaders are organizing to confront the APRA bureaucrats in power in the entire region. The peasants had shown me their evidence of graft, crumbling pieces of irrigation canals that had broken off because not enough cement had been added to the mix when the canals were constructed. While I was in Ayacucho for the presentation of the truth commission's report, I had attended a meeting with the president of the department of Ayacucho with his subordinates and told them the evidence of graft I had seen. The president admitted that graft was widespread, and he had said, "All officials steal a little off the top." He then told me what he thought was a funny story about APRA representatives meeting in Lima with their party's presidential hopeful, Alán García. He related that one official from Ayacucho got up and pointed a finger at another official and said, "I have a videotape of you taking a bribe from such and such a company." To which the other official replied, "Well, I've hidden a camera in your office and I have videotapes of you taking kickbacks from eight companies involved in the Rio Cachi Project!" A melee of accusations broke out into pandemonium until Alán García shouted, "Oh you venal boys, you, just quiet down; you're only stealing chickens!"

I then interjected with a sweet smile, "And then Alán said, if you really want to learn to steal, I can teach you!"

"You didn't!" laughed Florencia, "I take it you're not fond of one of our potential candidates."

"No, I'm not. I can't imagine how a man who stole millions and fled prosecution during a gun battle could return and run for president! And I understand that he stands a good chance of winning. But then, I shouldn't criticize any country's electoral politics when my own country re-elected an administration that lied to us about Iraqi involvement in 9/11. Bush was elected because of fear of attacks. And look at the mess we have created. Iraq is close to civil war."

General assent washed over the cab in a wave of relief. The Peruvians now understood where I stood on Bush's presidency, and that made it easier to relate to me.

Jorge, the driver, cut in, "How can U.S officials hold up their government as the model of democracy for everyone to adopt? Maybe we should invade Ecuador. But first we need a vice president who's been CEO of a powerful corporation like Halliburton, then he could give the company a contract to be in charge of everything from reconstruction of the country to transportation and meals for the troops. It's unbelievable. How can the people of the U.S. be so gullible?"

"Most people in the U.S. get their news from TV instead of reading papers."

We then discussed how Peru is a literate and informed society by comparison, even though the level of education is so much lower than in the United States. Everyone agreed that even during the last twenty years of warfare, Peru's press and media were not suppressed and managed. I allowed that in the United States, Fox News, owned by Murdoch, who backs Bush, is the source of the majority's news, and I described the phenomenal growth of the religious right on talk radio and TV.

I turned around in my seat to address the psychologists and asked, "Returning to Alán García, do you think he will win?"

"He's very popular right now, but then Toledo's presidency has been such a disappointment," Florencia answered.

Jorge announced, "We're in Toccto; let's stop for a bite to eat."

Margarita, rubbing the temples of her forehead, asked, "How high are we here? I don't feel so good. I have a splitting headache."

"You have sorroche, high altitude sickness," Jorge answered. "We're at 4,240 meters, the highest pass before we drop down into the River Pampas valley. Just take it easy and drink coca tea."

"Have you noticed that restaurants always seem to be located at high passes?" I asked as I got out of the truck. "I often don't feel like eating at this altitude either."

"How are you feeling, Florencia?" Margarita asked.

"I'm fine," answered Florencia. "I'm taking Diamox, which is a vascular dilator."

"I am too." I answered. "The first time I was prescribed that drug, my doctor gave me the wrong dosage and I was taking twice the amount recommended. I felt like I was inserting my fingers into wall sockets all the time. ZzZzZzZzZAP." I held out my fingers and shook them while making the sound of electricity zapping. "Luckily, my trip to Pumapunku that year lasted only for six weeks."

We all laughed while walking into the large, rustic restaurant filled with travelers. Three buses and five trucks were parked in front and most of the travelers were headed to the weekly market in Pumapunku. The trucks and buses were bursting with cases of beer and soda, drums of alcohol, bundles of clothing and hats, utensils, pots and pans, kerosene lamps and primus burners, cases of canned goods and cooking oil, and packaged rice and noodles. The vehicles would leave Pumapunku filled with livestock, small rounds of cheese, saddle blankets, hand-woven articles for the tourist market: ponchos, women's carrying cloths called llikllas, braided wool Christmas ornaments and knitted hats, gloves, and sweaters. I saw several market vendors I knew and made the rounds greeting people. Meanwhile my traveling companions settled themselves at an empty table and the driver ordered cuy, guinea pig. Margarita made a face and she and Florencia ordered mate de coca, coca tea. I joined them and ordered a mate as well. While we waited, I studied Margarita. Yes, she was even taller than I first thought, about five-feet-ten and very lean and muscular, probably works out. I noticed with relief that both of the psychologists had on sensible boots, jeans, and sweaters under their parkas, thank god. Years ago, women teachers would arrive in skirts and high heels as a sign of their status.

As I looked around the restaurant, I told my companions that I remembered the first time I ate here. When I asked what the specialty of the house was, everyone answered cuy. I didn't know what it was but ordered it anyway. When my plate came, I thought to myself, oh my God, they've cut off the tail of a very large rat and fried it, head and all! People at my table must have read my mind because they laughed and explained that it was a guinea pig. But why leave the head on, I asked, looking at the long rodent dentition and beady little eyes. Now I love cuy, but not this morning. It is definitely too early.

Jorge rubbed his hands together and tore apart the guinea pig's body and ate the crispy fried ears off the head. Margarita blanched and asked him for the keys to the truck. She excused herself, declaring that she would like to lie down in the back seat.

I turned to Florencia and asked, "Is this Margarita's first trip to Pumapunku? She mentioned having worked in the region before."

"Yes, she worked for a month interviewing victims, but she has a terrible time adjusting to the altitude. She's taking all the right precautions this time."

As we approached our pickup, several trucks and buses were pulling out, stirring up clouds of dust, and I was overwhelmed by the familiar sensation of being engulfed by the scent and sound of the ancestors who murmured their complaints in my ears. I looked around at the bone-dry landscape and joined in their lament. Tayta Razuwillka, we beseech you, please send the rains. Pachamama, have pity on us.

With the dry conditions and the newly paved road, we arrived in Puma-punku in an hour and a half. As we slowed on the descending hairpin turns that passed the cemetery, I noticed that several of the eucalyptus trees were bereft of leaves; their bony arms were raised in the attitude of prayer. They died from susto, fright, I thought; they have seen far too much.

Every space in the plaza was vibrating with commercial activity; make-shift food stalls filled one end of the plaza with each vendor specializing in local soups and dishes. I smelled the trout frying and my mouth watered. As long as I could remember, trout was brought up on market day from the River Pampas a thousand meters below. How in the world did Sendero think they could close down regional markets? When they attempted to, villagers revolted, asking, "Without markets, where would we get matches, kerosene, and all the things we need?" Sendero relented and let the trucks through their roadblocks.

The village mayor, Tomás Vilca Quispe, and a delegation of officials were waiting for our arrival in front of the municipal building. Tomás greeted me with the double embrace. He then turned and shook hands with Florencia and Margarita, motioning the varayoqkuna, the staff holders, to gather their visitors' luggage together. The men began to load the psychologists' suitcases, sleeping bags, and boxes on their backs, balancing them in their ponchos. A young boy held all their varas, their staffs of office, as they loaded their cargo. I told them to set my backpack aside, and I looked around and said:

"I don't see my compadre Gregorio or my comadre Clotilda."

"They're in Chicllarazo where their animals are pastured. They're driving several head of cattle down to the market to sell. We expect them any time now."

"Just leave my things here," I instructed. "I'll wait for their return and meanwhile, I'll have trout for lunch." I turned to Florencia and Margarita and asked, "Do either of you want to join me? The trout is fresh and delicious."

"Yes, I will," answered Florencia.

"No, I would like to lie down," responded Margarita.

The mayor instructed the varayoqkuna to accompany Margarita to the new health clinic with their luggage and to deliver coca tea to her immediately. They hurried off, backs bent under their cargo, holding their staffs in front of them to signify that they were on an official errand. The mayor then turned to me and said, "I'll join you for lunch and we can plan your activities here in Pumapunku." We made our way through the crowded market and I noticed that computer disks and CDs were a new item in the array of goods for sale. We settled into Doña Rosa's stall and the weathered face of the proprietress lit up when she saw me. "Doctora Alicia, we have been waiting for your return." She left her double primus stove to come to the serving side of her table and greeted me with the customary embrace that I have learned to love. Doña Rosa leaned close to my ear on our last embrace and whispered, "My cousin Benita would like to talk to you."

"Certainly, I'm staying with my compadres Gregorio and Clotilda. She can send me a message and tell me when it is convenient to visit her," I whispered in Rosa's ear as she finished the ritualized embrace.

"I'll tell her. And now, do you all want trout with papas fritas?" We all answered affirmatively in unison and Rosa set to work frying the fish. She was a round energetic widow in her forties dressed in the local style: a battered black hat that seemed a tad too small bobbing on top of her braided hair that hung to her hips, a bright pink satin ruffled blouse and long-sleeved black cardigan with holes at the elbows, and three long, ankle-length skirts, the black outer one decorated with cutout designs that showed the green cloth that made up the decorative inner layer. On her bare feet she wore rubber shoes that bore the popular brand name of Siete Vidas, seven lives. And of course, to top off this ensemble, she wore a long double-pocketed apron. Hurriedly dunking four dirty plates and forks in the pail of cold water sitting beside her table and extracting a cloth from one of her pockets, she dried them and heaped on them large helpings of fried potatoes, and balancing a whole trout on each plate. "Servidos," she said smiling as she set each plate in front of us. We seated ourselves on four wobbly stools and attacked our food.

Florencia looked at the plate apprehensively and whispered, "Aren't you afraid of communicable diseases? She just dunked these plates and forks in dirty cold water and wiped them off."

"I've not gotten anything yet," I answered, "except beriberi from eating only white noodles one year."

Florencia looked at me and laughed and was about to ask a question when Jorge cut in. "I love eating in the campo; everything always tastes better here."

Rosa nodded approvingly.

I turned to the mayor and asked, "How many houses have electricity? I noticed the electrical poles along the paved road."

"Only those around the central plaza. We haven't extended the lines up the hills to the outer barrios." The mayor then described other changes including the road that was paved for President Fujimori's visit, the new secondary school, and health clinic, but he emphasized that they were built with communal labor whereas the departmental government had not fulfilled its promises of providing desks, books, or teachers for the school or equipment and drugs for the health clinic. He ended his discussion by commenting that the reinstitution of the traditional authorities, the varayoqkuna, has greatly helped in organizing communal labor and meetings.

"Years ago, we anthropologists predicted that the traditional authorities, the varayoqkuna, would disappear altogether with modernization, and here they are reborn and as strong as ever," I said between bites of trout.

"But with several important changes," the mayor observed. "All the current holders of the staff are literate, except for the senior alcalde varayoq, who is over sixty years old. And all the other officials have lived outside of the community at one time or another and that means we have a very different relationship with the state. We now know how to make our demands known."

"I understand, Don Tomás, that you were chosen to participate in a travel program to various cities in the U.S. for a democratization program sponsored by the State Department. I'm sorry that I was not in Washington, D.C., during your visit."

"Yes, it was fascinating. You know that in the Hilton Hotel, I saw an employee who looked so Peruvian that I went up to him and spoke Quechua. He was from Huanta."

"So many people fled Peru during the war, but many are returning now, right?" I asked.

The mayor explained that returnees were becoming active in local politics and developing grassroots efforts to revitalize local communities. He hoped that the party that wins the next election realizes that their demands cannot be ignored as they have been in the past. He said that they were far more organized now. "We're not the humble Indians who hang our heads and plead with officials as if they were our patrones. We have rights and make demands." He looked determined as he declared, "The main question is whether the government will respond."

We paid Rosa for our meals, and just as I reached around Rosa's back to give her the second series of pats, a commotion in the plaza attracted our attention.

"It's my compadres Gregorio and Clotilda!" I exclaimed, grabbing my cane and making my way through the market crowd to meet them. Florencia and the mayor followed me to the corner of the plaza, where a cobblestone pathway from the northeast met the paved street around the town square.

Gregorio and Clotilda and one of their sons, my godson Gabriel, were herding three young steers and five sheep. They had walked the sixty kilometers from the high pasture of Chicllarazo.

I marveled at their stamina. I wouldn't be able to walk 120 kilometers up and down the mountain. Clotilda is my age and Gregorio is five years younger. I remember when he told me the sad story of not being able to marry the girl he had fallen in love with at one of the adolescent sexual competitions. While his sexual stamina was being tested by the young girls of the community, his social stamina was being tested by his parents, who were arranging a marriage with Clotilda's family. The two families had use of adjoining pastures and consolidating their holdings was the parents' first priority. Gregorio reluctantly agreed to the marriage. His only other option would have been to flee the community. The two have grown close over the years. Has that closeness developed into love?

Amazing! They both look younger than I do. Of course their hair won't go gray until they're about ninety years old and they don't eat sugar or processed foods and live primarily on grains. I'll never forget when I gave their children chocolate and Gregorio insisted on tasting it. His comment was "This cannot be good for you."

Now that they had converted to Protestantism, they didn't drink cane alcohol or even chicha anymore. As we completed our embrace, I smelled the acrid odor of coca leaves and thought. *Aha, they haven't given up chewing coca. I hope American missionaries don't notice and start a campaign of eliminating the "evil leaf" without realizing that coca leaf is not cocaine. For most gringos, coca leaf is equated with cocaine and my compadres would be arrested for chewing coca leaf in the United States.*

Gregorio interrupted my thoughts, saying, "Comadre, I see you brought your cane. I have finished your vara. You are now our gringa varayoq. We'll formally install you into your office tomorrow at our convocatorio, our communal meeting."

"The meeting should be of great interest to you also, Doctora Garces," commented Tomás Vilca, "and to your student, if she feels well enough to attend. Let me present one of our village elders, Don Gregorio Quispe Cabana and his wife, Clotilda Taipe Conde, and their son, Gabriel." They all shook hands and Gregorio repeated the invitation to Florencia to attend the communal meeting. Gabriel said he would deliver the cattle and sheep to the buyer who was waiting by her truck, and would meet them at home.

On the way up the steep hill, Florencia asked, "What is the meeting about?"

Gregorio responded, "Two former Senderistas have returned and petitioned to return to live in the village."

He paused and looked at the ground, embarrassed. "Also, we must deal with our own evangelical pastor."

As we entered the house, I saw the Timex wristwatch I had given Gregorio in 1980 hanging from a nail. I also noted that very little had changed in the house except that they were adding another room made of adobe bricks with a thatch roof. When we entered the kitchen hut, I was surprised to see a laptop computer sitting on the table in the center of the room. I asked, "And whose is this? It must run on a battery pack. There's no electricity in the house."

"Yes, it runs on batteries," responded Gregorio. He explained that my godson, Gabriel, studied compa (computing) at the university and now has a business "del web."

"Dios Mío! Que modernidad! Computers in Pumapunku!" Gabriel must be a webmaster. I wonder where the tower is for transmissions of signals? And how does he charge up the batteries?

Tomás Vilca was explaining to Florencia how the convocatorio worked. The community would hear from two petitioners who wanted to return to the village. He also informed us that they had to discuss how to handle the vultures circling over their lands; a Spanish mining company was trying to buy the communal pastureland in Chicllarazo, and the mayor was sure that no one would agree. I was alarmed when he said they were required to register their lands with the Institute of Culture in Lima and were told that they had to present a map, with all the landmarks and boundaries and the locations of all of the herding huts, within a month, or else the institute would grant the mining company a permit to explore the region.

"I can't believe that," I responded. "That'll be impossible to do."

"Yes, we know, and to top it all we have to hire the Institute of Culture's geographer to do the mapping, which will cost $750. We don't have the funds."

"I can provide the funds from my university research account, and with my godson's computer, I can e-mail the university to transfer the funds to the community's bank account immediately. You can also send a message to the Institute of Culture."

"Gracias comadre, may God repay you," Gregorio embraced me and wiped a tear from his cheek. "We've organized a delegation to visit the authorities in Ayacucho and demand teachers, books, and supplies for the health clinic.

We've completed our obligation of constructing the buildings and now they must complete theirs."

"May I videotape the meeting?" I whispered to Gregorio.

"I don't know. We'll have to see."

"Fine. I see that electricity has been installed in the plaza and in a few houses close to the square. Do any of the buildings or houses have running water as promised by the Rio Cachi Project?" I asked.

Gregorio and Clotilda both laughed and answered, "Dios Mío comadre, of course not. We don't even have enough water to irrigate, even though we cleaned the canals last August. The water has been diverted," Gregorio explained.

"Yes, I know. It's criminal!" I exclaimed.

"Yes, we'll probably have to sue to get anything done about it."

Incredible, no running water, no electricity, the same watch on the wall, but the web has arrived in Pumapunku. We anthropologists are lousy at predicting change. What other changes will I see tomorrow? But some things never change. I wonder who the mining company bribed in the Ministry of Culture to get a permit to explore the region.

CHAPTER 12

THE CONVOCATORIO

Tomás Vilca sent a young varayoq to ring the church bell at 9 A.M. for villagers to gather in front of the municipal building. Close to eight hundred people answered the call and congregated around the plaza. Young people perched on the wall that surrounded the padlocked church; some adults sat on the steps of the church and on the park benches in the pitiful plaza with its dead geraniums, but most adults stood around the cement plaza and in the circular street waiting for the officials to begin the meeting. The town officials arrived first and called the traditional authorities to come forward. The meeting was called to order by the two highest authorities in the community: the municipal mayor, Tomás Vilca, who had been elected, and the alcalde varayoq, Edmundo Pacotaype Llalle, who had ascended the ladder of twenty traditional positions to become the highest traditional authority of the community. He was the last eligible elder of his generation to serve. Sendero abolished all the varayoq positions in 1986, but the system of traditional authorities had been recently re-established. At almost seventy years old, Edmundo was the only traditional official who was still illiterate, but he spoke Spanish. He was also a powerful shaman and curer, serving not only Pumapunku but neighboring villages as well.

The two officials took their places on the second-floor balcony and addressed the assembled throng through a microphone and loudspeakers mounted on the outside wall of the municipal building. Tomás Vilca began the meeting by motioning to the village brass band to play the national anthem. A cacophony arose from the throng that must have made the mountain deities weep and Pachamama shudder because the national anthem was so badly performed. A difficult song for native Spanish speakers, it was particularly impossible for Quechua (and English) speakers. I, along with most of the women in the crowd, mouthed our way through the patriotic highs and lows of the anthem with the brass band doing its best to carry the difficult tune.

Tomás Vilca raised his arm and motioned for me to come to the balcony. I passed through the lower floor, ascended the staircase, and stepped onto the balcony with Gregorio at my heels.

The mayor announced that I would provide the funds for the mapping of their communal lands and that an e-mail had been sent to the Institute of Culture. There was applause from the crowd as Gregorio stepped forward and spoke in Quechua.

"My fellow villagers, my comadre Alicia is providing a great service to our community and to reward her, I want to present this vara to her. She will be our gringa alcalde varayoq."

Laughter and applause.

I stepped forward and kneeled with difficulty on my titanium knees to accept the vara. Wiping a tear from my cheek and taking the microphone to thank my compadre, I joked in Quechua, "Where are my aguaciles and regidores? I need subordinates to do my bidding." The crowd clapped.

I stared at the exquisite staff in a kind of trance. An entire annual cycle of rituals and festivals spiraled up the cane. And look, the year 1973 was carved into the bottom of the cane and 2005 in the top to commemorate the intervening years that I had been coming here. How marvelous! Tiny figures adorning the staff represented the annual cycle of rituals that I had studied and documented. The details were so exact that I imagined that I recognized individuals engaged in dancing during the yapuy, the planting ritual. And oh look! That must be Gregorio and Clotilda performing the Herranza, the fertility ritual for animals. And here—the harvest festival, Santa Cruz, in May! At the top near the 2005 date was the December solstice celebration when the sole male dancer dressed in a llama skin was pursued and encircled by young girls, women of child-bearing age, as well as old women, all dressed in blue. They were shown encircling the llama with their peculiar dance while banging their long decorated stripped poles on the ground. I could see the harpist playing the harp upside down and the crowd seemed to be shouting. I remembered they shouted, "Hurrah, they have mated!" when the women encircled the llama dancer.

A voice broke my concentration and I looked up.

The alcalde varayoq, Edmundo Pacotaype Llalle, stepped to the microphone, and the crowd became quiet and attentive. He asked, "Do you remember when the army Capitán and his soldiers came to Pumapunku searching for Senderistas?" General murmurs of assent rolled through the crowd. They had heard this story many times. Thus an oral tradition had been born.

"El Capitán was a brutal man who took me prisoner and beat me." The alcalde varayoq switched into Spanish and spoke in a high falsetto voice to imitate a maricón, which made the throng roar with laughter. His imitation of El Capitán became complete as he took a military stance. "We know Senderistas are here. Where are they? If you don't tell us we'll kill you and your family," the falsetto voice threatened as he brandished an imaginary pistol.

Don Edmundo switched back to Quechua and resumed his story in his normal voice. "They dragged me to the waterfall outside of the village on the path to Pomabamba and held my head under the water. But our brave young varayoqkuna ran to the top of the falls and blocked the flow of water with a boulder. That made El Capitán even more furious and he began to beat me with his pistol, but suddenly he was overcome with a violent fit! His eyes rolled back into his head. With his body twisting and turning with convulsions, he fell down unconscious. His soldiers were overcome with fear. 'What has happened to our Capitán?'"

In Spanish, imitating the frightened voice and expression of one of the soldiers, a sergeant, he continued. "Where is your curer? You must have one. Bring him here immediately to look after our Capitán." Pointing to the ground, he assumed another voice in Quechua and said, "But, mi Sargento, there is our curer, Don Edmundo, lying on the ground unconscious. The Capitán may have killed him." Not understanding Quechua, the sergeant said "What?" And then Don Roberto shouted a translation from the crowd. The alcalde varayoq feigned alarm and said in Spanish, "We have to revive the curer!"

In his own voice he continued in Quechua. "The sergeant began to dump water on my face and I was revived, but the Capitán remained unconscious. I ordered several varayoqkuna to go to my house and fetch my basket of herbs along with a large bucket." Giggles erupted from the crowd in anticipation. The alcalde varayoq waited a moment for dramatic effect, scanned the crowd and continued. "When the varayoqkuna returned I instructed each of them to piss into the bucket. Then I sprinkled herbs on top of the piss, lifted the head of the Capitán and helped him drink. He coughed and regained consciousness."

Now reverting to Spanish to imitate the voice of one of the soldiers, he asked in a high, nervous voice, "Is that a local cure?" He grinned at the crowd and answered in his own voice, "Of course! It cures susto! But you know what?" The alcalde varayoq leaned forward and as if in an aside declared in Quechua, "It was perfect vengeance." The plaza erupted in laughter and applause.

Yes, I thought to myself, *it is venganza perfecta. If only the alcalde varayoq could have called on Saint Francis to require El Capitán to drink piss throughout eternity so he could become the perpetual companion of the haciendado in Arguedas's story The Pongo. What a delicious image: The abusive landowner licking shit off his Indian servant and accompanied by El Capitán drinking Pumapuqueño piss throughout eternity.* I was smiling and deep in thought when Tomás Vilca turned to me and said, "Excuse me" as he walked to the microphone.

"Fellow villagers of Pumapunku, we have selected a committee of four to petition the authorities in Ayacucho to fulfill their obligation and provide the needed supplies and teachers for the school as well as the medicine and equipment for the health clinic."

As he read off the names selected, I was pleasantly surprised to hear Adriana Conde's name. Adriana was a young woman in her late twenties who migrated to Paterson, New Jersey, with her family as a small child during the late 1980s, with the flood of Peruvians fleeing the violence. Her parents returned to Pumapunku in 1997. Adriana stayed in New York City to finish her BA at New York University and then returned to Peru and enrolled in law school at the University of San Marcos in Lima. She just passed her law exams and she's going to represent Pumapunku! Que Maravilla! Even though we didn't see potable water or electricity, and the state and departmental bureaucrats were as corrupt as ever, an unanticipated consequence of the war was that people had become politicized through displacement. With legal representation from Adriana, hopefully their demands could no longer be ignored.

Gregorio appeared at my side and whispered, "You cannot videotape these proceedings. The former Senderistas do not want to be videotaped." He retreated quietly. I nodded that I understood. I probably shouldn't record it anyway.

Tension rippled through the crowd as two men and one woman made their way to the door of the municipal building. They joined the officials on the balcony, and Tomás Vilca addressed the assembled villagers. "We have serious decisions to make this morning. The first case we will consider concerns Pastor Jorge Vargas, who set fire to the Catholic chapel in Ranga Cruz. A meeting of the council has decided that Pastor Vargas must rebuild the chapel himself, brick by brick. He can commence today. Pastor Vargas, please come forward." The Protestant pastor stepped forward and kneeled in front of the municipal mayor. The alcalde varayoq mayor stood and gave the pastor three light lashings across his back with his chicote, the black whip with four straps made from the testicles of a bull. It always hung at his waist as the symbol of his authority.

"I yielded to the temptation put before me by Satan," the pastor pleaded, "I ask you and God Almighty to forgive me." He left the balcony, descended the stairs, and made his way through the crowd and up the path to Ranga Cruz followed by two young varayoqkuna in charge of watching him.

My God, it will take him months to rebuild that chapel. I understand that the two young varayoqkuna have to make sure no one helps him. I wonder how many villagers are Protestants. Gregorio said that perhaps 80 percent of the population has converted. No wonder people are hanging their heads in shame. Searching for solutions to the violence, many converted to Protestantism believing that only their prayers kept Sendero and the military at bay. Pumapunku was a Catholic community when I arrived in the 1970s, but the Catholic Church hasn't had a priest in residence for twenty-five years, ever since a guardia officer and some of his men came to the village to celebrate the priest's birthday. They got drunk and fired their pistols into the market crowd, wounding three people. Folks armed themselves with anything they could find and stormed the priest's residence. They captured the priest and his drunken friends, tied their hands behind their backs, and marched them barefoot 120 kilometers (75 miles) into the city of Ayacucho and turned them over to the prefect. The villagers padlocked the church and no priest has lived here since. Catholicism has failed them. The priest was a disgusting lout. He lived with his so-called housekeeper and his nephew. I wonder what happened to them?

Tomás Vilca took the microphone again and I returned my attention to the unfolding events. "The next case concerns Susana Conde, who will speak for herself."

Susana was in her early thirties, dressed in slacks, a sweater, no hat, and tennis shoes. She looked like many of the Senderista women that I had observed in the prisons: impoverished, a cholita from the highlands. Susana stood nervously in front of the microphone for a few moments before speaking. She cleared her throat and addressed the authorities first and then the crowd in Quechua.

"Señores autoriadades y llaqtamasikuna." *Interesting. She's addressing the crowd with the familiar "my fellow villagers." Let's see what else she has to say.*

"As most of you know I was kidnapped by Sendero when I was tending sheep in my family's pastures in Ranga Cruz. I was only twelve years old. They took me to a training camp where I attended classes every day and read Presidente Gonzalo's words. We marched and trained and I learned to shoot. Six months later I was ordered to participate in my first action, the assault on the National Guard post in Pomabamba. Several guardia were killed. Eventually I was trained to become part of an all-women hit squad. And I took part in the assassination of Romulo Rosetti here in Pumapunku in 1985."

Even the chattering green parrots that roosted in the lone tree in the plaza seemed to fall silent. Not one baby cried or whimpered; the children playing in the center of the plaza stopped and stared at Susana.

"After that I was transferred to Lima." Susana, clutching the front of her sweater nervously with her left hand, scanned the crowd and found her parents. She raised her right hand in a half-hearted greeting that looked like a plea for help. "Eventually I was able to escape after Guzmán was captured in 1992. I worked at various jobs in Lima, but now I want to come home. Tell me what I have to do to come home. I ask you to forgive me for the harm I've done."

I've got to talk to her! She can tell me where Cholita is! Who are her parents? Gregorio will know.

I wiped off the cold sweat that sprouted on my forehead and lips. Even the palms of my hands were damp. My heart was pounding so loud I was sure everyone could hear it. I waited for the reaction of the authorities and the crowd, but all that happened was that the mayor thanked Susana for her honesty and told her she would be informed of their decision very soon.

She left the balcony and I took note of her joining her parents in the plaza. *Oh yes, now I know who her parents are; they live in upper barrio. I'm not surprised that a decision is not being announced. The authorities, the varayoqkuna, the elders along with their wives, will receive anyone who wants to voice an opinion and then discuss it in private. The decision will be circulated through the community by word of mouth and a consensus will be reached. No voting, no public discussion. If they allow Susana Conde to return to the community then Teresa, Cholita's cousin, has a good chance of returning as well. I must deliver the taped letter to Teresa's parents and talk to Susana.*

Tomás Vilca was standing at the microphone with a thin man in his forties who looked vaguely familiar to me. He was introduced as Carlos Huamani, a former schoolteacher in Pumapunku. As the man took the microphone, a murmur rippled through the crowd that grew louder, like the rumble of an approaching earthquake.

His voice shook and his eyes darted back and forth, surveying the crowd. "Many of you know me from the years that I taught in the secondary school here. Yes, I was one of the early supporters of Sendero and I helped establish a base of support through indoctrination of secondary students. I truly believed we were going to establish a new democracy in Peru. I was wrong! Before the four Pumapunku authorities were shot, I and other teachers argued with the leadership in Ayacucho, but I realized that we could never influence their decisions. So I began to look for a way to get out of Sendero."

He stopped to wipe his brow and face nervously, then continued. "As you know, the only way we could leave Sendero once we joined was feet first. When the combined forces of the government launched a massive attack on the region and we retreated from Pumapunku, I was able to slip away because I knew the terrain. I eventually made my way to Lima and through a friend I was able to buy false identity papers with an assumed name. I got a job teaching in Villa Salvador, outside of Lima. I've been teaching there for years, but I've been informed that I've been recognized and now I'm afraid that I'll be killed."

He knelt and raised his hands in the attitude of prayer and continued. "I have embraced the Lord Jesus Christ and I'm a lay preacher in the Evangelical church. I beg for your forgiveness. As a son of Pumapunku, I want to return home."

Stony silence and then an eruption of palpable anger rose from the gathered throng. A man in the crowd shouted, "My father was one of the authorities shot! How can you show your face here! We don't want you teaching our children." People were getting riled. Several women and children bent over to pick up rocks. Tomás Vilca quickly stepped to the microphone and raised his arms for silence; a hush fell over the crowd.

"Fellow Pumapunqueños, we will consider Carlos Huamani's petition and come to a decision in good time. Let's return to our homes and think on the matters at hand. We cannot meet past violence with more violence. Perhaps if we can forgive our brothers and sisters, the rains will come." With that he dismissed the meeting, but Carlos Huamani put his face in his hands and began to sob. He stayed on the balcony, fearful of facing the crowd.

As I passed him, I heard him mutter, "I was so hopeful that they would forgive me. Where can I go now?"

I whispered, "They might still forgive you." I felt sorry for him. He was so young and idealistic in those days. I remembered him now; he was one of the first "hijos del pueblo," sons of the village, to attend the university. The words of Presidente Gonzalo must have fired him up to participate in the creation of the new Peru, and he probably even believed he would have a leadership role in the new revolutionary government. Instead he found himself hiding from a rigid, hierarchical death cult.

Gregorio and I arrived at the front door of the municipal building to find Florencia and Margarita waiting for us. "That was so interesting," Florencia declared. "We found someone to translate the Quechua for us. Do you think they will accept him back into the community? It seems clear that the young woman will be accepted back, but what about him? Even though they need teachers, the resentment and anger against him seems extremely high."

"I've given up predicting events, but I agree with you," I answered. "Resentment is high. However, we'll have to wait and see how things develop." I turned to Margarita to ask how she was feeling and whether she could walk up the side of the hill to my compadres' house. They had invited the psychologists to join us for lunch. She thought she could make it if she walked slowly.

"Here, use my new vara. Isn't it beautiful? My compadre Gregorio made it for me."

Margarita examined the staff with care and replied, "Thank you. The carving is exceptional."

We bid Tomás Vilca farewell, arranging a meeting later in the health clinic, and started up the stone path to Gregorio and Clotilda's house perched high on the hill overlooking the valley. My godson, Gabriel, joined us and we began to discuss the events of the meeting. Families returning to their homes were doing the same thing—discussing what decisions had to be made. The heads of the household would then tell the authorities, and that was how a consensus would be reached. No assembly with votes. It took me so long to understand this. We passed a small store where an elderly woman was sprawled across the path, drunk. An acrid, putrid odor wafted above her body. She had vomited all over her clothes.

"Oh, Dios Mío," Clotilda exclaimed. "That's poor Mama Justina. She's a widow. Her husband, son, and daughter were killed by the military at the wedding party massacre. You remember, don't you, comadre?"

"Yes, I do, but how did she survive? I thought they killed everyone."

"She had returned home to fetch more potatoes for the wedding dinner. She was the aunt of the bride. Look, she's clutching the stick that she keeps with her after all these years."

Aha, she carries her fetishes with her just like I do, I thought.

Clotilda recounted in Quechua that Mama Justina had returned for the wedding and found everyone gone, but there were boot prints all over the patio, so she got a stick and measured them. Then she went to Cangallo to the military garrison and presented the stick as her evidence that the military were responsible for the disappearance of the whole wedding party. The garrison commander threw her out, but she traveled to Ayacucho to file a report denouncing the military. She carries that tattered piece of paper—or what's left of it—in her pocket. She's gone a little mad. When the Truth and Reconciliation Commission excavated the mass grave outside of Pomabamba and identified the bodies as those of the wedding party, poor Mama Justina had to be carried away screaming. She has been like this ever since. Clotilda knelt beside Justina and looked up at us inquiringly. She asked what we should do. I translated for Florencia and Margarita. Then we propped Justina up on the steps of the store.

Florencia asked, "Doesn't she have any family who can look after her?"

"No," answered Gregorio, "she lives alone. Her only surviving daughter lives in Lima and Mama Justina refuses to move there. We can't carry her up the hill. I'll ask the storeowner to look after her until you return from lunch. I'll send food with you for her then."

Gregorio returned from speaking to the proprietress, shaking his head. "The owner agreed reluctantly to look after Mama Justina if she's left on the steps. The blasted woman is willing to sell Mama Justina cane alcohol but she isn't willing to have her in the store. We'll have to leave her here until you return from lunch. You can pick her up on your way to the health clinic."

"Where does she get the money to buy alcohol?" Margarita asked.

"Her daughter sends her money to buy food," Gregorio answered.

"We'll take her to the clinic. There are two other beds there," Florencia offered.

"It looks like you have your first mental health patient," I observed.

"And not an easy case either," Gabriel added. "She's been this way for years. We used to see an occasional drunk man after a fiesta, but it was scandalous for a woman to get fall-down drunk in public. Now we have elderly widows who are drunk all the time."

"We saw the same thing in so many communities. I'm surprised they haven't frozen to death. Does anyone at least cover them up at night if they are in the street?" Florencia asked.

"Yes," responded Gabriel. "The youngest of the varayoqkuna are charged with looking after them. They also bring them food and carry them home if they find them passed out. The varayoqkuna could carry Mama Justina home now."

"No," interjected Gregorio. "I told the owner of the store that the varay-oqkuna are to leave her here and that you will pick her up after lunch."

We climbed the path to the outer ring of stone, thatch-roofed houses with small garden plots around them where pigs, chickens, sheep, and the occasional cow were husbanded. Smoke was pouring out of the thatch roofs of most of the cooking huts where women were busy cooking lunch. The stone cooking huts stood like small smoked mushrooms alongside the houses. To reach Gregorio and Clotilda's house, we had to cross several fields, climbing over stone boundary fences and jumping across irrigation ditches devoid of water.

"The lack of rain is very worrisome," I commented. "I see that the irrigation ditches are dry but they look like they were cleaned in August. Why isn't there water flowing? Isn't water usually distributed this time of year if the rains are so late?"

"Yes, that's right," Gregorio said. "Usually water is distributed under the supervision of the varayoqkuna, but the Rio Cachi Project water has been diverted to the main canals that carry it to the valley of Ayacucho. We were told that feeder canals would deliver water to all the communities of the region, but that's a lie! We've inspected the main canals and feeder canals were not even planned. Some of the main canals are crumbling because not enough cement was used. Carajo, son ladrones."

His fists clinched, Gabriel cut in with anger in his voice. "When our representatives met with the president of the region and asked about the disappearance of the World Bank funds . . . And what about the feeder canals? His answer was that they were studying what their priorities had to be, canals or roads. Carajo!"

Clotilda hurried into the cooking hut with a handful of herbs she had picked in her kitchen garden. An elderly aunt had been left to prepare lunch. I helped her peel potatoes, noticing that they were wrinkled with age and some were sprouting. *God, I hope they have a decent harvest this year. I remember the terrible years when drought or early frosts killed the crops. Existence becomes like living on the edge of a razorblade.* Clotilda added quinua, potatoes, dried fava beans, and a few carrots, as well as the herbs to the soup pot. To accompany the soup, toasted corn, cancha, and hard cheese were set out in two large gourd bowls. Clotilda and I served everyone their bowl of soup in the portal area of the house. We accommodated ourselves around a small knee-high table that held the cheese and cancha.

"The soup is delicious," Margarita declared. Florencia added, "And I love cancha and cheese."

"Cancha, toasted corn, is the most popular snack around." I commented. "You'll see women and children with cancha in their skirts and aprons to munch on as they work or walk."

Conversation turned to the events of the morning, and Gregorio declared, "I think we are going to accept both Susana Conde and Carlos Huamani back into the community. The lack of rain means that Pachamama and the mountain deities are angry because we're not healing ourselves. We must forgive them. The question is what they must do to compensate the families they have harmed."

When I asked what he thought they would be required to do, Gregorio answered that he thought that Susana Conde had suffered enough. After all, he said, she was stolen from the community and forced into the ranks of Sendero. But Carlos Huamani chose to join Sendero and community authorities were killed. He will have to serve those families for at least a year. Gabriel wondered if Susana could take care of Mama Justina. His father thought that was a possibility. A discussion ensued concerning the wedding massacre and the lack of a legal means to require the military to compensate the victims, much less face justice.

"How much power does the military still have locally?" Margarita asked.

Gabriel, in a voice full of rage, explained that in nearby communities the military have brought repentidos, those who have given up names of their comrades in order to get released from prison, and required that their home communities install them in positions of power, as mayor or judge. He adamantly asked if we could imagine going before a judge who had killed a member of our own family. Clotilda asked if anyone wanted tea and we all answered yes. As she turned to the cooking pots, she declared in Quechua that she hoped no repentidos were ever imposed on Pumapunku. *She understands Spanish conversations perfectly,* I thought to myself.

"That's why there have been a number of revenge killings in the region," explained Gregorio. "At least we're in charge of our own reconciliation in Pumapunku. Except that we can do nothing about the guardia and military abuses."

"But a list of the guilty has been delivered by the Truth and Reconciliation Commission to the judiciary," commented Florencia. "The names of those involved in the wedding massacre are on the list. Hopefully, they will be brought to justice."

"I'm not very confident about that," I allowed. Everyone became quiet and I thought about what the judiciary would have to do. First, they would have to confront the military. When the Truth and Reconciliation Report came out, the general who had been commander in Huancayo during the years when more than 150 students disappeared from the Central University said that the report was vengeance against the military. He also said that the TRC was made up of "reds" and the legal left. Another general declared that the TRC was implementing a new strategy for the surviving remnants of Sendero. That same general made a statement to the press saying that the terrorists had wanted to destroy the Peruvian society and the state. The military believed they were only defending the state and in the process a few excesses were necessary.

Margarita interjected with vehemence, "Thirty percent of the fatalities were caused by the military. General Luis Arias, the military representative on the TRC, registered fifteen objections to the report that have been included in the final version. One of the objections was to the commission's move to forward cases to the judiciary. He declared the armed forces should judge their own, and we know what will happen if they do. The same thing that happened in Chile and Argentina, general amnesty."

"Nothing is happening with the cases that have been forwarded to the Peruvian judiciary," Florencia emphatically added.

"Let's hope it doesn't take thirty years for those cases to come to trial," I responded. I explained that Chile declared they would try Pinochet, but he'll probably die first. There is also the question of compensation to victims. Seventy thousand victims in Peru; where's the money going to come from? In addition, the rondas campesinas, the peasant patrols that were forced into service, are demanding compensation. Truth commissions all over the world have not fulfilled promises of compensation.

I turned to Gregorio and pleaded, "Compadre, I have been talking to women who have been gang raped and they have nowhere to turn; they didn't come forward when the TRC was interviewing victims, nor can they talk openly in convocatorios about what happened to them. I was thinking that with your help we could create hampi, medicine, that would heal them. They are probably suffering the most because of their isolation. Please help me think about what we could do."

Gregorio thought for a moment and I could see that the idea intrigued him. He went on to say that a pagapu to Pachamama, who is responsible for all things that have to do with birth and fertility, would be appropriate. He smiled and added that she could cure these women. As he rose to leave the lunch group, he turned and said, "Let me think about it."

"Could we observe and take notes?" Florencia whispered to me, giving Margarita a knowing look.

"I'll go down the hill with you to pick up Mama Justina," I told Florencia and Margarita, "but then I have to make two visits this afternoon. Gregorio and Clotilda have chores to do." I prepared to leave by making the rounds of good-byes. Pat, pat, pat, pause, pat, pat, pat.

Margarita stopped me in the pathway outside and inquired, "I keep noticing that you embrace people the same way when you first greet them and then when you part company, even if you've only chatted for a few minutes. Let me see, am I doing it right?" She put her right arm at the back of my waist and her left arm on my upper back, pat, pat, pat and then she switched arms and positions and repeated the gesture.

"Yes, by jove, I think you've got it!" I said, laughingly imitating a British accent. We walked down the hill and found two young varayoqkuna waiting for us. We helped carry Mama Justina to the new clinic. The old woman opened her eyes for a moment and stared at us uncomprehendingly. Then she began to sing in Quechua in the high falsetto typical of women's music:

> Señor Fiscal, great sir,
> in the middle of the day
> they kidnapped my family
> and the whole wedding party.
> I went to look at Infiernillo,
> but my beloved family is not there.
> I went to the garrison,
> but my beloved family is not there.
> Mr. district attorney of the great City of Huamanga,
> make my family reappear.
> I hope the government hears this song.

She fell silent and just stumbled along with the two varayoqkuna supporting her slight frame. She looked like a wounded black bird trying to take flight. When we reached the health clinic, the varayoqkuna deposited her on one of the beds, and Florencia and Margarita said they would try to feed her when she woke up.

Florencia requested that I translate the words of the song. She had understood the words in Spanish but didn't understand what Infiernillo referred to, so I explained that Infiernillo referred to Little Hell, a place outside the city of Ayacucho where bodies of the disappeared were dumped by the armed forces. As these places were discovered, they became part of a sacred geography. Mama Justina is using the song to declare that she went to Infiernillo to look for her family. The last lines of the song say: Mr. district attorney, make my family reappear / I hope the government hears this song. The original song included a male voice who sung the part of the district attorney who responded to the woman, Señora, run along and don't cry / I'll send a memo to the garrison to the investigators and inquire about your family.

Florencia listened to the song translation and then commented, "The song is so ironic."

"Yes, most of the protest songs are. Another song I recorded in Puma-punku is called 'Democracy and Liberty.' It goes like this."

> You keep insisting there is democracy and liberty.
> (Then switching to the suffix for direct experience, the female
>   singers claim):
> This good liberty comes to us with death,
> This good democracy puts us in jail.
> Whom have we offended?
> How have we caused harm?
> They arrived suddenly in my village
> and caused my loved ones to disappear.
> Some are in jail,
> others are in the ground,
> Some will be in prison,
> others will be buried.

I gave a quick exegesis of the song, telling them that the song was claiming what the singer has experienced in her flesh and in her blood but then accused her interlocutor by singing "you keep telling us lies." I told them I had first heard this song sung for Lima bureaucrats who spoke no Quechua and no one translated, so when a local pointed out that the song was about democracy and liberty, they made their own assumptions without realizing that the singers were representing an ironic dialogue with the state. Florencia had asked when I recorded the song and I answered that it was after Guzmán was captured in 1992.

"I wonder if songs like those are still sung." Margarita interjected. "When we conducted our interviews here last year, we found that people were waiting for the state to compensate victims. There are whole generations that lost the opportunity to go to school, not to mention the families of the disappeared." She looked so disheartened that I embraced her, saying her work would help. Jumping to my feet, I said I had to run because I wanted to make at least one visit that afternoon. I bade the two women good-bye, no embrace, just a wave of the hand calling back over my shoulder, "I'll stop by in the morning."

I must visit Teresa's parents and deliver her recorded letter. I am optimistic about the possibility of the community accepting her back into the fold. I wonder if Teresa is related to Tomás Vilca. Possibly; his mother's last name is Quispe. But Quispe is as common in the highlands of Peru as Jones or Smith is in the states. Half the population in the department of Ayacucho is named Quispe either on their mother's side or father's, including my comadre, Clotilda. The mayor could help get Teresa released from prison to return to the community. I hope he's Teresa's relative.

I found the Quispe house and delivered the taped letter and found out that Tomás Vilca was Teresa's second cousin. Her father and his mother are first cousins, classificatory siblings, and he is therefore obligated to help her. I inquired about Susana Conde's family and quickly sketched out a kinship chart to search for relationships that I could use to talk to Susana Conde. I discovered that Susana Conde's father, Nicario Conde, had married my compadre Gregorio's first cousin or classificatory sister, Maria Quispe. So Susana's full name was Susana Conde Quispe. *Students hate to study kinship but it comes in handy! I've got to get to Gregorio's and ask him to help me approach Susana. She can probably tell us where Cholita is.*

The sun was sinking fast behind the mountain to the west, and when the darkness is pulled down like a shade, the temperature drops immediately fifteen to twenty degrees. I looked up at the mountains across the River Pampas and saw a pair of condors circling. Was that a good sign? Condors are the mountain deities in alternate form. Have they heard our pleas?

The next morning I visited the two psychologists to see how they were getting along with Mama Justina. I arrived at 6 A.M. because Gregorio's household rose at 5 A.M. to have breakfast and collectively tell their dreams before assigning chores to various members of the family. Dreams are important prognosticators for the activities assigned to each member of the household.

I knocked on the door to the clinic and a voice inside mumbled, "Just a minute." Margarita came to the door in her rumpled clothes and socks. I burst out laughing, saying, "Sorry, I've done the same thing myself. Sleep in my clothes to keep warm."

"Its ice cold in here," she responded, shuddering.

"You know what I do? I sleep in silk long johns and a long sweatshirt and socks. Then I leave them on and put my jeans and a sweater on over them. I also sleep on my clothes to keep them warm. I know what you mean about the cold. It'll get warmer when the rains finally come." I touched Margarita's arm to reassure her.

"There's ice on the water pitcher! And all we have to heat water on is one little primus burner and I can't get it lit," Margarita said. She looked like she was going to cry.

Florencia, awake but huddled in her sleeping bag, peeked out and muttered, "Can someone please put water on for coffee?"

Mama Justina roused from her drunken stupor of the day before and declared loudly in Quechua, "I'm hungry!"

"I brought your breakfast!" I replied as I set the blackened pot of quinua porridge on the table and pulled a round cheese wrapped in straw from my pocket. I think the quinua is still warm and the cheese is good just mixed in, or you can add sugar and milk to the quinua and eat the cheese with the cancha." I untied a piece of cloth that had toasted cancha in it.

"We have only three cups, no bowls," Margarita said. She still looked like she was going to burst into tears.

"We'll use the cups for the porridge and then rinse them out for your coffee," I said. "I brought spoons. Margarita, do you want mate de coca, instead of coffee?"

"I'll have a mate after my coffee! I can't function without coffee." Margarita said. She had taken off her socks and was rummaging around in her duffel bag for clean socks while dancing from one foot to the other. Her bare feet emitted translucent blue waves as she danced. "How do the folks here wear those rubber tire sandals in this freezing cold?" Margarita demanded.

As I lit the primus stove and put water on to heat, I said I had wondered the same thing years ago but I learned that people who live in high altitudes have circulatory systems that are highly efficient and that their blood is not only thinner but they also have a pint or two extra. Our blood struggles just to get through our hearts and lungs, and when we eat it rushes to our stomachs and intestines and we feel sluggish and sleepy or we get headaches. I poured the water into the coffee and added that the hands and feet of these highland folks are always warm. I turned and held my hands up and told them that my nickname was chiri maki, snow hands.

Florencia, up and dressed, gave me the questionnaire and asked, "Will you look over these questions for us?"

"Sure, why don't you both come with me today to visit a woman who was gang raped. I'll ask her if you can be present when we talk. How are you going to configure your therapy sessions?"

"We thought we would interview women individually first and then form groups," Florencia answered.

Trying to be as diplomatic as possible, I said I didn't think that would work, and I went on to outline what was necessary for a Quechua speaker to tell a story. Usually, a speaker has to have someone present who has experienced the same events to validate or contradict the speaker's version, or at least relate some similar experience. I learned this the hard way years ago when I tried for years to tape record women's life histories but failed. I especially wanted to interview a famous storyteller named Victoria, but she always brushed me off, saying I didn't know enough for her to tell me her life story. Finally, I interviewed her with her daughter and granddaughter present. That worked—she needed someone present to provide a running commentary on her story as she told it. I also learned that Victoria understood everything we said in Spanish, even though she only spoke Quechua.

"That's interesting," Florencia said thoughtfully. "What a good defense mechanism." She went on to say that they had a woman native speaker who would work with them. She had been part of the truth commission team. She could help form group sessions first and then advise us when it would be appropriate to move to individual therapy. I agreed.

As we prepared breakfast, I continued my story about the famous storyteller, Victoria. "She told us a funny story about how in her youth she had shot a cattle thief in the leg and yelled at him as he got on his horse and rode away." I cupped my hands and yelled, "'Stay awhile, look what else I have for you,' lifting imaginary skirts. During Victoria's narrative, her daughter provided the required running commentary, such as, 'My mother is a very good shot' or, 'Everybody says that she really did that.' Then her daughter told a story about the death of her first-born and at one point, weeping, she grabbed both of her breasts and cried, 'Mi hijito, my poor little baby boy, died because I got an infection in my breasts and couldn't feed him. He shriveled up like a leaf and died!' At that point, her mother cut in; speaking in Quechua, she growled in a low voice, 'Your firstborn wasn't a boy; your firstborn was a girl.' Her daughter stopped crying for a moment, wiped her eyes, and said, 'Yes you're right; my firstborn was a girl.' So the point is—veracity is constructed dialogically."

"But the truth commission interviewed people individually," responded Florencia. "I've read the transcripts."

"Which worked for bilingual Spanish-Quechua speakers," I responded, "but the TRC teams eventually took testimonies in small groups for monolingual Quechua speakers so that dialogically, truth could emerge from the group's interactions." I dished up Mama Justina a bowl of quinua with cheese crumbled into it, asking, "Here you are, Mama Justina. How do you feel today?"

"My heart is so full of sadness that it has to work very hard. I can't move my legs properly either. Here, feel my heart." Mama Justina took my hand and placed it in the middle of her chest. I set down the bowl of cereal and placed my other hand on Mama Justina's back and began to massage the old woman's torso.

Her heart rate is very fast. Now it's slowing down a bit and I can feel the beat getting stronger. If I close my eyes, I can visualize the contractions of her heart beginning at the base, lub DUB, lub DUB, causing the heart to wobble. Lub, the blood is pumped to the lungs to be oxygenated, then the louder DUB as blood is being pumped through the left ventricle, spinning out to all parts of the body. The heart beats 100,000 times a day and pumps blood the distance from New York City to San Francisco. It's a swift river of vitality. What has gone wrong with Mama Justina's heart? Do women who have been gang raped have some malady of the heart? They all complain of their hearts being heavy and sluggish. Are their aortas constricted? Is the blood not being properly oxygenated? Is their adaptation to high altitude a factor? Larger lung capacity, thinner blood? Are they developing hypertension? Will they become victims of heart attacks?

Mama Justina closed her eyes, smiled, and almost crooned, "Oh ah, that does make me feel better," as she patted my hand on her heart. After a few moments, I stopped massaging her back and embraced the fragile old woman, rocking her back and forth like an infant. Then, giving Mama Justina the bowl of quinua, I watched the old woman eat parsimoniously, as though she was trying to make her cereal last forever.

The two psychologists had been silently watching the massage while eating their cereal. As Florencia served the coffee, she turned to me and inquired, "So that's how the massaging anthropologist works? What do you think that did for Mama Justina?"

I paused and thought for a while and then responded that in a culture where every social encounter begins and ends with an embrace, one of the worst things to endure would be to be treated like a pariah and never be touched. Wouldn't it be psychologically devastating for someone like Mama Justina not to be touched for years except to carry her when she is unconscious? They both nodded in agreement.

We climbed the hill to the north and reached lower barrio. I located Benita's house and knocked on the outer gate. A timid voice inquired in Quechua, "Who is it?"

I answered and we heard Benita approach with a slow, heavy step. She unlocked the gate and peered out cautiously. I examined her closely. Benita was perhaps thirty-five; her brow was furrowed in permanent worry and her eyes darted back and forth apprehensively. Her braids had come partly undone and strands of hair fell around her face. Her skirt and blouse were soiled and she emitted a peculiar odor I could not identify. She embraced me but looked suspiciously at Florencia and Margarita. I explained that they were colleagues who worked with the Truth and Reconciliation Commission. I pointed to Florencia and told Benita that Florencia was a doctor who might be able to help her. Benita nodded slowly and led us to the cooking hut where she had been peeling potatoes for lunch.

"My husband has gone up to the high pasture and my children are in school except for Joselito." She pointed to a bundle in the corner. I walked to the corner and inspected what looked like a bunch of old rags and found an undernourished, sickly looking infant who was only two or three weeks old.

"I can't nurse him," Benita proclaimed, "because he would get my nightmares. I've been feeding him potato and rice water. I try not to sleep, but the visions come to me even when I am awake." She began to silently sob, her shoulders heaving up and down violently. Turning to Florencia, she asked, "Does the doctora have a pill that will make me forget? That's what I need, a pill to forget."

I translated for Florencia and Margarita. Florencia asked me to tell Benita that she could give her something that could help, antidepressants, but she added, "They won't make her forget the rape."

I sat on a stool beside Benita, who was squatting in front of the fire, and translated. While getting out my tape recorder, I asked Benita if I could record her story and assured her that we wouldn't play it unless she gave me permission. I touched her hands, which were clenching her skirt, and added that even then we wouldn't use her name.

"Yes," Benita answered, but she turned her back to me as if to address the cooking pot. She began her narrative in a breathless whisper while staring into the cooking fire. "It was the year that the military disappeared our village officials"—plop, a potato hit the water in the cooking pot—"who refused to form the civil patrols." Two more potatoes hit the stew pot—plop, plop.

"That was in 1992," I added.

"The army officer who took our judge and municipal mayor away sent patrols to every house. They came to my house in the afternoon. I was here cooking and Louisa was asleep exactly where Joselito is sleeping now. She was older, almost five." She paused and added habas to the pot.

"Four soldiers drug me to the house and held me down across the table. They smelled of rum and tobacco. They took turns holding my arms and legs." Benita stopped and covered her eyes. "I keep seeing them, smelling them, hearing their voices. They kept calling me, 'Stupid chola, terruca! We should just shoot you.' I bit my lip and made it bleed so I wouldn't cry out and wake Louisa, because if they found her, they would . . .'"

Benita put her hands on her chest and rocked back and forth.

I asked, "Is that where you hurt?"

Still with her back toward me, Benita answered, "Yes, my heart and stomach are filled up with sadness. It starts in my stomach and rises up to my heart until I can't breathe. The sadness hovers over me like a large black bird ready to invade my body. I keep seeing those horrible men, jabbing, jabbing, dripping, dripping. I was all wet and sticky when they left. And I smelled of their semen. They filled me up with their semen . . . that's why I'm sick. After they left, I crawled over to the water bucket and washed myself off as best I could. Louisa started to cry and I picked her up and rocked her back and forth. My two older children came home from school and found me here in the kitchen, rocking and holding Louisa. The fire had gone out. When my husband came home from the pasture, he scolded me for not having dinner ready. I prepared dinner and never told them anything. I was so afraid that he would smell them on me. Please help me, Doctora Alicia. I know you have helped other women like me."

Reaching around Benita's body, I began to massage her sternum. Leaning against my body, Benita closed her eyes and moaned, "That feels better. I need to sleep but I can't close my eyes. Those men are carved on the inside of my eyelids."

"Imagine that we're looking at the western horizon. The sun is about to set. See how beautiful it is?" I said, still massaging Benita's chest.

Benita closed her eyes briefly but popped them open again, shouted, "No! I'm afraid!"

"Try. The sun, Tayta Inti, is about to travel behind the mountain, but look, he is crying for you. He says, 'Benita, I will watch over you. I'm going to sleep. Come, try to sleep with me.'" I began to rock Benita back and forth and to sing a lullaby in Quechua. Benita closed her eyes. "Tayta Inti is smiling on you," I whispered. "He is washing your eyelids clean of all those images. See? He takes one of his tears and wipes your eyes clean."

I could feel her heart slowing down and the rhythm getting stronger, lub DUB, lub DUB. Now the rhythm was slowing down in time with our rocking, back and forth, back and forth. *I'm exhausted. Oh no! Flash and sudden pain, men's bodies, faces, dicks, dripping, jabbing, jabbing.* I popped my eyes open in panic and stopped rocking Benita.

I looked at Florencia and whispered in Spanish, "Dios Mío, her images just flashed in front of my eyes! They overcame me. I could see, hear, and smell the rapists. Let's see if we can get her to rest a while." Even though it was cool, I was sweating. We led Benita outside onto the portal where she dropped like a wet rag onto the adobe and stone bench built into the outer wall.

"I am so tired. Maybe I can sleep now," Benita said as she curled up in a fetal position.

"Yes, try to sleep. I'll stay here with you," I assured her as I hit the stop button on my tape recorder.

"My God, that was incredible," Florencia said, wiping her face with a handkerchief. "I think I saw a manifest cloud as her images were transferred to you." Nervously she looked at Margarita, saying, "Have you ever seen anything like this?"

Margarita was visibly shaken as she said, "Last year when we were taking testimonies with the TRC, we were told over and over again that women were not nursing their babies out of fear that their nightmares would be transmitted in their milk to their infants. The result was an alarming rise in infant mortality and malnutrition. How do we convince these women that their memories and nightmares are not liquid that can be passed to their infants?"

"But for them, maybe their memories are liquid," I declared emphatically. "Sadness, they believe, is a liquid also, a heavy liquid that fills up the body cavity and can even stop the heart from functioning."

CHAPTER 13

THE CURE

Clotilda and Gregorio sat on low stools in the cooking hut waiting for their comadre and the two psychologists to arrive for the evening meal to discuss the cure that was planned for Tuesday. Gregorio turned to his wife and said, "Wife, do you think we can create a new pagapu for the women in the community who have been raped? Will Pachamama accept such an offering? I'm worried."

"Yes, husband, I believe that Our Mother will accept such an offering and perhaps the rains will come . . ." Her voice trailed off to a whisper, "if the women are cured of their nightmares. Maybe Pachamama and the Wamanis are angry because we have not helped these women."

"Yes, that's possible," Gregorio said. "But what do we do for them? We've never had women in our community violated like this." Gregorio looked down at the floor, embarrassed to be discussing such a matter with his wife.

Clotilda got up and put her hands on his shoulders and said, "Husband, it will be all right. Let's see what happens with the pagapu for Benita."

"I'm also worried about letting the two women from Lima attend. Will Pachamama accept them?"

"She has accepted our comadre Alicia."

"But our comadre Alicia changed after her visit with Pachamama. Don't you remember what she was like when she arrived?" asked Gregorio.

"Yes, she was always in such a hurry; she wouldn't just sit and be quiet. She wanted to talk and talk, always asking questions and writing in her little black notebook," answered Clotilda.

"I remember when we went to return Juana's organs to her body; I thought I was going to have to gag Alicia to keep her quiet. She kept babbling. I wondered if all gringos talked so much." Gregorio laughed as he asked, "Do you remember the first Herranza she attended? She took pictures of everything and was so interested when we performed the marriage of the young bull and heifer. She asked, 'Why have you tied them together like that?' And when we answered, 'so they can mate and have offspring.' She said, 'But cows and bulls don't copulate like that. Tied together front to front.' As if we don't know how cattle copulate. The next morning when it came time to go up to Lake Matuma to make the offerings to the Wamanis, we had to sneak out of the hut and leave her sleeping because she would have tried to follow us and women can't see the offerings. When we returned, we decided to play a joke on Alicia. Three men of our family called to her, 'Comadre, comadre come, come, we need you!' Then they pretended to mount her like a bull from the rear and asked, 'Is this how bulls do it?'"

"But she kept on talking and asking questions waving her hands and saying, 'Dios Mío, do you always do this? Am I supposed to be the heifer? Were the cattle representing humans yesterday when you tied them together?' And on and on," Clotilda said giggling.

Gregorio had been deep in thought. He confided that his biggest problem was where to have the hampi, the cure, for Benita. "Since women can't get near the cajas, the stone boxes, nor know what is in them, we can't perform the curing ritual there. Maybe we could perform it on the edge of Lake Matuma since Pachamama resides under the lake with her two-headed snake, the amaru." He turned to Clotilda and asked her opinion.

Clotilda put her hand up to her mouth to cover her laughter and told him that women know very well what is in those stone boxes. Growing serious, she told her husband that the sacred lake would be a good place. She told him that Alicia should be present; after all, she had talked to Pachamama years ago.

"Yes," responded Gregorio, "but the two psychologists shouldn't be there; they would offend Pachamama because they would never ask Pachamama or the Wamanis for help. Gabriel explained to me that they think they can cure our sadness with the help of one of their ancestors, called Wreud, and with their pills."

A knock at the gate interrupted their conversation, so Gregorio went to answer the door, and when Gabriel, Florencia, Margarita, and I stepped into the courtyard, he embraced us all, including Florencia and Margarita. Turning to Florencia, he asked in his most careful Spanish, "Who is Wreud? One of your ancestors?"

"What?" She looked to Gabriel and me for help.

Gabriel laughed and said, "Oh, Freud. My father is asking if Freud is one of your ancestors. I explained to him that you and Margarita thought you could cure the women who have been raped with the help of Freud. He wondered why you don't ask the help of Pachamama and the Wamanis and I explained that you don't believe in them."

Gregorio thought for a while and said, "My comadre Alicia didn't believe in them either when she arrived but she does now. She has seen Pachamama. Isn't that right comadre? You had a conversation with Pachamama, didn't you?"

I answered that I certainly did believe in Pachamama, who was beautiful and fearsome. I described my vision of years before and explained that I had been both attracted to Pachamama's kindness and afraid of her ferocity. She had two faces: one in the front with all the beneficial animals at her feet and one in the back with the animals that announce bad omens. There were potatoes and other tubers growing out of her body and she was dressed in the most beautiful long dress made with a shimmering silver warp. Live creatures moved in the golden weft of the cloth. I told them that often when I closed my eyes, I could still see her huge, round figure with all the native Andean animals sitting around her.

Florencia and Margarita looked at each and Florencia suppressed a smile. "Please explain to Gregorio that Freud is not one of our ancestors. Besides, I'm a Jungian." She suggested that we take a two-pronged approach: Gregorio could conduct the cure and they would try to convince the women to agree to meet with them in group therapy sessions. We all turned to Gregorio, who anticipated our questions and said that the pagapu should take place at Lake Matuma with offerings to Pachamama. When I asked what kind of offerings, he told us the usual: coca, bread, fruit, cognac, adding that we should all wear new clean clothing. I then asked whether we should make an offering to Pachamama by burning a bit of Benita's hair, and he agreed. He dug around in his bag of paraphernalia and found a small alabaster Inca period llama that had a hole in the top that was charred black from centuries of burned offerings. He announced that he would use it, his most powerful illa, or messenger.

As we were discussing the best strategy for convincing Benita's husband and his family to attend, Florencia interrupted our conversation in Quechua and asked for a translation, which I gave in summary form. Florencia asked if they could attend the ritual. Gregorio turned to them and said no, that he was afraid they would offend Pachamama.

"Why?" Florencia and Margarita asked in unison.

"Because you don't recognize her," explained Gregorio.

Everyone fell silent for several moments. Feeling uncomfortable, I explained that Benita was such a good candidate for our first cure but Gregorio did not want to run the risk of offending Pachamama. I quickly changed the subject to Benita and said that when I had spoken to her yesterday, she was eager for the cure to take place. She even gave me permission to play her tape during the ceremony, but we'll have to convince her husband, her in-laws, and her children to attend. I asked whether Gregorio needed Benita's brothers-in-law and sisters-in law as helpers and he answered that indeed for the hampi to work, they had to be his assistants. We discussed Benita's as well as her husband's kin groups and Gregorio and Clotilda found common relatives that they could approach. Gregorio said that Benita's husband was a distant relative of his and he would approach him and his family to ask for their help.

"Maybe Doña Rosa, Benita's cousin, could be recruited as well," I said. "Rosa must know about the rape because she asked me to visit Benita, so that means Benita must have talked to her about how much she is suffering."

We agreed, and plans were made to buy the necessary items and to make the trip to Lake Matuma the following Tuesday, a propitious day for offerings to Pachamama. I turned to Florencia and Margarita and outlined what the sequence of events would be. I emphasized that even if they could not witness the cure, they would be able to accompany the group up the mountain and wait in one of the herder's huts nearby until the ritual was over. Besides, I explained, a group of women will remain behind to prepare a meal and you can talk to them.

I bid Florencia and Margarita good-bye and told them that everything would work out all right because even if you can't attend the cure, you will have access to all the relatives present and perhaps you can set up sessions with some of the women. They agreed, but I could see that they were not happy about the outcome of the meeting.

Before we retired for the evening, Gregorio and Clotilda agreed to accompany me to the home of Susana Conde, the young former Senderista who pleaded her case at the convocatorio. I could hardly sleep thinking about the possibility of finally locating Cholita. The visit to Susana Conde's home was planned for the next day at four o'clock in the afternoon when the family returned for the evening meal. Gifts always lubricate social gears when a favor is involved. Clotilda would take a live chicken in her shawl and I would give them a large flashlight and extra batteries. I was extremely nervous about the meeting. "What if Susana doesn't want to talk to us about Cholita?" Perhaps she had sworn silence. I kept up a running commentary about my worries as we proceeded to the outskirts of lower barrio. Gregorio and Clotilda reassured me that Susana would cooperate because her parents, Felix and Patricia, were their compadres. Gregorio and Clotilda were baptismal godparents to Susana's brother, Jorge, and through extension godparents to Susana as well. Also, Gregorio emphasized, Cholita was his niece. We're all family, including you, Alicia. This is a matter for family members to discuss, he declared as he and Clotilda spread the sheep hides on the adobe, built-in seating area of their roofed portal that served as their bed.

"But what if she has sworn an oath to Cholita?" I asked as I picked up my things and made my way to the store room where I slept. I opened my mouth to ask another question when Gregorio, already tucked in under a mound of hand-woven blankets with Clotilda, suddenly raised up on his elbows and softly, but with authority, told me that Susana's loyalties have to be with her family if she wanted to return to Pumapunku. Showing rare irritation in his voice, Gregorio demanded no more questions please. He emphasized that he would initiate the discussion tomorrow. Gregorio had dismissed me and I felt chastised. I moved dejectedly toward my dark, dank room that smelled of corn and potatoes when I heard Clotilda muttering under her breath, "At last, peace and quiet."

We reached the house and the Conde family was waiting for us with a prepared meal. The round of embraces, exchange of formal greetings, and presentations of gifts went smoothly and I began to relax. Perhaps Susana was ready to talk to us after all. Word had reached the Condes through rumors that I was trying to locate Cholita, and they anticipated the motive for our visit when they received the news that their compadres were coming.

I knew that I had to follow my compadre Gregorio's lead, but I could hardly wait to talk to Susana. First we had to engage in small talk about the lack of rain, the convocatorio, and news from family members who are living elsewhere. I couldn't stand it, but I was patient.

Patricia came out of the cooking hut with two large bottles of Fanta and one glass. She poured each of us a large portion and said "salud" as Gregorio, Clotilda, and I drained the glass in turn and returned the salutation. *Felix and Patricia must be Protestants. Or maybe they are serving Fanta out of respect for Gregorio and Clotilda.* After a large bowl of soup, Patricia and her sister-in-law served each of us cuy, guinea pig, and fried potatoes. This was indeed a special occasion; cuy is usually reserved for baptisms or weddings or for dignitaries at village banquets. We were being given special treatment—that meant that they, too, wanted something from Gregorio and Clotilda. They knew that my compadres could influence the decision about Susana's return.

After two hours of eating, drinking, and polite chitchat, Gregorio broached the subject of Cholita by turning to Susana and asking directly, "When was the last time you saw my niece, Cholita?"

"It was four years ago when we discussed how we were going to escape from Sendero. I planned to go to Lima and she said she was going to a new community that was being formed in Victor Fajardo. I hear that she is there, teaching school."

I broke in excitedly, "What community? Where?"

Gregorio gave me a look as if to say, "I'll handle this." He continued. "We are willing to help you return to Pumapunku. Can you help us contact Cholita?"

"I hear that she is using the name Juana Quispe," I said, unable to contain myself.

"Yes, that's true, she has identity papers that say she is Juana Quispe and she is living and teaching in Paradiso, Victor Fajardo, not far from the community of Sarhua."

That's only a day's walk from here! We have to go there immediately. I turned to Gregorio excitedly and started to say, compadre . . . but he cut me off and directed his attention to Susana and asked how we could get in touch with her. Susana informed us that we could send a message with a market vendor who is in touch with her. Gregorio nodded in agreement.

"But compadre—" I attempted to object. Gregorio held up his hand to stop me and simply said, "Paciencia, comadre."

He's right. I have to be patient. After all these years of searching for Cholita, I can't blow it now. We'll send a message and wait for an answer. I'd like to set out tomorrow, but I'll wait.

Gregorio stood, signaling that our visit was concluded. Patricia went to the cooking hut and brought a new bottle of Fanta and served everyone once more. *If they don't stop giving me this stuff, I'm going to commit Fantacide!*

We filed through the gate of the Conde compound and walked through the community and back up the hill without exchanging a word. Every time I attempted to talk, Gregorio raised his hand and motioned for me to be silent.

The next day I visited Rosa, Benita's cousin, pleading with her to come with me to talk to Benita's family about curing her nightmares. Rosa had already heard that Gregorio would perform the ceremony at Lake Matuma next Tuesday and she also knew that it was essential that members of Benita's family, as well as her husband and his family, help with the cure. She agreed to contact the necessary family members and asked who was buying the gifts for them. I told her that the gifts would be my contribution. She asked that Gregorio accompany her on the official visits and I said that I was sure he would. We arranged to meet and visit Benita after lunch. I hurried toward the store to buy gifts for the families but then changed my mind and decided to stop by the clinic and ask Florencia for antidepressants for Benita. I raced to the clinic and found Florencia and Margarita preparing breakfast with Mama Justina's help. I explained that the cure would take place tomorrow and that they would be allowed to accompany us on the procession to Lake Matuma. We'd leave at five in the morning from Gregorio's house; dress warmly, I advised, but be able to put on extra layers as we climb. The ritual will take place at sunset. Then we'll spend the night nearby at La Union. We'll return to Pumapunku on Wednesday morning. Bring only the absolute essentials. It's quite a climb.

"I wish we could see the cure," Florencia said as she looked dejected, but then she added, "I understand. They don't want to offend Pachamama."

"But you'll get to know members of several of the major kin groups of the community. Observing everyone before and after the ceremony will be a way to begin to organize group therapy sessions."

A long silence ensued. Hoping to cheer them up, I told them that I had been excluded from many rituals when I arrived, but I was able to learn a lot by talking to the women who stayed behind to prepare the food. Over the years, I added, they have let me observe more and more.

Margarita said, "Well, I don't have thirty years to wait to finish my doctorate."

"True," I laughed. "I assure you, you'll have enough data for a thesis in a year."

I said, "Florencia, I wanted to ask you if you think that Benita should be taking antidepressants. Could they help her?"

"Yes, she probably would not feel the effects immediately. She certainly does appear to be suffering from posttraumatic stress disorder. Paxil is a fairly new selective seratonin reuptake inhibitor that relieves the three major symptoms of PTSD: depression, phobias, and flashbacks. We saw the flashback. Does she suffer from phobias?"

"Yes," I answered. I related that Benita had told me that she's afraid of leaving her house. "We have to convince her that it is safe to come with us to Lake Matuma. I've asked Doña Rosa to go with me to convince her. For this to work, everything has to come together. I think Benita will agree to make the trip. The difficulty will be to convince her husband and his family to attend. Rosa tells me that her husband and practically everyone else in the community know about the gang rape but they don't know how to talk about it. Maybe our task should be to represent the gang rape and her flashbacks without verbalizing. That would mean calling up her flashbacks and using them ritually. That's tricky. God, this isn't doing anthropology, so what are we doing?" Margarita and Florencia laughed nervously and shook their heads to say they weren't sure either.

On the walk up the hill to Gregorio and Clotilda's house, I recounted the transformations in my wall-building dream. "The wall didn't crumble last night and the dead victims came closer."

"It seems that your memorial project is making progress," Florencia commented.

I helped my compadres string the necklaces of bread and fruit for everyone to wear as offerings to Pachamama. Clotilda organized the food. Gregorio had assembled a group of women to play the tiña, a small ceremonial drum played only by women who have borne children. The elderly drummers spent the night and slept with the family on the stone benches in the portal. Before they went to sleep, Gregorio explained to them that the repetitive drumming and singing should evoke memories and bring out the demons that haunted Benita.

Gregorio checked his hampi bundle and I observed with amusement that he had included several large bottles of 90 proof cane alcohol, trago, and small bottles of cognac as well as the ubiquitous Fanta. Aha! Pachamama has not converted to Protestantism! She still drinks alcohol. Gregorio also included double ears of corn and potatoes that have odd shapes as offerings. But no computer discs or CDs have made it into the hampi bundle. Pachamama hasn't gone high tech yet.

The two psychologists, Gregorio, Gabriel, and I discussed how to configure the cure with stimuli so that Benita would experience a flashback that would enable Gregorio to dispel her demons. We decided that rhythmic drumming while someone held and rocked Benita would be good while I played the tape of Benita recounting the gang rape.

Florencia pointed out, "Smell is a powerful stimuli to memory. Benita repeatedly experiences the smell of the men's semen when she has flashbacks. Perhaps we could provide that stimulus along with the sound of the tape and the drumming. Multiple sensory stimuli would be ideal."

Gregorio had to ask for a translation into Quechua and when Gabriel provided it, he jumped to his feet and exclaimed, "Impossible, we can't do that! Have our sperm remind her of her rapists!"

Gabriel thought for a moment and offered a solution. He had a classmate who was studying agronomy and working with the herders in La Union on artificial insemination of cattle to improve the herds. He has cattle sperm. We'll pass right through La Union, so Gabriel said he would e-mail his classmate and ask him to provide enough sperm for our needs. He looked at the psychologists and asked, "We need only enough for her to smell? Right?"

"Yes," answered Florencia. "Just enough to evoke memories."

Gregorio left the room, mumbling under his breath while Gabriel headed for the cooking hut to send the e-mail on his computer. I followed him and asked, "How do you charge up the batteries?"

"I hook them up to my cousin's truck. He's here twice a week."

"And where's the tower for transmitting signals?"

"Just south of here. President Toledo's government installed it. He had a plan to supply computers to schools, but that hasn't happened."

"Fantastic," I said. "Pumapunku has really entered the computer age and you're a webmaster!"

At four o'clock in the morning, I was awakened by Clotilda's call for help in the cooking hut. We had to prepare a hearty soup with cheeses and cancha for the entire entourage. Relatives began to arrive and I couldn't distinguish the Catholics from the Protestants because Fanta was the preferred social lubricant for the entire gathering in deference to Gregorio and Clotilda's new religion. However, several families had small bottles of trago in their bundles.

All the participants arrived wearing new, or almost new, clothing in hues of blue. We're translating a major pagapu to Pachamama, like the Yarqa Aspiy, the cleaning of the irrigation canals. Both male and female supreme deities should be given offerings for the sake of equilibrium, but what should we do when male power has destroyed that equilibrium? Which is the case with gang rape. Should the Wamanis, the male deities, be propitiated? That was the real issue.

I continued to mull over these questions as I prepared for the four-hour trek up the mountain to the sacred lake. I rolled up my sleeping bag and packed extra wool socks, toothbrush, and several medications (growing old was such a drag). I included batteries for my digital camera and tape recorder and finally selected a wool hat called a chullu with earflaps to wear under my felt-brimmed hat. I searched for my wool gloves without fingertips—such a practical invention, keeping your hands warm while working with your fingertips. I also threw into my blue backpack extra bottles of boiled water. I laced up my Gortex boots and put on my rain parka and went into the courtyard to observe the preparations and discussions.

Gregorio was in command. He reminded me of an orchestra leader preparing for a major performance. Each section had to play its particular part perfectly. Benita's in-laws were especially important; two brothers-in-law and two sisters-in-law had the responsibility of acting as Gregorio's assistants in the cure. Usually the two brothers-in-law provided comic relief for the assembled participants. But would they engage in the usual buffoonery expected of them? Probably not, given the objective of this ceremony. Gregorio checked again with the four elderly women about when to begin the ritual drumming.

Gregorio and Clotilda distributed the bread and fruit necklaces to the twenty assembled participants. When he came to Benita, he carefully placed two necklaces around her neck and blessed her, making the sign of the cross. Everyone brought bottles of cane alcohol, cognac, or Fanta as gifts. Women carried bundles of food to prepare at La Union. All rituals were sealed by sharing food and drink.

I approached Gabriel with a delicate question. "Godson," using the formal greeting in Quechua, "did you get a message back from the agronomist?"

Gabriel looked embarrassed, lowered his head to avoid my eyes, and whispered, "Yes, I'll pick it up."

Twenty minutes outside of the village, the procession stopped at a stone table and grotto that were used during the cleaning of the irrigation canals, the Yarqa Aspiy. Two women came forward with chicha, corn beer, from ceremonial wooden vessels that I recognized as Inca period qeros, carved wooden drinking beakers, and poured the libations onto the stone. A man stepped forward and placed coca leaves on the stone after blowing on them and intoning an incantation.

Wow, they're pulling out all of the stops! Bringing out the sacred qeros found in burial caves! We're retracing the path of the ritual that I think symbolized the irrigation water as the semen of the Wamanis, the Mountain Deities. They're propitiating the male Mountain Deities as well as Pachamama. I wonder how much of this is conscious. Or are they merely repeating a pattern from the Yarqa Aspiy, the cleaning of the irrigation canals?

I had learned that during the cleaning of the irrigation canals in August, the pagapus, the offerings to Pachamama, were made at several stone tables that demarked ecological zones of productions as we ascended the mountain. The journey up the mountain encoded the transition of the upper limits of corn production to potatoes and other root crops; and further up, we would probably stop at the stone table that marked the upper limit of potato and root crop production. The last zone, the puna, dedicated to herding, was our final destination at four thousand meters (13,100 feet) in altitude. We would stop at each stone table and grotto and repeat the offerings.

Different kin groups provided the offerings at the three stone tables. At the last stop, Gregorio asked me to pour the chicha that his family provided. I stepped forward, using the staff Gregorio had made for me for support, and poured the corn beer from a qero that had plants carved into its surface. Human, animal, and crop reproduction were intricately linked. Gang rapes damaged the human soul and endangered agriculture and herding.

As I poured the libation for Pachamama and Gregorio intoned the prayer, I looked out over the valley below. How spectacular! I could see the patchwork of fields that clung to the hillsides. Some were so steep that they looked impossible to till and plant. But every bit of available land was utilized. All the fields were bone dry. Benita's kin groups were probably thinking that if they restored Benita to health and sanity, then the rains would come. No wonder we had such a good turnout.

We climbed the one thousand feet to La Union in five hours, stopping several times to chew coca. At four thousand meters, the thin air meant that we gringas had to stop and rest more often than the other participants, who joked about the poor foreigners who needed help up the mountain. We had surrendered our backpacks to others more acclimated, and to my shame, the woman who carried my backpack was at least sixty years old. But she nevertheless bounded up the steep rocky path like a mountain goat.

Florencia and Margarita sought me out for an explanation of the ceremonies they had observed on the journey up the mountain. I explained while Gabriel listened, then I asked him to comment on whether my interpretation seemed correct.

"Yes, basically," Gabriel said, "but the bit about the irrigation water being the semen of the Wamanis, the Mountain Deities, might be overinterpretation. Anthropologists sometimes get carried away with symbolism. I took an anthropology course at the university last year, madrina, and we read your ethnography on Pumapunku." Gabriel grinned impishly, but then, becoming serious, he added, "Speaking of semen, I have to go over to the agricultural station and pick up the bull semen for the cure tonight."

"It's great when the natives talk back," I commented and laughed. "Does that ever happen with your patients?"

"Yes," Florencia responded. "And then they stop coming to the therapy sessions."

"When are you going to give the Paxil to Benita?" I asked.

"I think at the conclusion of the cure. What do you think?"

"Seems O.K. to me, but we are operating in uncharted waters, aren't we?"

Before Florencia could answer, a young boy announced that lunch was ready. We walked over to the herding hut that belonged to Gregorio and Clotilda where two large cooking pots were balanced on stones with small fires under them. Dried llama dung was used for fuel, and people believed that llamas were very considerate of their human owners because they deposited the dung in one place near their owner's hut, making it easier to collect. Five women were preparing the soup for our lunch in one of the pots and three other women were putting dried corn in the second pot of water for mote, boiled corn similar to hominy. Tin bowls were lined up on the ground ready for serving. I explained that we would have to eat in shifts. "As guests, we will be served in the first group, along with Benita, Gregorio, and Clotilda. After us, all the men attending will be served, and finally the women who are preparing the food will serve themselves last."

"Are women always last?" Margarita asked plaintively.

"Yes, but these women have been eating all the time that they have been cooking." I answered.

We sat on the ground or stone outcroppings to eat. Lake Matuma was visible in the distance. Herds of alpacas and llamas were feeding on the short grass near the lake. The high-altitude marshes were dry and cracked, and I pointed to the marshes and noted that at this time of year those marshes were usually filled with water. Gabriel looked in the direction of the marshes and said, "This year herders had to drive their alpacas, llamas, and cattle closer to the lake for water. This area is part of the land held communally that the Spanish mining company is trying to either buy or rent from Pumapunku. But that'll never happen. These marshes are ecologically very fragile and they act as natural filters as the water passes through the ichu grass before draining into the rivers below."

Florencia asked, "How does that happen?"

"Ichu grasses are natural purifiers. Pollutants attach to the roots and are absorbed by the plants." Gabriel looked proud and he went on to say, "The marshes would be destroyed if mining operations were to move in here.

The geographer from the Ministry of Culture should arrive soon to do the mapping."

"Good, that means that this fragile environment will be saved from the destruction of mining," I commented.

"This landscape is spectacular," exclaimed Margarita. "Everything except for the mountains and the lakes is in miniature. The clumps of tiny plants, the mosses and grasses, even the huts look like they're hugging the ground."

"Comadre, please come with us to set up for the cure," called Gregorio. "Rosa and Benita's sisters and cousins will bring her later."

Getting up to leave, I called to the psychologists and reminded them that even though Gregorio has decided that they couldn't be present that I would tell them everything that happened. I suggested that they talk to Benita while we were setting up for the ceremony. Suddenly, I remembered something important and said, "If you decide to take a nap, don't lie down directly on the ground. Everyone believes that the Wamanis or Pachamama can capture your soul if you sleep in the wrong places up here."

At dusk, people began to gather at the edge of the lake at the place where a waterspout had been sighted several times. People believed that the waterspout was the amaru, the giant snake with a head on each end that lived in the underworld with Pachamama. Benita was brought to the lake's edge by her sisters and cousins. The elder women commenced drumming and a chorus of high-pitched falsetto voices filled the air. Gabriel arrived with a small plastic container and gave me a nod to say, "Here's the semen."

Gregorio had laid a ritual table that looked much like those I had seen before. His bundle of paraphernalia sat in the center of a beautiful woman's shawl, a lliklla, with a special design called pawsa, consisting of a series of double scrolls. The small carved stone alpaca offertory, an illa, with a hollow in its back for burning offerings, sat to the right of the basket. A bundle consisting of ground powders and seeds was untied, with its contents visible.

The medicine bundle was called kimsa pawsa, "three double scrolls," I reflected. And the women were singing,

> I have been led from high Matuma
> A clean, pure woman, pawsa lliklla.
> Owner of a beautiful shawl,
> owner of a beautiful shawl.

Benita was led by two classificatory sisters to the ritual scene. One of the women placed a chair facing the ritual table, and Gregorio instructed Benita to kneel in front of the chair and a second identical pawsa shawl was placed around her shoulders by her women kinfolk. She was dressed in a new blue skirt and blouse; the pawsa shawl also looked new. Did one of her kinfolk give them as gifts for this occasion? That would be the expected pattern. And why the chair? I had never seen a chair placed in such a way for a pagapu to Pachamama.

The old women quickened the pace of the drumming, and to my surprise, Benita's husband came forward and sat on the chair; Gregorio instructed Benita to sit on her husband's lap. Her husband put his arms around her waist and began to rock her back and forth. Good Lord, that's the birthing position. When a woman was ready to deliver, she sat on her husband's lap and he pushed down on her belly. The midwife knelt in front of the pregnant woman to assist in the delivery, cut the umbilical cord, and catch the afterbirth. The placenta was considered powerful and dangerous; the midwife usually gave it to the husband to bury. Gregorio knelt in front of Benita as if he were the midwife and nodded to me to start the tape recorder. Dios Mío, this was brilliant! Benita was going to give birth to her own affliction! Or perhaps the affliction is the afterbirth that must be buried later. Sitting in the front row of participants, I pressed the play button of my tape recorder.

Gregorio gave Benita a pink seashell filled with chicha with several powders from his medicine bundle sprinkled on top. He instructed her to drink it while he intoned another prayer to Pachamama. I knew that one of those powders was a powerful hallucinogen. I wondered what effect it would have on her.

Benita's sad story rose from the tape recorder and startled her for a moment. She looked as though she wanted to flee, but her husband held her firmly and continued to rock her back and forth. The drumming increased in tempo and volume. Gabriel stepped forward as Benita's story was recounting the rapes—"jabbing, jabbing, dripping, dripping." Several women began to moan and keen as if they were at a funeral. Gabriel passed the container of semen in front of Benita's face. She screamed and her body convulsed; her eyes rolled back into her head and she looked as though she had passed out, but she was speaking along with the tape recorder. She was having a flashback! Gregorio called one of her sisters-in-law to his side and instructed her to take the pawsa lliklla, the beautiful shawl, from Benita's shoulders and spread it on the ground at Benita's feet. Then she placed her hands under Benita's skirt. Of course, a woman had to be the midwife.

Gregorio knelt behind the midwife and put his hands on her shoulders and whispered instructions into her ear. As Benita continued to struggle with her phantoms, Gregorio and her sister-in-law waited for the birth. Benita's husband massaged her stomach and continued to rock her back and forth. She let out a cry of pain and fell back against him, unconscious. Gregorio took out a knife from his ritual bundle and cut a swath of Benita's hair from the end of one of her braids. He laid the hair in the illa, the stone llama offertory, and set it afire. Gregorio whispered something to the midwife, and she folded the shawl, rose, and handed the small bundle to Gregorio. She then walked with Gregorio to the edge of the lake. While Gregorio chanted a prayer to Pachamama, they made the motions of throwing the contents of the shawl into the lake. Was that a splash? Yes, I definitely heard a splash. Then Gregorio threw the burnt offering of Benita's hair and the small bundle into the lake. He knelt and pulled something out of his bundle. I peered through the dusk and saw that it was a toy boat with pages of a written supplication mounted as sails.

A written petition to Pachamama! That's a new twist. I guess she has learned to read and write Spanish. I peered through the dim twilight and saw an apparition rise from the lake. The assembled family members gasped; several women began keening as a swirling waterspout rose offshore. I heard a chorus of excited voices exclaiming, "It's the amaru from the underworld. Pachamama has accepted the offering!" Women's voices rose in unison:

I have been led from high Matuma
A clean, pure woman, pawsa lliklla.
Owner of a beautiful shawl,
owner of a beautiful shawl.

Gregorio returned to Benita's side and tenderly replaced the beautiful shawl that had held the offerings around her shoulders; her husband held her against his body and her sisters-in-law poured her another libation of trago in Gregorio's pink seashell cup. As Benita drank, several of her women kinfolk came forward and knelt around Benita and her husband. Gregorio poured himself Fanta and drank it. I picked up my tape recorder and pressed stop and looked at the scene. Benita and her husband were being helped to walk; Gregorio looked like the cat that ate the canary, sooo pleased with himself as he gave me a smile. Gabriel came to my side and whispered, "Did you see the amaru? Did you hear the splash? I know I heard a splash."

"Me, too," I responded. That clever devil! Gregorio probably pulled the oldest shamanic trick in the book; he slipped something in the shawl before he made the motion of throwing the contents into the lake. But the appearance of the waterspout, the amaru, Pachamama's familiar companion, there's no way that he could have manufactured that. And the small bundle he threw into the lake, I'll bet that was the "afterbirth" that must be buried. I remembered my own encounter with Pachamama and found myself thrust into the familiar space between belief and disbelief. I know that I saw and talked to Pachamama years ago, just as I know that I saw the amaru rise from the lake tonight.

The congregated participants headed back to Gregorio and Clotilda's hut, where a group of women were waiting to serve them food and Fanta. Some of the other family members had their own libations, chicha and trago. I decided to help with the cooking and serving so I could put off drinking anything for a while.

Florencia and Margarita were waiting to hear what had happened at the edge of the lake. I related the entire sequence of events to them and they looked at each other with incredulity. "But it's all so impossible!" exclaimed Margarita.

"Is it? Look around you. Look at Benita." I pointed to Benita and said quietly, "She's sitting among her women kinfolk who are serving her chicha. She looks revived and almost radiant as she recounts her experience of the cure. She's nursing her infant for the first time in months, no longer afraid that her nightmares will be transmitted in her breast milk. Her husband and children are relieved."

Several people were drinking Fanta with Gregorio, toasting him on his success. His prestige as a curer would skyrocket with the retelling of this story. Clotilda and Gabriel both looked proud as they served the assembled guests. I accepted one glass of the orange sugar and then begged off, saying I was going to help with the serving. The festivities lasted well into the night. I went to sleep and dreamed of the amaru, who carried me upward on the waterspout and then down to the underworld to Pachamama's feet. The two sets of eyes of the amaru glowed green. Pachamama pointed to my unfinished wall; it had not crumbled and the participants of the cure were helping me build it. As I woke with a start, I realized that the crowd of victims had drawn closer.

Festivities continued the next day with the public slaughter of a sheep that belonged to Benita's husband's family. His brother cut the animal's throat and the blood was collected to make a special offering to the Wamanis. He cut up the meat and gave it to the women to prepare. It was almost midday when one of the sisters-in-law assigned the job to cook and serve approached Gregorio with a huge washbasin of soup with a whole leg of mutton balanced across the top. I remember the first time I was served such a portion; I thought I had to eat it all, but finally an old woman approached me with a bucket and indicated that I was expected to eat some and take the rest home.

The gifts of food were delivered with great ceremony, and Benita's husband gave a flowery speech of appreciation on behalf of Benita's in-laws. Benita's family presented Gregorio with a sack of potatoes and a smaller bag of quinua. I observed that more Fanta was consumed than chicha or cane alcohol as the congregated participants were served in hierarchical order according to age and status. We three gringas were served after Gregorio and Gabriel. We each had a small piece of meat in our soups. And so it would go; each person was served according to their relationship to Gregorio and Clotilda.

As Florencia received her soup, she turned to me and said, "I gave Benita the Paxil this morning."

"Good," I responded. "It doesn't hurt to cover all bases."

Before leaving Lake Matuma, everyone, except Florencia and Margarita, approached the site of the cure and threw their bread and fruit into the water. Early that morning, just as dawn was breaking, Gregorio, accompanied by a small group of men, took offerings to the Wamanis. He buried the offerings in the stone boxes that are passed down from father to son and used for pagapus to the Wamanis.

On our return to the village, the procession stopped again at the three stone tables and Benita poured chicha offerings to Pachamama while women sang the pawsa song. As Benita was offering the last and final pagapu at the offertory designating the boundary between the zones of corn production and herding, it started to rain. The jubilation of the procession echoed like an angelic chorus down to the village. We arrived at the plaza in the late afternoon. The crowd that greeted us joined in our celebration to thank Pachamama for the rain. They already knew what had happened at Lake Matuma and thus a new oral tradition and perhaps a new ritual was born.

CHAPTER 14

FINDING CHOLITA

I slept fitfully; my mind swirled with images and dreams. The wall construction advanced quickly with a large contingent of villagers helping me. The dead victims drew closer and smiled. I woke with a start with one task on my mind: I had to write the letter to Cholita to give it to the market vendor tomorrow. I sat with pen and paper and contemplated how to start.

To Juana Quispe:
Paradiso, Victor Fajardo, Peru
December 23, 2005

Dear Juana:

This is your godmother, Alicia, writing. I've been searching for you for years and I finally have word of your whereabouts. I hope you are well and happy in your teaching position in Paradiso. Susana Conde gave a presentation at a convocatorio in Pumapunku and asked the community to allow her to return and I think they will. She told me you were in Paradiso and that is why I'm writing.

I also talked to Teresa Quispe, your cousin, who is in Santa Monica Prison in Lima. I delivered a taped letter from her parents and carried an answer back to Pumapunku. Perhaps we can get her released so that she can live in Pumapunku. Carlos Huamani also spoke to the community. Do you remember him at all? He taught in the secondary school and was one of the first Senderistas to arrive. He was born in Pumapunku and was evidently chosen to return to begin indoctrination in the secondary school when he completed his university training as a teacher. There is a lot of resentment against him, but your uncle, Gregorio, thinks he has a good chance of being allowed to return.

Your aunt Clotilda and uncle Gregorio are well. Your cousin Gabriel is in his last year at the university studying computer science. He has a small web business. He has his laptop in Pumapunku. You can communicate with us via e-mail at Gabriel's address, wamani@terra.com.pe. We would like to visit you in Paradiso. Would that be possible?

I anxiously wait for your answer,

Your Godmother, Alicia Woodsley
Pumapunku

I read the letter several times before sealing it. *Will she allow me to visit? To finally locate her and then have her say she doesn't want to see me would drive me nuts! Gregorio says be patient; he insists that Cholita will eventually contact us and want to see her family. I hope so.* I signed the letter with a shaking hand, sealed the envelope, and set out for Benita's house.

At Benita's house, I joined a group of women kinfolk preparing the noon meal and made the usual rounds of greetings. Florencia and Margarita, with a young woman university student who had arrived on one of the market trucks from Ayacucho acting as translator, were talking to Benita.

"How have you been sleeping since our return from Lake Matuma? Have your nightmares returned?" Margarita asked.

"No. I slept through the entire night, no nightmares and my heart doesn't feel so heavy either," Benita answered, holding her hand on her heart.

"Are you continuing to take the medication that I gave you?" Florencia inquired.

Benita answered that yes, she was taking the medication but wondered if she had to continue because Pachamama had cured her. Florencia told the student to tell her in Quechua that she should continue taking the pills at least for a while.

One of Benita's cousins excitedly interjected, "Pachamama accepted our offerings and sent the rain. It rained all last night and looks like it'll rain again this afternoon. We're planning another pagapu soon." The women started talking all at once about the cure, the rains, Benita's recovery, and the planned offering.

We retreated to the portal area of the house. "What if Benita decides she doesn't need medication?" Florencia asked. "If she's not medicated, I'm sure that her nightmares and flashbacks will return. What do I say when she insists that Pachamama has cured her?" Florencia looked at us questioningly.

"Well, why not explain that doing the pagapus, as well as taking the medication, will both be helpful. The villagers understand multiple strategies to solve a problem," I answered.

Florencia turned to Margarita and said it was an opportune time to organize group sessions of women who had been gang raped and perhaps another group for their husbands and relatives. The news of Benita's cure was spreading through the community like wildfire. Margarita looked perplexed and declared that she was not sure how to interpret the curing ceremony.

I offered the observation that it doesn't matter what you think of the ceremony. Benita and her kin believe she has been cured. Isn't it essential for patients to believe they can be cured? We sat in silence for several moments and I finally looked at both of them and asked whether improved health was more likely if people have a positive attitude. Florencia agreed, but I could see skepticism in her eyes. She started to say, "Well, yes, but—"

Margarita interrupted, "Why not take this opportunity to ask these women if they know of any other victims like Benita and bring them together."

Margarita and Florencia looked at each other and finally Florencia answered, "I'd be willing to do that."

Margarita brightened and said excitedly, "It could be the focus of my thesis."

"I may leave Pumapunku for a while," I said. "I'm sure that Gregorio, Clotilda and their kin will help you. You could also approach the mayor, Tomás Vilca, to help organize the groups." I headed for the cooking hut to say good-bye to each woman with the required embrace.

I followed the path down to the center of the village and stopped in the plaza to chat with groups of people talking excitedly about the arrival of the rains. Everyone had a version of the cure. But those who had been present held sway in the discussions. Their versions were validated by that special suffix that says: I know what happened. I saw it. I was there. I saw the amaru. When people stopped me and asked if I had seen the giant snake come out of the lake, I answered that yes I had, using the same validation suffix. Curious linguistic requirement, experiential validation. I wonder how university professors would give lectures if we had to differentiate between hearsay and personal experience. How would we mark that we read such and such authority on a subject? Quechua doesn't give the written word any special status whatsoever. Will conversion to Protestantism change what is validated? Probably the weight of the written word will find its way into the linguistic and cultural systems.

Susana Conde was waiting just inside the gate and rushed to embrace me. *This is a good sign; she's greeting me with the customary embrace and not just a handshake. This means that she's willing to talk to me.* Susana had heard about Benita's cure and we talked for a while about her chances for recovery.

"I feel guilty about what has happened to my people in Pumapunku. I feel responsible for bringing such disaster on my own village," Susana declared while staring at the ground as we settled onto the stone bench built along the wall of the covered portal.

"You were kidnapped and forced to join Sendero!" I declared emphatically.

She whispered, "Yes, but I was converted. By the time I was fifteen, I really believed in the revolution." I took her hand and silence wrapped us in its protective cloak as we both gazed out at Razuwillka; snow was falling on the peaks and rain was making its way down the mountainside. Razuwillka was the highest mountain in the region and the most revered Wamani. The powerful mountain god responded to our thoughtful silence with a flash of lighting and a loud clap of thunder. The lighting flash streaked across the sky and landed in the puna above Pumapunku. The stone house reverberated and a hoe fell with a clatter from its place on the wall.

"I hope no one was struck," Susana said.

"Me, too," I responded, continuing to look at the mountain peak. "Anyone who was struck would be endowed with special powers, right?"

"Yes, and be rendered hunchbacked by the lord of lightning."

If Gregorio were here, this would be the moment he would pull out his coca bag and offer us coca and lime to chew. We would sit in silence and watch the rain approach across the valley until it finally arrived at our doorstep. Susana didn't offer me coca, but we continued to watch in silence as the spectacular rainstorm raced toward us. I felt comfortable, dry and warm sitting on the llama skins that covered the stone bench. The ichu grass roof gave off a pungent odor as it soaked up the rain. Susana rose and said, "I've put water on for tea. Do you want a mate?"

"Yes, please, that would be great." *Do I just ask her directly about Cholita, I mean Juana Quispe? Or should we discuss her potential return to Pumapunku first?*

Susana solved that dilemma when she came back with the tea and asked, "What do you think my chances are for being able to return to Pumapunku?"

"Excellent. I think the village has already decided to let you return. I'm not so sure about Carlos Huamani, the former schoolteacher. However, my compadre Gregorio thinks the community will allow him to return as well."

"He was one of our trainers."

"Oh, were you and Cholita trained together?"

"No, she and Teresa had already gone through training and were part of a cadre when I arrived. She had become famous by the time I was given my first assignment. She earned the name of Comrade Runtuta Kachuyoq."

"Comrade Ball-Biter? Good grief! How did she get that name?"

"She was captured by a military patrol and one of the men tried to force her to . . . you know . . ."

"Suck on his dick?"

"Yes! And his balls! When he pushed her face into his crotch, she bit off one of his balls and escaped. That's how she got the nickname."

I covered my mouth but could not stifle my laughter as I said, "My goddaughter, Comrade Ball-Biter!"

"Only Quechua speakers called her that," continued Susana, also laughing. "Men would say, 'Don't piss that one off, or you'll lose your huevos, your balls!' But after her initiation, you know, her first kill, she was given another name, Comrade Victoria. That was the custom; our first kill was considered the end of our training and we were given a new name. My name was changed to Comrade Constancia and after my first . . . you know . . . I was assigned to Comrade Felicia's all-women hit squad and your goddaughter was told to train me. She had already gone on several successful assignments. The Sendero command thought we could get into places that men couldn't. They were right. Especially if we dressed in school uniforms, we could move around city streets without difficulty and carry bombs in our school satchels."

I wonder if Susana and Cholita knew the two kids the taxi driver shot in Huanta? We sat in silence for a while.

The rain reached Pumapunku and mist rose from the valley, obscuring our view of Razuwillka and the lower peaks. The powerful mountain was considered the general and the peaks that surrounded him were his army. It made me remember the myths I had heard in which the mountains marched as giant soldiers against the invading Spanish. Who would they have marched against in this last war? Against Sendero or the armed forces? Susana and I continued to watch the rain as it soaked the dry fields.

Finally I said, "I'm hoping to visit Cholita, alias Ball-Biter, alias Comrade Victoria, now known as Juana Quispe. I can almost make out the route to Paradiso from here: down the mountain to the River Pampas, then up the other side toward Sarhua. I've written a letter asking if I could come for a visit. They say that ex-Senderistas, former members of civil patrols, and even former soldiers from the armed forces are living together in Paradiso. Is that true?"

Susana looked at me, puzzled, and answered, "I can't imagine how that's possible. Can you? But that's what people say. They are all born-again Christians who had to confess publicly before being allowed into the community."

"Well, it does sound impossible," I responded. "I'm anxious to visit the community and see for myself. I hope that Cholita, I mean Juana, will allow me to come."

"I think she will. It's important to try to connect with your family. That's what I'm trying to do." Susana looked hopefully at the community of Pumapunku below drinking in the blessed rain. We sat in silence, savoring the rain, and finally I turned to Susana and asked, "What kind of person is Juana? What can I expect to find in Paradiso?"

"Comrade Victoria was filled with rage and she commanded the assassination squad without fear, but I don't know the born-again Juana. I have no idea what she's like. But I do know that once we were transferred to Lima and were assigned as bodyguards for the leadership, we both began to lose faith in the revolution. Close up, the leadership didn't look so good."

When I asked her to explain, Susana told me that the leadership drank and partied all the time. She and Cholita escaped in 1992 because they were sent out to buy more beer for one of the leadership's parties. When they approached the house, it was surrounded by cops, so they went into hiding. That was just before Guzmán was captured. They melted into the refugee settlements. Both of them worked in the day and went to school at night. That was about the time Teresa was captured.

"Teresa wants to return to Pumapunku, and her family is willing to take her in. I hope she can return. She's ready to start a new life. All of you are still so young," I said softly, looking into Susana's tormented eyes.

"Yes, but at times I feel ancient," Susana said with a sad smile. "How is Teresa? She was named by one of the repentidos, wasn't she?"

"Yes, but she refuses to name any of her comrades to gain her freedom. Besides, she says she is being watched."

Susana looked alarmed and said, "Yes, I sometimes feel like I am being watched too. You never know who they are."

We returned our attention to the rainstorm. The rain had arrived at our doorstep and was coming down in torrents; I pulled my parka tighter around me and wondered out loud if Cholita has been able to forgive herself. As we embraced, Susana whispered in my ear, "I don't know, but I haven't been able to."

I turned after ducking through the low gate and looked back at the forlorn figure. It's hard to imagine her as an assassin. Susana had tears in her eyes as she dissolutely raised her hand to wave good-bye and called, "Good luck." I heaved a sigh and waved back. "Good luck to you as well." I used my vara to make my way carefully down the slippery stone path to the central plaza and then up the other side to Gregorio and Clotilda's house.

The next morning at six, I descended to the plaza and searched for Miguel, the vendor of school supplies. I found him setting up his merchandise. He was in his thirties with a hard, determined face; dark, penetrating eyes; and the short, powerful physique of highlanders.

"My name is Alicia Woodsley and I'm hoping that you can deliver this letter to Juana Quispe in Paradiso. I am her godmother and I'm hoping to visit her soon," I explained, smiling but sure he could smell my nervousness.

"Yes, I know who you are. You've worked here for years, haven't you?"

"Yes, I have, since 1975. My compadres are Gregorio Quispe Cabana and his wife, Clotilda Taipe Conde, Juana's aunt and uncle. I haven't seen Juana for years and I'm anxious to visit her. She must be a customer of yours. I hear that she's teaching school."

"That's right. She's an excellent teacher, very dedicated. I will deliver your letter."

"When will you be in Paradiso?"

"Tomorrow."

I told him that I had included my godson Gabriel's e-mail address and asked if there was a computer in Paradiso.

"Yes, I believe so," answered Miguel as he pocketed the letter. We shook hands and I tried to appear nonchalant as I ambled over to Doña Rosa's stall. I glanced back and Miguel's eyes were following me. *I wonder if he had been a member of Sendero? Probably so. He's the right age and he has that hard yet haunted look in his eyes, as if he has seen too much.* I gave an involuntary shudder as I sat down at Doña Rosa's table to have a cup of coca tea and trout for breakfast. Several vendors were having breakfast and the topic of discussion was Benita's cure. I became the center of attention as one of the principal actors in the cure and I verified that, yes, we had seen the amaru rise out of the lake. Years ago I would have hedged and answered that a waterspout had appeared. But now, well, I am living in the world where anything's possible.

I decided to visit the cemetery before the rains started, so I quickly took the path down to the hill as a gust of wind carried the scent of eucalyptus toward me, I looked up at the tall, straight trees. Several were barren of leaves and looked like tall thin men raising their arms in prayerful gratitude to Pachamama for bringing the rain. I found Cholita's mother's grave by the simple, crude wooden cross Gregorio had erected. Gregorio had carved: Juana Quispe Cabana born 1956 — died 1980. I pictured the elaborate headstone I had imagined erecting for her so many years ago. Gregorio told me he had dug up Juana's bones from the periphery of the cemetery and reburied them in the space occupied by his ancestors. He had removed some of their bones and arranged them in floral designs on top of Juana's grave. He told me that Juana's bones had not been disturbed, and he took that to be a sign of her successful arrival into the underworld domain of the dead.

Careful not to disturb the bones of the ancestors adorning Juana's grave, I eased myself onto the grave with the help of my staff and addressed myself to the young woman who had committed suicide so many years ago. "Well, Juana, I hope I see Cholita soon. It's pretty clear that she assassinated Romulo and God knows how many others. Do you think he deserved to die that way? Do you feel vindicated by your daughter? Or are your Catholic morals outraged? You wanted to become a nun and teacher, remember? Well, your daughter has assumed your name and is a born-again Christian who is teaching school in Paradiso. That's poetic justice, isn't it?" A drop of rain fell on my cheek and I looked up, expecting Juana's form to be floating above me again, but all I saw were thick cumulous clouds rolling toward me, so I picked up my vara and hurried up the hill to Gregorio and Clotilda's house.

Waiting for a reply from Cholita was excruciating: I had not learned the forbearance that Gregorio and Clotilda had to exercise every day. The reply arrived on Christmas Day over Gabriel's computer in the form of an e-mail. I couldn't get used to having e-mail in Clotilda's cooking hut hooked up to a battery. The message simply read, "Godmother Alicia, it would be a pleasure to see you again after all these years. Is anyone else coming with you? You can reach me by e-mail at: soldiersforchrist@terra.com.pe." The email ended with "Your sister in Christ, Juana Quispe."

Soldiersforchrist? What does that mean? Who could travel with me? Gregorio says he has to officiate at the Navidad celebration. I'll ask Gabriel.

I attended the Christmas celebration with Gregorio and his family in the Protestant chapel with the repentant pastor presiding. Benita's family was there and several members rose and thanked God for her cure. Perhaps they were converting and abandoning Catholicism like so many in the community.

Meanwhile at the ancient colonial Catholic Church, a visiting priest, a Spaniard, had to wait until a village official unlocked the door so he could deliver Mass. No flowers adorned the altar and only a handful of elderly Catholics attended, but the church smelled as though all the ancestors had come for Mass. The itinerant priest departed immediately after Mass to attend to the few parishioners in nearby Pomabamba. After Mass, the Pumapunku church was padlocked again until the next traveling priest appeared.

What a contrast from the Navidad celebrations I used to attend in the 1970s, with the procession of the Christ child around the plaza and the entire community kneeling on the stone floor of the ancient church with the resident priest and his so-called nephew presiding. The mestizo officials always sponsored an elaborate luncheon for the priest and his guests. Lines of indigenous families with gifts of meat, corn beer, potatoes, quinua, vegetables, and herbs waited to give their "donations" for the feast that indigenous women prepared.

The Catholic church has been closed for thirty years and evangelical Protestants are in the majority. The pastor's peccadillo of burning down the Catholic chapel doesn't seem to have affected his popularity. I just can't get used to hearing all those familiar hymns sung by Quechua speakers in Spanish. I never would have predicted this massive conversion to Protestantism, but I wouldn't be surprised if some event caused a wave of Catholicism to return and overcome the current trend. Will villagers continue to propitiate the Wamanis and Pachamama? Even though he's Protestant, Gregorio is still supervising the Dance of the Machu for Navidad that echoes the ancient December solstice celebration and animal fertility rites.

Gabriel agreed to accompany me to Paradiso; he was anxious to meet Juana because he had been only an infant when she fled the village. They were first cousins and therefore considered siblings, so he felt he should represent his family and invite his sister to Pumapunku. He was also curious about Paradiso; it had a mythical reputation as a born-again community of ex-combatants.

Gabriel and I found a truck leaving for the communities along the river bottomlands the following Wednesday. We arrived in Incamarca, a community famous for several standing Inca portals and walls as well as an Ushñu, a ceremonial pyramid for the Inca administrator on his official visits. The truck deposited us in the plaza where market day was in high gear under the six palm trees that stood guard over the lush garden. We walked to the Inca baths located at the edge of the village, now a commercial venture run by the town council. The trip from Pumapunku had taken two hours and it was only eight o'clock in the morning, but the temperature was already eighty degrees. We peeled off our jackets and sweaters and were walking languidly along the Inca period cobblestone road to the baths when I heard a sound and looked up as a flock of green parrots swooped overhead as if they were one connected body and landed, chattering, in a peach tree.

It was so amazing that within a two-hour descent we had arrived in a totally different environment. We were perhaps two thousand meters (6,500 feet) lower than Pumapunku and it felt like we were in the tropics: I could hear the roar of the River Pampas another thousand meters below. The Incas probably built this place to control access across the River Pampas. The smells of the mineral water, with sulfur predominating, assailed us as we neared the bath entrance. An Inca square cut stone wall with hot spring water pouring out of a stone channel in the top of the wall was stained with years of mineral sedimentation: yellow, orange, and blue shone on the stone. On the back side and off to the south of the wall, an adobe building with a thatch roof had been built to house the changing rooms and cover the original stone baths. A crowd was waiting to enter the bath and I joined the line to buy a ticket. I looked around and saw a few hardy European tourists, but most of the customers were market vendors or locals conversing in Quechua. Everyone was talking about the arrival of the rains, and several of the vendors waved in our direction. One man came over and asked about the cure of the Pumapuqueña woman. Now the story had entered the market circuit, so it would circulate quickly in the region. What would future anthropologists be told about the cure?

Inside the bathhouse, three square stone tubs had separate pipes feeding them and were labeled as appropriate for the treatment of specific diseases: arthritis, heart and liver diseases, and eye, ear, nose, and throat maladies. The fourth and largest stone pool was labeled for general health, with waters from all three sources being fed into it. Only one of the stone pools was original to the Incas. It looked as if Inca stones, some of them three feet square, had been robbed from nearby ruins to expand the baths. Only the Inca royalty and their retinue had been allowed to use the original baths. I wonder who was allowed to use the baths in colonial times. Perhaps the indigenous elite.

I looked around and saw an array of human diversity filing into the baths: Market women and men taking a break from their grueling rounds of travel, young women with babies, men and women of all ages. I entered the dressing room and was fascinated as women stripped to the waist and let their multiple skirts fall to the floor, then, reaching through their legs, they drew up their gathered underskirts and tied them into knots in the front, to fashion makeshift pants. I, on the other hand, took off my jeans, stripped down to my aqua silk underwear, entered the shower, and soaped them down. I entered the public area in my long underwear. What a contrast! Their bulbous butts and bare breasts and my covered skinny butt were testimony to the fact that culture determines sexual mores—breasts are not sexual here, but butts are, and the bigger the better. I couldn't go into a public area with my breasts uncovered even though I know it's a common practice here. Ah ha, direct evidence—look at how that toddler is playing with her mother's breasts. The little girl was slapping them back and forth and ouch, that must hurt! She just yanked one straight down with all her might. The mother didn't even stop talking.

The bathing tubs were filling up with all shapes and ages. As I eased myself into the arthritis tub, I noticed that one market woman had kept on her white, felt, broad-brimmed hat. I had to stifle a giggle as I found a space in the crowded pool. I attempted to make my way to the outflow but a fat woman had her back to the jet of water, moving up and down so that it massaged her spine. "That looks like it feels good," I commented in Quechua. The woman replied in Spanish, "Yes, it takes away the pain in my back. Come and try it." I moved closer and she reached out with a strong, broad hand and pulled me forward, her breasts bobbing and my body making waves. She planted me squarely in front of the outflow and smiled. I thanked her and assumed the same position with my back to the outflow. "Ah, yes, that does feel good."

By the time I left the arthritis pool, it was so crowded that people couldn't move at all. I climbed the steps to the dressing room and looked back. The bathing tubs looked like they were packed with vegetables being steamed for canning. Perhaps asparagus? No, wrong color, carrots. I passed the eye, nose, and throat pool and noted that people were cupping their hands and pouring the water into their eyes. Dios Mío, the eye is an entry to the river of blood that flows swiftly to all parts of the body. There must be twenty people jammed in there exchanging God knows what!

Gabriel was waiting for me outside and we decided to eat lunch in the market before embarking on the walk to Paradiso. Several vendors had set up food stalls at the entrance to the baths, offering papaya, bananas, the usual soups, and of course trout. Later, walking to the suspension bridge below the village, I remembered the ethnographic accounts of how the fiber ropes of the bridge were repaired. The village directly on the other side of the roaring River Pampas had two territorial halves that divided them into "foreigners" and "original inhabitants," and once a year the two halves of the village took up positions on either side of the bridge and hurled insults and stones at each other. It was important that no one be seriously injured, but if a little blood was spilled, the harvest would be abundant. The "foreigners" were required to complete the maguey fiber ropes and repair their half of the bridge on the far side, while the "original ones" worked on their ropes on the village side. When the two sides met in the middle, the "foreigners" were reincorporated into the community with a three-day fiesta of drinking, feasting, and dancing. The social division was centuries old and no one could remember where the "foreigners" had come from, but after the Incas conquered the region they moved distinct ethnic groups from as far away as Ecuador and Bolivia and organized communities on their Cuzco model, with the ruling elite living in the administrative center of Incamarca. Sons and daughters of the conquered chiefs were taken captive and educated in the religion, administration, and customs of the empire.

As we walked through the magnificent geography lesson with rapidly changing flora and fauna every hundred feet, my imagination carried me to the time of the Inca Empire, and I wondered how many royal retinues had traveled this road? How many chaskikuna, the trained runners who crossed the great expanse of the empire with everything from fresh fish to battle plans, had raced across this bridge? How many official rememberers carried their knotted string accounts, the qhipus, to the administration in Incamarca? How many "virgins" had been delivered to Incamarca for sacrifice or initiation into the house of the chosen women, the Acllakuna, dedicated to the cult of the moon, the sister and wife of the sun?

My thoughts were interrupted when Gabriel asked, "Madrina, how are you doing? Do you want to stop and rest before we cross the bridge?"

"Yes, let's stop here for a few moments. Besides, it is so beautiful."

"But remember, it will rain before long and the road will become slippery. We should stop only for a few minutes."

"I'm fine but I am so glad that I brought along the vara that your father made for me. It helps. Just give me a few moments to rest. I'm not too tired. The trail has been downhill, but after we cross the bridge, it's all uphill. Just let me catch my breath."

I found a large square cut stone, probably of Inca origin, and sat looking at the river raging below. The roar was deafening. I gazed at the suspension bridge constructed by thousands of hands over the centuries. I counted twenty people trudging across the bridge one hundred feet above the river. The plants around the river were lush: giant ferns, angel wing begonias, and various species of fruit trees. Mosses covered the rocks and I noticed that the air was thicker and carried a fragrance unfamiliar to me. "Let's go," I said, getting up with a groan. "My bones tell me the rains are coming."

We gingerly made our way down the Inca cobblestone road onto the bridge, which swayed with the rhythm of the traffic. "Wow, what a view down of the river," I shouted over the roar of the river. The flock of green parrots I had spotted before swooped under the bridge and landed like a giant green cloud on top of one of the fruit trees. I hung onto the rope railing, pushing through the market traffic coming in the opposite direction. They didn't need the railing; rather they walked bent over with loads on their backs as if they were stepping on dry land. Reaching the other side, we stopped and asked for directions to Paradiso.

"Good, they say it's only a half hour up the mountain. That means it will take me an hour. Let's hurry, I'd like to get there before the downpour," I told Gabriel. "But before we start out I want to put on my parka and pack my long underwear. Look, they're dry. I can sleep in them tonight." I untied my long underwear from my backpack.

Gabriel laughed and said, "Here, let me carry your pack."

"Thanks, Gabriel, I won't argue."

Why am I carrying my portfolio of horrors with me? Do I think Cholita and I will sit down and review the articles?

The climb was excruciating. My feet hurt and I had to stop frequently. The early market travelers were returning from Incamarca and everyone spoke as they hurried past us, but only a few stopped and chatted. "We're going to Paradiso," Gabriel would explain, and I would take the opportunity to catch my breath. The journey took an hour and a half, but Gabriel didn't complain; rather he complimented me on making the climb.

When we arrived, I looked around and thought that Paradiso is definitely not Paradise. Thirty or so adobe and stone houses were scattered on either side of the path. In the center of the community stood a chapel with an attached one-room school, both constructed of adobe with tin roofs. A fenced-in, well-kept vegetable garden stood beside the school and a composting latrine was located at the appropriate distance from the school. In front of the chapel, a six-foot-tall, bare wooden cross shared the space with a tall light pole.

I took a deep breath and stepped into the school. Seated at the front, an attractive woman with dark curly hair, a broad, freckled face, and large doleful eyes was reading to the class. She rose and came forward to greet us. "Madrina Alicia, Gabriel, my brother, it is good to welcome you to Paradiso. May God bless you." She embraced us.

"May God bless you," echoed the class of thirty children. The classroom was barren except for a large colored poster of Jesus Christ, not with the bleeding heart common to Catholic iconography, but depicting a blond, blue-eyed Jesus Christ, smiling with his hands outreached. Jesus Christ Loves Each of Us was written in large letters at the bottom of the poster. In the poster, children dressed in clean shirts, pants, and skirts sporting shiny black leather shoes were seated at his feet. In contrast, the children in the classroom, sitting on crude benches or on the dirt floor with their workbooks on their laps, wore ragged homespun wool pants and skirts and either had rubber tire sandals or were barefoot. They looked up at their visitors with clean, expectant smiles.

Juana Quispe explained to the class that the visitors were members of her family from Pumapunku, and as she turned her head, I spotted the purple, hourglass s-shaped birthmark on her neck. With a shock I remembered having noticed it on her when she was a child, crouching under her father's table and grabbing any scraps of food that he flung to her. She's Cholita all right. She has her mother's eyes and freckles and her father's hair. She is about thirty-four or thirty-five now, but she looks older. No surprise.

Juana genuinely seemed pleased to see us. The embrace swept the years away and I felt transported to 1980 and saw a ten-year-old, freckle-faced child standing before me. An awkward silence prevailed for a few moments while Juana dismissed the class. She turned and invited us to have lunch at her house.

"I live adjacent to the school. Please come, we've prepared a special lunch for you." Juana's home consisted of two rooms with a cooking hut in the back; another composting latrine stood some distance from the house, and a large vegetable garden with a fenced-in corral was located between the cooking hut and the house. Smoke was bellowing from the cooking hut where an elderly woman was cooking lunch on an open fire. A small girl about three years old was seated beside her, peeling potatoes. She looked like Juana, curly hair and freckles.

"I've always been amazed to see small children peeling potatoes," I said. "We would never give a knife to a child that young but children here learn early and I've never seen children cut themselves." I turned to Juana and asked, "How old is she?"

"She's three and she's my daughter." Juana hugged the girl and said, "Her name is Carmela Huanca Quispe. Her father's the vendor you gave the letter to in the market in Pumapunku, Miguel Huanca Tomaylla. We've been married for four years and we came to Paradiso three years ago with the first group that organized the community."

"Tell us how this community got started," Gabriel requested as he pulled a chair out for me and took a seat opposite Juana.

Juana related that the idea came out of discussions in Lima in an evangelical church made up of Ayacuchanos who had fled the violence. At first no one revealed which side they had been on, only that they all had suffered because of the war. Bit by bit, with the pastor's encouragement, each of them told their story, and they realized that they had all turned to Jesus Christ, although they had fought on both sides of the war—for Sendero or for the military, and some members of the church were former ronderos who had been forced by the military to march against their neighbors. Since they were born again in Christ, what mattered was how they lived today—forgiving, vigilant, and repentant. One couple had just inherited the use of his parents' land, so they decided as a group to move here and form a community.

"Some of the community members are ex-soldiers and others are former Senderistas and others are ronderos? Is that right?" I asked. Juana nodded affirmatively. "That's amazing. There are no disagreements about the war?"

"No, we all feel that the war was wrong," answered Juana. "Everyone here killed someone during the war and every day we ask for forgiveness and repent our sins." "We're having a prayer meeting this evening. You can come and see for yourselves."

"Thanks, we will," I answered, looking at Gabriel for confirmation. He nodded yes.

Juana and the old woman served lunch: Soup, chicken and rice, and, to my surprise, a green salad. When I hesitated over the salad, Juana told me not to worry, that the greens had been washed in mild bleach to kill the microbes. She had learned to do that at the church center in Lima. She proudly told us that they grew all of their own food. Each household had a vegetable garden and she loved working in it. She told us we would see the communal fields.

Gabriel asked, "Who's the old woman in the kitchen?"

We were told that she was Mama Florentina, the widow of the mayor of Cancha Cancha. Juana looked at the floor and wrung her hands together in a manner that made me think of her mother. She finally looked up at us and said, "I killed him and I have vowed to support her for the rest of her life. I also confessed to her in Cancha Cancha. We feel that public confessions are important for our salvation. She's been living with us for six months. She was all alone in Cancha Cancha and had no family to look after her. I think she's content here." Juana leaned over and embraced Mama Florentina, who beamed at her.

Extraordinary. Seeing this as a chance to open our conversation to Romulo's death, I commented that confession seemed to be an important element in healing, and I went on to describe the convocatorio in Pumapunku. I described how Susana had confessed that she had been a member of the hit squad that killed Romulo and that she was asking for forgiveness from the community to be able to return to Pumapunku. I looked at Juana for some sign of recognition in her eyes.

With a sad smile, she said that she knew about the convocatorio and that I had talked to Susana. So she was aware that I knew she was part of hit squad, along with Teresa, that killed Romulo. She then told me she had seen the newspaper report, and as if to read my mind said, "It was Teresa who turned to me and said, 'Well, Cholita, we've finally killed the old bastard.'" Juana looked directly at me and her eyes did not waver. She continued, "At the time I felt elated but later I began to regret my actions. It all seemed so pointless. It didn't bring my mother back. The revolution hadn't brought lasting changes. And in the end, Sendero commanders were as corrupt as the politicians we were fighting to replace. They never listened to any of us. We were there to carry out their orders, nothing else. When I killed Mama Florentina's husband, I began to have doubts about the revolution, but it wasn't until months later that I began to look for a way out."

I started to ask another question, but Juana interrupted and said, "I must return to school. We'll talk more this evening."

I was stunned by her candor. Did she always readily reveal her past like this? Or is it because I'm her godmother? Juana left for school and Gabriel and I decided to walk around the community before the rains started. We found the fields where ten people were repairing the irrigation canals. They stopped and waved to us and called out, "God Bless you! Welcome to Paradiso!" They were obviously expecting us. I noticed that they were growing tarwi, a bean of the lupine family that can be either harvested for food or plowed under as green fertilizer to increase nitrogen. I asked if they were going to harvest the beans.

"No," a tall man in his forties answered. "We're going to plow it under as fertilizer."

"Oh, then you are using organic techniques?" I asked.

"Yes, that's correct," a woman answered. "We don't use chemical fertilizers or pesticides."

Gabriel and I were both impressed. We talked for a while and they showed us the fields. They were intercropping corn, beans, and squash and using the material from the composting latrines mixed with animal manures. Someone here was well-versed in organic farming. I was intrigued. As we were talking, three men carrying rifles marched by and asked if everyone had attended the noon prayers. A woman responded that yes, everyone has been to noon prayers.

I looked inquiringly at Gabriel and he asked, "Who are they?"

"The prayer patrol," a woman with a lined face and hard eyes answered. "We rotate and everyone serves on the patrol to remind people to attend prayers three times a day."

"What happens if someone misses prayers?" I asked.

"If they miss three prayer sessions, they are expelled from the community," explained the tall man. "We've expelled only one person since the community was formed."

A dark woman in her late thirties explained that a community member was given the chance of asking for forgiveness in an evening prayer meeting before expulsion was carried out. She then turned to another woman and instructed her to show us the clinic. A mestiza woman in her thirties stepped forward and told us she was called Marta. We were led down a path to a building that was still under construction. Inside the clinic, three patients were seated against the wall and about twenty children were receiving inoculations from a young man, who smiled and motioned for us to enter. He introduced himself as Emilio García, the health provider of Paradiso. We shook hands and told him we didn't wish to interrupt his work. He showed us the sparse clinic and I noticed boxes of medications from several Protestant nongovernmental organizations. When I pointed to the boxes and asked if they were receiving aid from all of those organizations, he answered affirmatively with a smile. Moreover, he added with a chuckle that they seemed to be competing with each other to keep the community healthy and born again.

"You have a very impressive clinic for such a small community," I responded, thinking of several larger communities in the region with no clinics at all.

"Well, thank you, we'll you see this evening," the health provider said as he returned to the children and coaxed a reluctant girl to come forward for her inoculation.

As we returned to Juana's house, I said to Gabriel, "This is a very intriguing place. What do you make of the three men on the prayer patrol? Why are they armed? Protecting themselves? Against whom? Sendero? Government forces?"

"I don't know. Maybe government arrests?" Gabriel answered but looked puzzled.

Juana returned from school in the late afternoon and I was so anxious to talk to her that I felt pools of sweat forming under my breasts. Juana went into the cooking hut to greet Mama Florentina. I followed her but I couldn't concentrate on her conversation with Mama Florentina. Juana left the house to look for Carmela, and I impatiently watched a beetle crossing the kitchen floor while I absent-mindedly peeled potatoes and held a desultory conversation with Mama Florentina and Gabriel. When Juana returned and entered the cooking hut, I jumped as if startled. "Juana, you're back! Good! Do you think we can talk?" I asked anxiously.

"Of course. I'm sure that you want to hear my story. But first I want to go into the garden with Carmela to pick vegetables and herbs for soup. Do you want to come?"

Another lesson in patience—when will I learn? I followed Carmela and Juana into the garden. We worked in silence for about an hour and returned to the kitchen to give our bounty to Mama Florentina. Juana turned to us and said, "Let's go into the bedroom so that Mama Florentina and Carmela can set the table for dinner."

In the bedroom, Juana indicated that Gabriel and I should take the two chairs and she would sit on the bed. The other piece of furniture in the small room was a small bedside table. A large wooden cross hung over the bed; a kerosene lamp, an alarm clock, and a Bible stood on the bedside table. I felt as if I were in a monastery bedroom: I expected to find a place to kneel before the cross but of course there was none. Another poster of a smiling, blond Jesus was on the wall opposite the bed with an inscription that read: Come Unto Me All Ye Who Have Suffered. Again, Jesus was depicted with open arms beckoning the viewer. So different from the Catholic iconographic focus on death, with Christ nailed to the cross, with his bleeding crown of thorns, spear wounds and red bleeding heart. *I'm curious to see what happens in the prayer meeting this evening. I wonder—* Juana's voice brought my attention back to the room.

"I left Pumapunku the afternoon of my mother's burial and went up to the puna where Teresa was herding sheep. I stayed with her for several days and then we decided to go to Ayacucho—"

I interrupted her and asked, "May I record your story?"

Juana looked worried and thought for several moments but finally said, "Yes, but don't use my name." She recounted that in Ayacucho, they slept in the market and did odd jobs for the market women. She saw Mama Jesús but didn't approach her. Teresa knew several university students from the Cangallo province who were living in a rented room and they let them share the room. One night the students invited Juana and Teresa to a meeting. The students said that several members of Shining Path who had gone to China were going to speak as well as several cadre commanders. Perhaps Presidente Gonzalo, Abimael Guzmán, would make an appearance even though he was in hiding. The meeting was in a barrio Juana had not been to before up above the city. There were almost a hundred people present. A cadre commander, a woman holding a machine gun, opened the meeting. She impressed Juana and Teresa a lot. They later learned that the commander was Edith Lagos, who recounted how she led the prison break and escaped. The other speakers held the group spellbound with their stories of training and experiences in China. Mao's teachings were a shining light for Peru.

Mama Florentina interrupted her story when she entered the bedroom with cups of herbal tea. We thanked her and she hurried back to the kitchen. Juana returned to her story. She remembered how this meeting gave form to her rage over her mother's barbaric death. She said she had been eating that rage all those months and suffering from stomach problems that she now knew were the beginning of ulcers. She said that if you eat your rage long enough, you get ulcers. But she went on to say that her symptoms went away once she was indoctrinated and believed that they could build a new Peru with no hunger, where no one was higher or lower than anyone else, but equal. When Edith Lagos spoke, Juana identified with her immediately even though she was a university student, a mestiza from a good family with a Catholic school education. Lagos had become a follower of Presidente Gonzalo in the university. Edith Lagos became Juana's inspiration. After the speech, a couple of women approached Juana and Teresa and asked if they were interested in training for consciousness-raising campaigns in their home territory. She and Teresa said yes, definitely. They thought that their lives would finally have purpose.

She said that they left that night for a training camp in Satipo on the edge of the jungle and that she had never seen anything like it, two hundred people who were determined and disciplined with one goal—to overthrow the corrupt regime and put in its place a just government and society where they, los olvidados, the forgotten ones, would have a place. She was hooked. She threw herself into training and learning. Even though she was just a child, she tried to read Marx, Mao, Presidente Gonzalo, and Mariategui, and she surrendered totally to the cause. Some of the texts became magical chants for her. She trained in military tactics and listened, listened and learned.

"How long were you in the training camp?" I asked.

"Six months," Juana answered, taking a long sip from her teacup. She looked pained when she told us about the episode of "paying the quota." She described how she would never forget the words they were taught about the quota. They were told that their blood was the stamp of commitment to the revolution, to the world revolution. They were adding their blood to a river of blood that had to be crossed to create a new Peru. The river of blood was flowing, they were told, like a purifying river of fire. It would not harm them; but rather it would make them stronger. She marched with other recruits to her first engagement ready to die. She was thirteen years old and Teresa was fourteen. They were perfect recruits. They were the vanguard of the world proletarian revolution. They attacked a guardia post and about half of their comrades were killed, all very young kids under a woman commander who was also killed. Juana believed she had been saved for special service to Shining Path, and evidently those in command believed so too because they assigned Teresa and Juana to an all-women hit squad; they became experts in bombings and assassinations.

She continued her story and said that her first trip to Lima was a bombing assignment. She was overwhelmed by the city but her commander, Comrade Karina, only eighteen years old, kept a tight rein on the new recruits and didn't let them out of her sight. They blew up the Bayer manufacturing plant in Ventanilla in May of 1983. She looked down at the hands that had thrown the bombs, turned them over, and inspected them as she said she could almost feel the weight of the bombs. Karina was captured, but she and her cousin escaped. She then looked up at us and asked, "Do you know that the dynamite was stolen from mining companies? We had all the dynamite we needed."

"You were eventually captured, weren't you?"

"Yes, I was, but I escaped," Juana answered.

"Susana told me that after your escape, you were given the name of 'Ball-Biter' because you bit the balls off the military guy who was holding you prisoner. Good Lord!" I waited for an answer, raising my teacup slowly to my lips.

"Yes, but I managed to bite off only one of his balls," Juana answered, smothering a laugh. "I'm sure he'll never forget it. I won't either. There are some things that I do not repent doing. So many women were raped during the war."

"Speaking of balls, what did you do with Romulo's genitals?" I asked.

"I nailed them to the school door." Juana answered, looking slightly embarrassed. We remained silent. All of us stared at the floor. Gabriel instinctively covered his crouch with his hands.

Finally Juana resumed her story. "In 1990 I was already beginning to doubt what we were doing. I had been fighting for ten years and we were no closer to creating the 'new democracy' that Presidente Gonzalo promised. I returned to one of the Sendero camps but I began to think of trying to escape. But as you know the only way to leave was to die in combat. If you fled the movement, you were hunted down and killed. Sendero has a thousand eyes and ears."

"Yes, we've heard that from the Senderistas who've returned and asked to live in Pumapunku again," Gabriel said.

I got up and walked across the room and found my backpack. I dug through my portfolio to find the picture published in Caretas in 1985, along with an interview called Criaturas del Terror, Children of Terror. All the children were smiling and the caption read "committed to gaining power while playing and killing." Among them were three girls, and one looked like Juana. "Here." I handed her the picture and pointed to a smiling, curly-headed, freckle-faced girl in the back row whose eyes were blocked out by a black strip. "Is that you?" I asked.

"Yes, that's me. That was taken right after we killed Romulo. I had submitted his name for five years, and I was thrilled when the committee decided that he was finally going to be punished and I would be a part of his trial. I have repented for that killing and asked God for forgiveness, but I still need to confess to Mama Jesús and ask her to forgive me. At the time I felt like it was justified—that's why I'm smiling in the photograph. We had just returned from Pumapunku and I felt I had finally achieved revenge for my mother's death."

Again I reached into the portfolio and handed her Romulo's letter and told her that he wrote it just before he was killed. "He said he regretted how he treated you and your mother and he felt responsible for pushing you into Sendero." She took the letter slowly from my hand and I could see tears welling up in her eyes. She turned away from us and wiped her tears away with her apron. Again I had a flash of her mother. She read it and wrung her hands and with a deep sigh said, "It's all so sad, isn't it? We're really not masters of our own fates, are we?"

I said I thought Romulo was captive of his history, just as you, Juana, were captive of yours. I thought to myself: *And I'm captive of mine, my obsession to find you.* But I said nothing as each of us remained wrapped in our cloak of memories. Finally Gabriel, breaking the uneasy silence, asked if Juana thought conditions had changed. Juana took Gabriel's hand in hers and looked directly into his eyes and declared that yes, she thought conditions were getting better all the time: Education was more attainable for one thing. She said, "Look at you, Gabriel," — she held out her arms as if to inspect him — "You're getting a university education and you've started your own web-page business. Also many people realize that they have the power to demand accountability from the government. You, Gabriel and your generation, are our future." Gabriel straightened his back and smiled proudly.

Gabriel told Juana how Pumapunku was organizing to demand accountability for the corruption of the irrigation project, the Rio Cachi boondoggle. "But there is still so much corruption in all levels of government, and the military has not been held accountable for the human rights abuses they committed," he declared, his voice rising as he stood up and jabbed at the air with his right forefinger as if pointing at an imaginary general. Pointing, he said, "They're responsible for half of the civilian deaths and should be tried."

Juana voiced doubts about the judiciary's ability to try the military personnel responsible for disappearances and massacres.

"But," I interjected, "it's the first time that a truth commission anywhere has given to their country's judiciary names of military or government officials responsible for atrocities."

Still standing, Gabriel turned to us and asked if we had read about Montesinos's coming to trial for human rights abuses and drug trafficking. Montesinos was also accused of smuggling ten thousand rifles to the FARC guerrillas in Colombia. "For twenty years, he successfully played all sides against each other. It's incredible that his own practice of secretly videotaping all transactions in his office became the most powerful evidence against him. When he was Fujimori's head of intelligence, he videotaped congressmen, judges, and high-ranking military as he bribed them. Now those tapes are being used in his trial."

I shook my head and observed that Montesinos was so slippery I wouldn't be surprised if he beats these charges. He was the lawyer for the drug cartel in Peru and was involved in drug trafficking even though he was the CIA's darling. Also, he was jailed by the military early in his career and discharged from the army, yet he rose to become the man behind President Fujimori's throne. Do you remember the national scandal that followed? The horrible Cayara massacre by the army in 1988? General José Valdivia raced around with his soldiers, digging up the victims and reburying them, trying to keep one step ahead of the official investigation. Montesinos was the mastermind in covering up that case and directing the murder of forty witnesses.

Juana reminded us that those were the kinds of abuses that were presented to them in their Sendero meetings. When she was part of the popular army, before she was trained as an assassin, she attended two meetings a week where leaders talked to them about corruption in the government—how they stole millions of dollars, murdered, and couldn't even feed the country. She was taught that the country depended on peasants in the highlands who were growing all the food for the cities. It was explained that the plan was to surround the cities and starve them into submission. When someone asked, "What about the poor people in the cities?" she was told that the poor would leave the cities and join them in the battle for a new democracy. Instead, more and more of the poor swelled the ranks of refugee camps in the cities.

"That's true. I worked in those camps in Lima," I said.

Juana recounted that in Sendero meetings, they were always told to bring a trusted friend to recruit. At each meeting they submitted lists of public enemies of the new Peru—for example, names of cattle thieves or of criminals in local governments who stole funds. She always submitted Romulo Rosetti's name as a rapist and thief. For two years, she was given jobs like distributing pamphlets and recruiting members, but toward the end of the second year, she became part of a team that warned people who were targeted for assassination. They would arrive at the door of, say, a cattle thief, and, hooded and armed, warn him that if he continued to steal, he would be tried at a popular trial and executed. She felt like an avenging angel. Juana looked at us with the hope that we would understand.

"What did the pamphlets say?" I asked as I reached toward Juana and touched her arm reassuringly. "Tell us about the pamphlets."

"One that we read out loud all the time was called War: Proverbs and Quotes. It was twenty-four pages long and our bible. I remember the phrase 'War is sacred, a divine institution, and one of the world's sacred laws.' Another phrase that stayed with me was 'War is humanity's most invigorating iron cure.' I felt that I was curing Peruvian society of all of its ills. We were successful in those first two years. The guardias were easy to fight and we were gaining support in the countryside. I also admired Presidente Gonzalo's book I was given to study because I thought that it had been written by Presidente Gonzalo, but later I learned he was using the words of the Germans during WWII!"

"When was the first time that you started to have doubts?" Gabriel asked.

She said she was very troubled by the attack on Lucanamarca in 1983, when men, women, and children were hacked to death, and it was said that Presidente Gonzalo gave the order directly to teach peasants that Sendero's ferocity would be felt by any community that dared to rise up against them.

When I asked if she voiced her misgivings even though she was only fourteen years old, she answered that yes, she and her comrades had long discussions about the attack on Lucanamarca in our meetings and many of the rank and file who were from Quechua communities were against it, but they were told that Presidente Gonzalo declared that Sendero must teach the peasants never to rise up against their leadership and that Lucanamarca would stay in people's memories as a reminder of their power. Juana plaintively said that Lucanamarca haunted her memory. She thought for a moment and added that Lucanamarca was a turning point. When the army entered the war, many communities pulled back their support for Sendero and formed civil patrols voluntarily. They attacked more and more communities and met more and more resistance. When the army stopped their campaign of suppression, it became even harder to count on the support from communities. She said that's why the focus was shifted to Lima. She was transferred to Lima to reaffirm her loyalty.

"But you stayed in the movement," Gabriel commented, looking worried.

"Yes," Juana said. "The only way to leave was feet first, but my doubts kept re-emerging as Sendero became more rigid and brutal against anyone who opposed us. For me, the final disillusion came with the brutal killing of María Elena Moyano. Do you remember her, Mother Courage, the leader of the poor in Villa El Salvador?" We nodded yes, and Juana continued. "She had organized a peace march against the strike called for by Sendero in February of 1992. A Sendero squad riddled her with bullets and then they blew up her body with two kilos of dynamite. Also I opposed the killing of the evangelists who worked with the poor—almost 550 were killed." Juana fell silent again and wrung her hands in her lap and looked down at the floor.

After several minutes, Gabriel asked, "Did you ever meet Guzmán?"

"No, he was considered a remote god for us to revere but never see, hear, or touch. I began to realize that those of us from highland communities would never advance in the hierarchy of Sendero and we were being used as cannon fodder. I also realized that we would never achieve the new democracy that Sendero promised."

"Many women were leaders in Sendero. Isn't that true?" I asked.

Juana turned to me and answered yes, women in positions of leadership were mostly educated mestizas from the coast. Very few Quechua speakers were advanced to leadership positions. But it was true that half of the Sendero was made up of women. They had equality—to be killed, she whispered—then her voice rose and she asked, "Do you know that Guzmán never learned Quechua in all those years he was in Ayacucho?" She doubted whether he had ever visited a small community. Before he was captured in 1992, she began to seriously plan how to escape after she and Susana were almost arrested when they were bodyguards of Sendero leaders in Lima.

"Yes, Susana told me that story. How you had gone out for more beer and came back to find the house surrounded."

"Yes, we were able slip away and take on the identity of refugees in Lima. We went to school at night and worked as maids during the day. But I became alarmed when someone took advantage of the National Repentance Law passed in 1992 and turned Teresa's name into the authorities and she was imprisoned. I was afraid that I would be next."

"What did you do?"

"Well, it's easy to get fake identity papers and that's what I did. Then I studied to be a teacher. After all, I was only twenty-two and most of the refugees who fled the highlands had experienced the interruption of their education. I was just one among many going to night school. But I had to be on guard all the time."

"When did you convert to evangelical Protestantism?" I asked.

"Do you mean, when was I born again? In 1995 I began to attend services in one of the refugee settlements on the outskirts of the city, and within six months I was born again, which has been my salvation. I also met my husband there; he was born again at the same time."

Juana looked relieved. Her story had been told. She breathed a deep sigh and rose, but I put my hand on her arm and asked, "What does it feel like to tell your story?"

"Every time I tell my story, the burden in my heart seems to get lighter and lighter and I can breathe better. Now it's time for dinner or we will be late to evening prayers and the patrol will be after us!" Juana said with a laugh.

We attended the prayer meeting that evening, accompanying Juana, little Carmela, and Mama Florentina, along with Juana's husband, Miguel, who had returned from the market in Incamarca. About forty adults were in attendance, and some thirty children of all ages, including Carmela, were running and playing in the chapel. One of the members of the patrol called the meeting to order by announcing loudly, "Brother and sisters, God loves you!" The assembled worshipers responded with "God loves us." They began singing "Jesus Loves Me, This I Know." The leader of the meeting asked if anyone wanted to speak to the congregation.

A woman stood up and began. "Brothers and sisters, I got angry with Sister Gloria today and shouted at her. I beg her forgiveness and the forgiveness of everyone."

Gloria stood up and walked over to the woman. She embraced her and said, "You are forgiven, sister." The congregation repeated, "You are forgiven."

Next, a man and woman came forward and the leader explained that they were petitioning to become members of the congregation. The man said that when he was a member of the civil patrol of his community, he had burned the house of his neighbor. "I coveted his cattle. May God forgive me, I told the military that this man was a Sendero sympathizer and he disappeared." The man knelt and cried. Several people of the congregation, including Juana, came forward and knelt beside him and said, "God forgives you. We forgive you. We welcome you both to Paradiso."

A woman rose and led the congregation in prayer and another hymn. Everyone bowed and held hands in silence. The three men on patrol rose from the last row and marched up the center aisle of the chapel. After propping their guns against the base of the altar, they turned and announced that no one was in violation of the prayer rules.

"My God," I whispered to Gabriel, "they have militarized religion. The Senderistas have exchanged one religion for another. What about ex-soldiers?" I could imagine the ex-marine taxi driver receiving absolution here. I looked at Juana and Miguel, who were holding hands. Juana was carrying Carmela in her arms and she smiled at me. I could tell that by recounting her story to us, her suffering had moved further away from her psyche. In time, her suffering would become remote. Her story was becoming crystallized, a bounded event that would allow her to forget, and forgetfulness was necessary for survival. But first she must tell her story over and over until she no longer relives the events. She was looking into the abyss and was beginning to see beyond it.

We returned to Juana's house and after embracing everyone and bidding them good night, I was ushered into Mama Florentina's room that she shared with the baby. A bed had been made on the floor and I fell onto the pallet exhausted but exhilarated. Immediately I feel asleep and the dream overtook me as if it had been waiting to emerge. The community of Paradiso was gathered beside a completed wall that was covered with the posters of victims of the war. Juana and Cholita, as the freckle-faced child of ten, pointed to the completed wall and smiled.

GLOSSARY

(SP) Spanish; (Q) Quechua

alcalde (SP). Mayor, bureaucratic official of a town
alcalde varayoq mayor (Q). Highest position in the varayoq system
alguaciles (SP). Lowest position in varayoq system
amaru (Q). Underworld two-headed snake
APRA (SP). Popular Revolutionary Alliance
aclla (Q). Chosen
aclla wasi (Q). House of the chosen women
ayrampito (Q). Little Ayrampu, Berberis lutea medical uses, dye
ayudante (S). Helper
barranco (SP). Ravine
cacique (SP). Colonial Indian chief
cancha (SP). Toasted corn
carajo (SP). God damn it, or go to hell
carajo son ladrones (SP). God damn it, they're thieves
cargo (SP). Official obligation
chaskikuna (Q). Messengers
chicha (Q). Fermented corn beer
chicote (SP). Whip
cholo (a) (SP). Person of upward mobility, person not to be trusted;
    "chola" can also refer to market women
cholos de mierda (SP). Shitty cholos
chullu (Q). Woolen hat with ear flaps
coca. Plant in the *Erythroxylacea* family
cochino (SP). piggish, dirty, filthy
comadre (SP). Term of address to a woman, co-parent
compadre (SP). Term of address to a man, co-parent
condenado (SP). Condemned

convocatorio (SP). Communal meeting

criaturas de terror (SP). Children of terror, damned

curandero (SP). Curer, shaman

cuy (Q). Guinea pig

dance of the machumachu (Q). Male animal-fertility dance

encomienda (SP). Land and inhabiting Indians during colonial period

fiscal (SP). District attorney

herranza (SP). Fertility ritual for herds

hijos del pueblo (SP). Sons of the village

huevos (SP). Eggs, slang for testicles

huayno (Q). Popular dance music

ichu (Q). *Stipa ichu,* high altitude grass of the puna

illa (Q). Messenger, offertory vessel

kimsa pawsa (Q). Three double scrolls

lecha fresca (SP). Fresh milk

liklla (Q). Woman's shawl

llaqtamasikuna (Q). Fellow villagers

madrina (SP). Godmother

maricón (SP). Male homosexual, queer

marineros (SP). Marine personnel

mate (SP). Tea

mestizo (SP). Someone who identifies with the national culture

molle (SP). Schinus molle red pepper tree

mote (SP). Cooked corn, hominy

multa (SP). A penalty or fine

pachamama (Q). Mother Earth

pagapu (Q). From SP pagar, to pay, offering

patrones (SP). Bosses

pawsa (Q). Beautiful, purified

pongo (SP). Indian servant

puna (SP). Tropical alpine region 3,300 to 5,000 meters (10,800 to 16,400 feet) above sea level

qarqacha (Q). Condemned person who has committed incest

qero (Q). Carved or painted wooden drinking vessel

quinua (SP Q). High-altitude grain Chenopodium quinoa

la raza (S). The racial or ethnic group

regidor (SP). Middle rank official in varayoq system

repentidos (SP). Those who have repented

ronderos campesinos (SP). Members of civil patrols

runtuta kachuyoq (Q). Ball biter

Santa Cruz (SP). Feast of the Cross, harvest festival in May

serranos (SP). Highlanders

susto (SP). An illness caused by fright

tarwi (Q). Bean *Lupinus mutabilis*

takisunchik (SP). Let's dance

Tayta Inti (Q). Father Sun

terruca (SP). Slang for female terrorist

tiña (Q). Small ceremonial drum played by women

trago (SP). Raw cane alcohol

TRC (SP). Truth and Reconciliation Commission

usñu (Q). Inca ceremonial pyramid

vaquita (SP). Calf

vara (SP). Staff of office

varayoq (Q). Traditional authority (singular)

varayoqkuna (Q). Traditional authorities (plural)

Vecinos Mundiales (SP). World Neighbors, Protestant
nongovernmental organization

visitador real (SP). Royal inspector

watan misa (Q SP). Watan (Q) annual; Misa (SP), Mass

wamanis (Q). Mountain deities

yarqa aspiy (Q). Ritual to clean irrigation canals

yapuy (Q). Planting ritual

yaravi (Q). Ceremonial music, e.g., for harvest and planting

SUGGESTED READINGS AND RESOURCES

Books and Articles

Allen, Catherine. *The Hold Life Has: Coca and Cultural Identity in an Andean Community.* Washington: Smithsonian Institution Press. 2002. This is a beautifully written, sensitive ethnography of a small community near Cuzco. Allen is present in the account, especially in the postscript of this second edition where she documents changes she found twenty years after the original work was conducted.

Allen, Catherine, and Nathan Garner. *Condor Qatay: Anthropology in Performance.* Prospect Heights, Ill.: Waveland Press. 1997. This ethnographic drama captures the tensions between indigenous peasants and mestizos dramatized in the form of a myth.

Arguedas, José María. *Deep Rivers.* Translated by Frances H. Barraclough. Austin: University of Texas Press. 1978. Originally published as *Los ríos profundos.* Buenos Aires: Editorial Losada. 1958. This widely read novel on the Andes relates the life story of a mestizo boy who identifies with the Quechua-speaking people that he is separated from by social conventions.

Bandelier, Adolph. *The Delight Makers: A Novel of Prehistoric Pueblo Indians.* New York: Harcourt, Brace, and Jovanovich. 1970 [1890]. The first ethnographic novel published by an anthropologist.

Behar, Ruth, and Deborah Gordon, eds. *Women Writing Culture.* Berkeley: University of California Press. 1995. Bringing together autobiography, ethnography, historical analysis, criticism, and experimental essays, this feminist critique brings together new reflections of the racial and gender politics of writing.

Bowen, Elenore Smith (Laura Bohannan). *Return to Laughter.* New York: Doubleday Anchor. 1964. Bohannan's novel is widely considered the most influential and widely read anthropological novel.

Caretas. *El Perú en los tiempos del terror: Las verdad sobre el espanto. Dossier 2003 fotográfico de Caretas.* Lima: Empresa Editora Multimedia SAC. 2003. Beginning with photos from 1981 and ending in 2003, this collection of photos tells the pictorial history of twenty years of terror.

Geertz, Clifford. *The Interpretation of Cultures: Selected Essays.* New York: Basic Books. 2000 [1973]. With the publication of this foundational volume in 1973, Geertz turned cultural anthropology away from a holistic discipline in search of scientific, universal explanations toward an interpretive one engaged in "thick descriptions," a now widely used term he introduced in the first chapter. The chapter titled "Deep Play: Notes on a Balinese Cockfight" is an example of "thick description" in practice and one of the most cited articles in current anthropological literature. One of the major criticisms of Geertz's approach is that it ignores dialogical aspects of conducting ethnographical research (see Dennis Tedlock, "Poetry and Ethnology").

———. "A Life of Learning." *American Council of Learned Societies* 45 (1999). An entertaining and reveling memoir that will help readers understand Geertz's motivations for developing a new paradigm for anthropology.

———. *Works and Lives: The Anthropologist as Author.* Stanford, Calif.: Stanford University Press. 1988. Geertz analyzes the rhetorical styles of representation of several founding figures of American and British anthropology as the bases for establishing an authoritative voice. It was awarded the Critics Circle Prize for criticism in 1989.

Gorriti, Gustavo. *The Shining Path: A History of the Millenarian War in Peru.* Translated by Robin Kirk. Chapel Hill: University of North Carolina Press. 1999. Originally published as *Sendero: Historia de la guerra milenaria en el Perú.* Lima: Editorial Apoyo. 1990. This is a highly readable comprehensive history of the development of the Communist Party of Peru, Shining Path (Sendero), the Peruvian Maoist movement. Gorriti, a journalist in Lima, begins the story in 1979 with the arrest of Abimael Guzmán during a general strike in Lima and ends it before Guzmán's arrest in 1990.

Guzmán, Reynoso Abimael. *Guerra Popular en el Peru: El Pensamiento Gonzalo.* Edited by Luis Arce Borja. Bruxelles (Lima): El Diario. 1989. Published from exile in Brussels with a forty-page prologue by Luis Arce, this is a compendium of writings of Guzmán (Presidente Gonzalo).

Isbell, Billie Jean. *Para Defendernos: Ecología y ritual en un pueblo andino.* Cuzco: Centro Bartolomé de las Casas. 2005. This is a Spanish translation of *To Defend Ourselves* (see below) with a new preface by Enrique Mayer and two new chapters dealing with the aftermath of the war.

———. "Protest Arts from Ayacucho, Peru: Song and Visual Artworks as Validation of Experience." In *Quechua Expresivo Quechua: La Inscripción de Voces Andinas*, edited by G. Delgado and J. M. Schechter. 237–62. Bonn: Bonn Americanist Studies. 2004. This is a revision of the 1998 *American Anthropologist* article *Violence in Peru* (see below).

———. "Public Secrets from Peru." 1994. This is an unpublished drama based on interviews with victims during the war that is available on the isbell/andes Web site.

———. *To Defend Ourselves: Ecology and Ritual in an Andean Village*. Austin: University of Texas Press. 1978. This ethnography of Chuschi, a village in the River Pampas region where *Finding Cholita* is set, will be informative to interested readers who want to explore the field of Andean studies. This edition is available online along with 1500 photographs of the region on the isbell/andes Web site listed below.

———. *To Defend Ourselves: Ecology and Ritual in an Andean Village*. Prospect Heights, Ill.: Waveland Press. 1985. Second edition with a new introduction that reflects on the war.

———. "Violence in Peru: Performances and Dialogues." *American Anthropologist* 100.2 (1998): 283–92. This article is an analysis of protest music and art. Transcriptions of the Quechua texts and recordings of the songs as well as the full corpus of protest art can be accessed on the isbell/andes Web site listed below.

———. "Women's Voices, Lima 1975." In *The Dialogic Emergence of Culture,* edited by Bruce Mannheim and Dennis Tedlock, 54–74. Urbana: University of Illinois Press. 1995. Three generations of women tell me the stories of their lives. This article is dialogical, as I am present in the representation of the text.

———. "Written on My Body." In *Violence: Anthropological Encounters*, edited by Parvis Ghassem-Fachandi. London: Berg Press. In press. In this short memoir I explore the impact on my body of working on violence for twenty years.

Kirk, Robin. *Grabado en piedra: las mujeres de Sendero Luminoso.* Lima: Instituto de Estudios Peruanos. 1993. With this slim volume Kirk brought attention to the importance of women in Shining Path's movement. A shorter version in English is published in *The Monkey's Paw*.

———. *The Monkey's Paw: New Chronicles from Peru*. Amherst: University of Massachusetts Press. 1995. This is a compelling chronicle of the war that puts a human face on the diverse segments of the Peruvian population affected by the war. Kirk, a journalist, sets out to interview Guzmán. She fails to do so but along the way provides an acute analysis of Shining Path.

La Farge, Oliver. *Laughing Boy: A Navajo Love Story.* New York: A Signet Classic, Penguin Books. 1971 [1929]. This Pulitzer Prize–winning novel is regarded as the most successful anthropological novel written. Oliver chose to set this story in the Navajo reservation in 1915. It details the love story of two young Navajo, and death of the heroine, as their culture confronts barriers and obstacles as whites begin to arrive in large numbers.

Lifton, Robert Jay. *The Nazi Doctors: Medical Killers and the Psychology of Genocide*. New York: Basic Books. 2000 [1986]. This edition has a new introduction by the author.

Based on ten years of interviews with Nazi doctors, Lifton develops the theory of doubling that is cited in *Finding Cholita.*

Martin, David. *Tongues of Fire: The Explosion of Protestantism in Latin America.* London: Blackwell. 1995. This is a good introduction to the study of the extraordinary rise of Protestantism in Latin America.

Mayer, Enrique. *The Articulated Peasant: Household Economies in the Andes.* Boulder, Colo.: Westview Press. 2002. Based on thirty years of research, Mayer examines household economies and changing systems of land use and agricultural production and economic exchange.

Montejo, Victor. *Testimony: Death of a Guatemalan Village.* Willimantic, Conn.: Curbstone Press. 1999 [1987]. This is one of the most compelling firsthand testimonies in print. Montejo, a schoolteacher, relates the story of the attack and massacre of a village by the military. Montejo escaped to the United States and became an activist and anthropologist.

Norstrom, Carolyn, and Antonius C. G. M. Robben, eds. *Fieldwork under Fire: Contemporary Studies of Violence and Survival.* Berkeley: University of California Press. 1995. One of the few volumes that characterize what it is like to do anthropological fieldwork in dangerous places.

Narayan, Kirin. "Ethnography and Fiction: Where Is the Border?" *Anthropology and Humanism* 24:2 (1999): 134–47. Narayan provides an excellent, historically grounded discussion of the place of fiction in anthropology.

Orlove, Ben. *Lines in the Water: Nature and Culture at Lake Titicaca.* Berkeley: University of California Press. 2002. Written in autobiographical style, Orlove documents twenty years of research among the indigenous fisher folk whose livelihood depends on the lake. He focuses on enduring memory and knowledge of the indigenous lake communities.

Parsons, Elsie Clews, ed. *American Indian Life.* Lincoln: University of Nebraska Press. 1991 [1922]. The new publication of this collection of short stories about American Indian life by twenty-seven prominent anthropologists of the time has a new introduction by Joan Mark.

Partnoy, Alicia. *The Little School: Tales of Disappearance and Survival in Argentina.* Pittsburgh: Cleis Press. 1992 [1986]. This firsthand account of being disappeared is unique because Partnoy's experiences of being held in a school during the dirty war are described from her view from out from under her blindfold. It is the unique and compelling writing of a first-rate novelist.

Poole, Deborah, and Gerardo Rénique. *Peru: Time of Fear.* London: Latin America Bureau. 1992. This well-documented volume provides a compelling analysis of the success of Shining Path that is historically grounded to explore the conditions that led to the development of Shining Path. It also takes the reader beyond the capture of Guzmán to examine the dictatorial policies of Fujimori as well as to explicate coca capitalism.

Shakespeare, Nicholas. *The Dancer Upstairs.* London: Harvill Press. 1995. This detective thriller is based on Guzmán's capture in Lima in 1992. Shakespeare also wrote the screenplay for John Malkovich's film of the same name. The book won the American Library Association Award.

Starn, Orin, Carlos DeGregori, and Robin Kirk, eds. *The Peru Reader: History, Culture, Politics.* Durham, N.C.: Duke University Press. 1995. This comprehensive collection offers the reader a wide array of voices to explore the complexity of Peruvian society and the rise of Shining Path. The full text of Arguedas's *The Pongo's Dream*, excerpts of which are featured in chapter 2 of *Finding Cholita*, is included.

Stern, Steve J., ed. *Shining and Other Paths: War and Society in Peru, 1980–1995.* Durham: Duke University Press. 1997. By bringing together essays by historians, social scientists, and human rights activists from the United States and Peru, Stern provides in-depth analyses of the development of Shining Path.

Tedlock, Barbara. *The Beautiful and the Dangerous: Encounters with the Zuni Indians.* New York: Viking Penguin. 1992. As one of the early readers of Tedlock's engaging dialogical narrative ethnography that draws on her twenty years of experiences among the Zuni, I was encouraged to continue experimentation with ethnography and fiction, which resulted in *Finding Cholita.*

Tedlock, Dennis. "Poetry and Ethnography." *Anthropology and Humanism* 24:2 (1999): 155–67. In Tedlock's comments on Narayan's essay in the same volume of *Anthropology and Humanism*, he states, "Every act of speech or writing has a poetic dimension" (155). His emphasis on dialogics and poetics has given me the final push across the border to write fiction and include poetic passages in *Finding Cholita.*

Theidon, Kimberly. *Entre prójimos: el conflicto armado interno y la política de la reconciliación el el Perú.* Lima: Instituto de Estudios Peruanos. 2004. This study of six communities in the zones of conflict in the department of Ayacucho will give the reader an extraordinary account and analysis of the impact of the violence in the region where *Finding Cholita* takes place.

Vonnegut, Kurt. *Cat's Cradle.* Penguin Books: New York. 1999 [1963]. Vonnegut's early novel is considered one of the great satires of American fiction. This science-fiction story was accepted in 1971 by the University of Chicago for his master's thesis in anthropology after they had turned down his original thesis.

Wachtel, Nathan. *Gods and Vampires: Return to Chipaya.* Chicago: University of Chicago Press. 1994. The author returns to Chipaya, Bolivia, sixteen years after his first fieldwork and finds that the Uru are being killed and tortured as vampires responsible for misfortunes in the region. He also finds widespread conversion to Protestantism as well as conversion of Protestants back to Catholicism. This engaging volume is written like a detective story.

Zorn, Elaine. *Weaving a Future: Tourism, Cloth, and Culture on an Andean Island.* Iowa City: University of Iowa Press. 2004. An in-depth study of the inhabitants of Taquili, famous weavers on an island community in Lake Titicaca, and their struggles to control their tourism. The study covers a twenty-year period that allows the reader to understand the nature of change.

Web Sites and Films

Web site of Isbell's research in the River Pampas region of Ayacucho provides background print, visual and tape-recorded resources on the region where *Finding Cholita* is set. http://isbellandes.library.cornell.edu/

Also of potential interest is another web site: http://courses.cit.cornell.edu

Peruvian Truth and Reconciliation Commission Report: http://www.cverdad.org .pe/

The Dancer Upstairs. Feature film by Fox Searchlight Pictures. John Malkovich makes his directing debut and the screenplay is written by Nicholas Shakespeare, author of the novel *The Dancer Upstairs.*

State of Fear. 94 minutes. A Skylight Pictures Film. Contact: Paco@skylightpictures .com

Interpretations of Culture in the New Millennium

BILLIE JEAN ISBELL is an emeritus professor of anthropology at Cornell University. She is the author of *To Defend Ourselves: Ecology and Ritual in an Andean Village.*

The University of Illinois Press
is a founding member of the
Association of American University Presses.

Composed in 10/13.75 Hoefler Text
with Univers display
by Jim Proefrock
at the University of Illinois Press
Designed by Kelly Gray
Manufactured by Cushing-Malloy, Inc.

University of Illinois Press
1325 South Oak Street
Champaign, IL 61820-6903
www.press.uillinois.edu